CHANGING
POLICE
CULTURE

CHANGING POLICE CULTURE

Policing in a Multicultural Society

JANET B. L. CHAN
University of New South Wales

CAMBRIDGE
UNIVERSITY PRESS

PUBLISHED BY THE PRESS SYNDICATE OF THE UNIVERSITY OF CAMBRIDGE
The Pitt Building, Trumpington Street, Cambridge CB2 1RP, United Kingdom

CAMBRIDGE UNIVERSITY PRESS
The Edinburgh Building, Cambridge CB2 2RU, United Kingdom
40 West 20th Street, New York, NY 10011–4211, USA
10 Stamford Road, Oakleigh, Melbourne 3166, Australia

© Janet B. L. Chan 1997

First published 1997

Printed in Australia by Print Synergy

Typeset in Baskerville 10/12 pt

National Library of Australia Cataloguing in Publication data
Chan, Janet B. L. (Janet Bick Lai)
Changing police culture: policing in a multicultural society.
Bibliography.
Includes index.
1. Criminal justice, Administration of – Australia.
2. Discrimination in criminal justice administration –
Australia. 3. Police – Australia. 4. Police – Australia –
Public relations. I. Title.
363.20994

Library of Congress Cataloguing in Publication data
Chan, Janet B. L.
Changing police culture: policing in a multicultural society.
Janet B. L. Chan.
p.   cm.
Includes bibliographical references and index.
1. Police – Australia. 2. Public relations – Police – Australia.
3. Minorities – Australia. I. Title.
HV8280.A2C43 1997
363.2' 0994 – DC20   96 – 28734

A *catalogue record for this book is available from the British Library*

ISBN 0 521 56420 4 hardback

Contents

Figures

Tables

Acknowledgements

This research was partly funded by the 1990 Sir Maurice Byers Fellowship offered by the New South Wales Police Service. I would also like to thank the School of Social Science and Policy, University of New South Wales, for supporting this research through the granting of leave from teaching from 1 July 1991 to 30 June 1992.

Many people currently or previously employed in the New South Wales Police Service made significant contributions to this research. Special thanks are due to Leela Smith and Geoff Bell for their support throughout the initial phase of the project. I would also like to thank the following people for their valuable contributions at various stages of the project: Gerard Banister, David Bradley, Neil Bridge, Brad Cable, Michael Egan, Warren Fletcher, Alison Jaffee, Jeff Jarratt, John McDonald, Peter Miller, Leo Raiti, Paul Talbot and Barrie Thorley. I would also like to thank everyone who participated in the survey and those who consented to be interviewed. I appreciate the time that you took to answer my numerous questions and the frankness with which you expressed your opinions.

I am also grateful for the cooperation and information provided by the Commissioners and contact officers of the Australian Federal Police, the Northern Territory Police, the Queensland Police Service, the South Australian Police Department, the Tasmanian Police, the Victoria Police and the Western Australia Police Department. Their responses to the national survey were enthusiastic and helpful.

Emma Bathie deserves special mention for assisting with several aspects of the project, including the onerous task of data processing. Sally Doran provided valuable editorial assistance to the final manuscript. I would also like to thank Lynne Barnes, Mary Christopher, Rose Egerton, Susanna Lok, Janelle Stevens and John Turner, for assisting with the transcription of the interviews.

I have benefited from my study leave in England and Canada during 1993, especially comments on this research by colleagues who attended my seminars at the Centre for Criminological Research, University of Oxford; Centre for the Study of Public Order, University of Leicester; and the School of Criminology, Simon Fraser University.

Various people have generously provided comments on earlier drafts of selected chapters: Richard Ericson, David Dixon, Andrew Goldsmith, Simon Holdaway, Peter Manning, Peter Saunders, Joanna Shapland, and anonymous reviewers from the Cambridge University Press and the *British Journal of Criminology*. I am indebted to their insightful suggestions and constructive criticisms. My only concern is that I may not have adequately addressed the issues they raised.

I would also like to thank Phillipa McGuinness of Cambridge University Press for her kind support and encouragement throughout the conceptualisation and production of this book, Jane Farago and Janet Mackenzie for their editorial support, and Diana Encel for compiling the index.

My personal thanks go to Peter Saunders who is always positive and supportive even when I falter, and to my children Karen and Kenneth who never complain that I spend too much time on my work. I am also grateful for Karen's editorial help when I needed it most. This book would not have been possible without the loving environment you have all contributed to.

J. B. L. CHAN
Sydney

Some of the material in this book has appeared in J. Chan (1996) 'Police Racism: Experiences and Reforms' in E. Vasta and S. Castles (eds) *The Teeth are Smiling: The Persistence of Racism in Multicultural Australia* Sydney: Allen & Unwin. Chapter 4 contains a revised version of part of a paper by J. Chan, 'Changing Police Culture', published in the *British Journal of Criminology* (1996) volume 36, number 1, used with permission from Oxford University Press. Chapter 8 is a revised version of a paper by J. Chan, 'Damage Control: Media Representation and Responses to Police Deviance', published in *Law/Text/Culture* (1996) volume 2, used with permission from the publisher of the journal. Extracts from other sources are reproduced by permission of the Police Association of New South Wales, the New South Wales Police Service, the *Sydney Morning Herald*, and Mr Tom Gilling.

Abbreviations

ABMF	Australian Bicentennial Multicultural Foundation
ABS	Australian Bureau of Statistics
ACLO	Aboriginal Community Liaison Officer
ALRC	Australian Law Reform Commission
ATSI	Aboriginal and Torres Strait Islander
CAGD	Australia. Commonwealth Attorney-General's Department
CARE	Centre for Applied Research in Education, University of East Anglia
CCC	Community Consultative Committee
EAPS	Ethnic Affairs Policy Statement
ECLO	Ethnic Community Liaison Officer
EEO	Equal Employment Opportunity
HREOC	Human Rights and Equal Opportunity Commission
NESB	non-English-speaking background
NSWEAC	New South Wales Ethnic Affairs Commission
NSWLRC	New South Wales Law Reform Commission
NSWPD	New South Wales Police Department
NSWPS	New South Wales Police Service
PREP	Police Recruit Education Programme
QCJC	Queensland. Criminal Justice Commission
SMH	*Sydney Morning Herald*

Introduction

This is a book about change in Australian policing. As it turns out, it is also a book about resistance to change. The conduct of police officers and the performance of police organisations are increasingly under public scrutiny in recent years, following revelations of systemic corruption and malpractice in some police forces (Fitzgerald Report 1989, and the current Wood Royal Commission into the New South Wales Police Service). Reforming the police has become an urgent item on the political agenda of governments. At a time when the necessity for change seems most pressing, it is important to consider our state of knowledge about change. While political urgency may have created unique opportunities and a favourable climate for wide-ranging reforms, there is considerable danger in pushing change for the sake of change. There is much to learn from experience.

This book examines the dynamics of change and resistance within a police organisation when reforms were introduced to improve relations between police and minorities. It captures the complexity and unpredictability of the change process. For example, radical change, though politically risky and unpopular, can be more successful in transforming organisational directions than incremental change, which requires a long period of sustained organisational and political commitment to produce effects. On the other hand, change introduced from the top of the organisation is often resisted by those at the bottom. Similarly, externally imposed change can be sabotaged by members within the organisation. Overall, the path of change is never straightforward: change can lead to further change in the intended direction, it can bring about unintended consequences, or it can suffer setbacks and reversals. What is intended in this book is not to create a manual for change management, but an awareness of the contingencies and vagaries of reform.

Police Racism and Police Reform

The problem of relations between police and minorities in Australia is in many ways no different from that of other Western countries such as Britain, Canada and the United States, where tension and conflict often exist between the police and visible racial minorities (Reiner 1985). Minorities complain of racist stereotyping, unfair targeting and at times harassment and violent treatment by police officers. Many members of minority groups are afraid of the police and do not trust them. Some are reluctant to report crime or cooperate with police investigation. However, the problem is not uniformly serious across all visible minority groups. In Australia, relations are historically poor between police and Aboriginal people, although a few ethnic groups such as the Vietnamese are beginning to voice concerns about abusive police treatment. Relations are also poor between police and young people, with homeless or unemployed youth from visible minority groups being the most vulnerable targets of police harassment.

While racial tension and hostility have led to the eruption of major urban riots in Britain and the United States (Scarman Report 1981; Skolnick and Fyfe 1993), police racism in Australia has largely remained simmering in the background of public consciousness. In fact, police–Aboriginal relations did not emerge as a critical public issue in Australia until the late 1960s and early 1970s (Lucas 1995). Since then, allegations of police brutality and heavy-handed tactics against Aboriginal communities have occasionally attracted media attention and government inquiries. The Royal Commission into Aboriginal Deaths in Custody in the 1980s certainly elevated issues of the criminalisation and incarceration of Aboriginal people to national prominence. The National Inquiry into Racist Violence also brought police racism to the front pages of newspapers in 1991. It took, however, a 1992 television documentary for police racism to really 'hit home' in the living-rooms of many Australians and, more significantly, in the boardrooms of Australian police commissioners and executives.

The documentary *Cop It Sweet* was filmed over a six-week period in Redfern, one of the most socially disadvantaged areas of inner Sydney, with a high concentration of Aboriginal population. It portrayed in graphic detail the harsh reality of police race relations in Redfern, and immediately drew powerful public condemnations against police racism. Compared with the weekly diet of action-oriented police dramas on television, *Cop It Sweet* was unexceptional viewing. As a real-life exposé of police deviance, it paled against the brutal beating of Rodney King. What shocked the audience, however, was not so much the crude and uncompromising message. It was true that the New South Wales police officers depicted were racist, sexist, ignorant, insensitive and hypocritical, but what was most disturbing of all, in the words of a viewer, was that the police were 'on their best behaviour for the cameras' (*Sydney Morning Herald*, Letters, 7 March 1992). This gave the impression that what was presented was 'business as usual'.

For practitioners and analysts of the criminal justice system, the documentary offered nothing new or shocking. Relations between Aborigines and police in Redfern have been a problem for at least twenty years (Cunneen 1990b). Among the problems documented in the late 1960s and early 1970s were the complaints that Aborigines were regularly arrested without cause and were subjected to a police-imposed curfew. Police–Aboriginal relations did not improve in the 1970s and 1980s. Constant complaints were made regarding police harassment and bashing of Aborigines; in addition, there were numerous 'large-scale police incursions' into Redfern involving riot police on several occasions (*ibid.*; Landa Report 1991). Indeed, the treatment of Aborigines by the criminal justice system throughout Australia has been the subject of numerous research studies, all of which have highlighted policing as the most problematic stage of the criminal justice process (e.g. Luke and Cunneen 1995; Cunneen and Robb 1987; Gale *et al.* 1990).

The irony of the public disgrace of the New South Wales police in 1992 is that it came at a time when the force had been undergoing major organisational and cultural reforms for some years. In 1984 a new Police Board was created and John Avery, a dedicated reformer, was appointed Police Commissioner. Avery's mission was to rid the force of institutionalised corruption and open the door to a new police culture in which service to the community is a major motivation for police work. Many sweeping changes were introduced, including a complete reorganisation of the command structure, the implementation of new recruitment criteria and training programs, and the adoption of community-based policing as the principal operational strategy. Some initiatives were specifically aimed at improving police–minority relations; others were simply blanket reforms for building a more professional, accountable and open police force.

The significance of *Cop It Sweet*, then, was not so much that it said anything new about police race relations, but that it raised serious questions about the effectiveness of police reforms. Not only did it question the force's policy direction, the quality of training, and the effectiveness of supervision, but it cast grave doubts on the entire reform program. Even though many New South Wales police officers publicly expressed abhorrence and disgust at the behaviour of their colleagues, and vehemently dissociated themselves from the image conveyed by the documentary, critics of the police saw the film as a scathing indictment of police racism and a vindication of their long-standing criticisms of police practice in Aboriginal communities. They were quick to point out that 'nothing's changed' after eight years of reform. Some blamed the wider Australian culture as the basis for racist attitudes among police officers. Others were impatient with the lack of progress in police reforms, advocating immediate action and more drastic measures.

Research Question

The purpose of this book is to examine a crucial question raised by the New South Wales experience: why did years of police reform make so little difference to police racism? This is not a uniquely Australian concern; the same question could well be asked in Los Angeles, where the videotaped beating of Rodney King brought shame to a police department said to be 'a shining example of the best in reform policing' (Sparrow *et al.* 1990: 60). To explain the failure of reform, it is useful to examine the original 'problem' the reform was meant to address. It is also important to scrutinise the intentions of reform, its implementation and outcomes. The New South Wales experience provides the main empirical foundation of this scrutiny, although relevant materials from other States are also consulted.

The use of the New South Wales Police Service as the basis of the case study was originally dictated more by opportunity than by choice. In 1990 I was awarded the inaugural Sir Maurice Byers Fellowship, which was established by the NSW Police Service to provide opportunities for academic research into policing issues.[1] The aim of the original research was to examine the NSW Police Service's policy in relation to ethnic minorities, how the policy was implemented, and the extent to which the policy was successful in improving police–minorities relations. The fellowship provided a unique opportunity for research, both in terms of making information accessible and securing formal organisational commitments to the project.

As it turns out, the New South Wales experience provides an ideal case study for a number of reasons. Firstly, New South Wales is a significant police jurisdiction in Australia. The NSW Police Service, with approximately 13,000 police officers and 3000 civilian staff, is the largest of the eight police forces in Australia, responsible for the most populous and ethnically diverse State in Australia. Secondly, police racism is a matter of great concern in New South Wales: relations between the police and the Aboriginal population have historically been strained, while the massive post-war influx of immigrants from non-English-speaking countries has created a rapidly changing environment for policing. Thirdly, New South Wales is considered a leader in police reform in Australia.

Since 1984, the NSW Police Service has undergone a period of substantial and continual reform, following the appointment of John Avery as the Police Commissioner. The reform initiatives introduced by Avery were seen as radical and innovative by international standards (Sparrow *et al.* 1990: 72–7). New South Wales was one of the first police forces in Australia to adopt 'community policing' as its main operational strategy. Its recruit training was rated as having the potential to be the best in the world by a team of overseas researchers (Centre for Applied Research in Education 1990). Finally, in spite of being a leader in police reform, the New South Wales Police Service has had the most visible and damaging public displays of its failures, including a string of government inquiries, the documentary *Cop It Sweet*, and the recent revelations from the Wood Royal Commission on police corruption. The New South Wales experience, then, represents an important social experiment; the reasons for its lack of success are of great interest to those concerned with police reform.

Research Methods

The methodology of the research was limited both by the duration of the fellowship and by the available resources,[2] although a substantial amount of additional work was carried out beyond the original project. The case study was based on three sources of data:[3] a survey of police officers by means of a questionnaire; semi-structured interviews with key informants; and a content analysis of a large number of official documents. Although I was a participant-observer in a number of meetings on minority issues at police headquarters, both the time-frame of the research and the policy of the Police Service at the time precluded any systematic observation of operational police work.

The survey was conducted on a random sample of police officers working in areas of relatively high ethnic population. The advantage of a sample survey using self-administered questionnaires is that it is a relatively efficient way of obtaining an overview of the police organisation, given the size of the NSW Police Service and the lack of available systematic data. The main purpose of the survey was to obtain information on the nature and frequency of police contacts with visible minorities,[4] as well as to canvass the views of officers on a number of related issues. A sample of 590 officers was randomly chosen from fifty-six patrol areas which, according to the 1986 Census, had over 15 per cent NESB (non-English-speaking background) population. These patrol areas were targeted for special attention by the Police Service's Ethnic Affairs Policy Statement in 1988 (see Chapter 7). The sample was stratified by rank. The sampling ratios were: one out of eight officers below the rank of senior sergeant, and one out of two officers at or above the rank of senior sergeant. The reason for using a larger sampling ratio for the senior ranks was to obtain a reasonable number of senior officers, who comprised only 7 per cent of the population of police officers, so that comparisons can be made between officers at different ranks.

A draft questionnaire was constructed and revised following consultation with a number of people in the Police Service. The revised instrument was then tested on more than forty officers of various ranks who attended classes at the NSW Police Academy. The final questionnaires were posted through the Police Service internal mail to the selected officers on 22 October 1991. Two covering letters, one signed by the State Commander and one signed by the researcher, explained the objectives of the survey and assured officers of the confidentiality and anonymity of their responses. Officers were asked to complete the questionnaire and return it within one week directly to the University of New South Wales, using the addressed, pre-paid envelopes provided. To maximise the response rate, an article was published in the *Police Service Weekly*, an internal publication of the Police Service, shortly after the questionnaires were distributed to announce the research project and to provide additional details of its objectives. Two weeks after the posting of the survey, a small poster was sent to each patrol area with a request for this to be put on the notice board to remind officers to return the questionnaires.

The average response rate of the survey was 56 per cent (332 responses), with the highest response rate among the most senior officers at the rank of inspector and above (69 per cent) and the lowest response rate from sergeants (42 per cent). A number of factors could be responsible for the low response. I was told that officers had been inundated with departmental surveys over the years and were becoming tired of filling out questionnaires. The questionnaire was fifteen pages long, with more than thirty questions, many of which consisted of a dozen or more items. Police officers, especially those in busy patrol areas, were likely to see the completion of questionnaires as additional paperwork they did not need. However, a 23-page survey on 'organisational issues' sponsored by the Police Service and carried out by commercial consultants obtained a response rate of 67.6 per cent in 1990 (Performance Diagnostics 1990). Apathy or lack of interest in multicultural issues could have been another reason for officers not responding. In any case, response rates for mail surveys are notoriously low. A response rate of 50 per cent is often considered adequate for analysis, although researchers must be aware of any sample bias resulting from non-response (Babbie 1992: 267).

When the sample of responses was analysed in terms of key

demographic and organisational variables, it was found to be reasonably representative of the population of police officers in New South Wales.[5] For example, 87 per cent of the sample were male officers, compared with 89 per cent in the population. Fifty-nine per cent of the sample were in general-duty policing, compared with 58 per cent in the population. While the median age group was the same (25 to 29 years) for both the sample and the population, the under-25 group was over-represented in the sample, while the 30-to-39 group was under-represented. This over-representation of young officers was similarly reflected in the distribution of respondents by rank and number of years of service. Officers with one to five years' service in the Police Service were over-represented, while those with eleven to twenty years' service were under-represented. Officers with more than twenty years of service and those at the rank of senior sergeant and above were over-represented as a result of the decision to over-sample senior officers.

Semi-structured face-to-face interviews were conducted by the author with selected members of the police organisation and a small number of non-police sources. Access to top management was made possible through the cooperation of the Police Board and top-level management in the Police Service. Before fieldwork began, the researcher presented a brief outline of the project to the State Executive Group, the highest-ranking officers of the Police Service, who showed enthusiastic support for the project. Many of the police personnel interviewed were chosen because they had played some part in the restructuring and transformation of the organisation in recent years. Others were chosen because they had direct contact with, or responsibility for the servicing of, visible minorities. The few non-police sources were selected because of their interest or involvement in police–minorities issues. Informal interviews also took place as part of the researcher's participation at various meetings. The objectives of the interviews were to collect information on the philosophical and historical basis of the NSW Police Service's ethnic and Aboriginal affairs policy, to canvass the issues relevant for the evaluation of the policy initiatives, and to provide contextual details to complement the survey results. A number of interviews were directed at general and specific policy issues and managerial strategies. Other interviews focused on detailed aspects of day-to-day operations. In total forty-one individuals and a group of about ten young people of Asian origin were interviewed. Most interviews were conducted between mid-1991 and early 1992. Each interview was about one hour in duration. Most were tape-recorded and transcripts of the interviews were prepared.

The research results are informed and complemented by a large number of official documents collected by the researcher during the course of the study. These include official reports, publications, internal documents, newspaper clippings and research reports. In addition, a survey of all Australian police forces (except New South Wales) was carried out in 1993. This provided additional documentary material for comparison. The documentary sources provide valuable background information as well as additional evidence to round out the data from the questionnaire and the interviews.

While the use of multiple sources of data can help to strengthen the findings of the case study, very often they yield contradictory results which must be explained (see Yin 1984; Patton 1980). For example, the majority of police personnel that I interviewed were fairly optimistic about the change initiatives, but non-police sources were scathing in their criticisms of police practice. Such contradictory results often reveal interesting aspects of the police organisation and its relationship with the environment. Though it may not be possible to resolve all contradictory findings satisfactorily, the search for explanation can often generate richer and better theories, which is precisely the purpose of any case study.

Ethical and Political Issues

Any discussion of the research project is incomplete without some reflection on the ethical and political issues in doing so-called 'race relations' research. Although the main concern of this study is the police, its findings have potential implications for members of visible minorities, whether or not they have come into contact with the police. Several aspects of the research raise important questions about the role of the researcher.

The first issue concerns the funding of the research. Since the major portion of funding for at least the main phase of data collection came from the NSW Police Service, doubts are inevitably raised about the capacity of the research to be independent. It is worth noting, however, that under the terms of the fellowship, the researcher has copyright over, and freedom to publish, all research findings. Unlike the antipathy towards academic research that Young (1991) encountered among British police forces, I was met during my fieldwork by a high degree of cooperation and even enthusiasm for social research within the NSW Police Service. Although a few of the questionnaire respondents criticised the research project as being a waste of time, the reception I got was overwhelmingly positive. This is not to imply that the research project was a public-relations exercise on the part of the Police Service. Certainly many critical comments were related to me during interviews and many of these comments were quoted in the final report (Chan 1992a). One academic colleague referred to the granting of the fellowship as a great source of legitimation for the Police Service. Indeed, the funding of the study was repeatedly cited by the Police Board and the Police Service as evidence that minority issues were being taken seriously. In reality, however, the findings of the study were not what the organisation would have been eager to put out in press releases. The final report contained many criticisms, but there was not a single attempt by anyone to ask me to change any part of the report. In fact, the report was widely circulated, both formally and informally, within the organisation. The Police Board wrote to congratulate me on the report, while the Inspector-General of the Police Service initiated a meeting to discuss the findings with me. Certainly, events surrounding the documentary *Cop It Sweet*—a sobering reminder of the police racism still untouched by reforms—brought a major change to the political climate. The Police Service was eager to fix up its tattered public image and be seen as doing something.

One incident was particularly revealing. After the completion of the original project, I delivered a paper at a national conference on immigration in 1992. The paper contained some negative findings from the research project and attracted some press coverage. There was an immediate suggestion by a civilian staff member within the Police Service that I should be required to submit all future papers based on the research study to the organisation for approval. I was rather offended by the suggestion and rang the senior police executive who was supposed to be approving my papers. I was told by the executive to ignore the suggestion. While I was relieved by the openness of this executive, the incident was telling in terms of the variation in attitudes to openness within the organisation (see Chapter 8).

Even though the research contract did not contain any censorship clauses, there is always the possibility that researchers might consciously or unconsciously censor themselves, not wanting to bite the hand that feeds them. It is therefore important to clarify my own values and pre-conceptions prior to the research project. I have for many years been interested in understanding why reforms so often fail to achieve their objectives. My work on penal reform (Chan 1992b) was clearly critical of the rhetoric of reform but nevertheless recognised the political and ideological power of this rhetoric. My interest in police research dates back to my work at the Centre of Criminology at the University of Toronto in the 1970s and early 1980s. I was much influenced by the critical traditions of police researchers such as Richard Ericson, Clifford Shearing and Philip Stenning. In 1978 I was co-investigator with Tony Doob in a Canadian project on decision-making by youth bureau police in 1978 (see Doob and Chan 1982), during which I spent over 300 hours with police officers. One observation that stuck in my mind for many years was the racist attitudes of many of the police officers I came across. While they were always polite to me, there was a widely accepted practice of denigrating minorities and telling racist jokes within the station, even in front of an 'ethnic' like me. Some ten years later when I was teaching at the University of Sydney, a female student walked out of my class in anger when I made a comment that police could not help being racist because of the occupational culture. I found out afterwards that the student's brother was a police officer, and she resented my generalisation. It was a lesson on the hazards of cross-cultural generalisations.

It took a few more years, however, before I conducted any research on an Australian police force. I must admit that I was genuinely surprised by many of the people within the NSW Police Service that I met in the course of this research. Even though it was presumptuous of me to compare the police of the 1990s in New South Wales with what I saw in the late 1970s in Canada, I was nevertheless impressed with the 'change'. I was shocked to find that not only was university education not denigrated by police officers, but a substantial proportion of officers in New South Wales either held a university degree or were in the process of pursuing one. I was amazed at the intelligence and openness of many of the senior officers that I interviewed. The thoughtfulness and sincerity of many of the Avery reforms also surprised me. The question, therefore, is not whether I had censored myself consciously or unconsciously, but how I could pull away sufficiently from the 'razzle-dazzle' of the organisational changes to assess in a relatively detached way the nature and quality of these changes. So it was, in the end, a matter of judgment, as I weighed up the research evidence as carefully and as responsibly as I could. My final report spoke volumes about the gap between what was intended and what was achieved, but the findings were not totally negative, because I did see more than a glimmer of hope among the police personnel that I met. It was noteworthy that the NSW Ombudsman's inquiry on police race relations quoted my report at great length (NSW Ombudsman 1994), while the conclusions of its final report (Landa Report 1995) substantially agreed with mine.

A final point concerns the politics of police–minorities research. Solomos (1988) has discussed the politicisation of 'race' in the British context and the problematic separation of research from political and policy consequences. Researchers in 'race relations' topics are often confronted with the question 'Whose side are you on?' It is therefore important for me to declare my position. Many in Australia would argue that it is impossible to de-politicise social research, especially research on oppressed minorities. I agree with this view in the sense that all research work is carried out in a particular political and institutional context, and all research workers carry with them particular personal and political perspectives. To the extent that a clear distinction can be drawn between the 'two sides' – the oppressed minorities and the racist police – my answer to the question 'Whose side are you on?' is unequivocally that I am on the side of the oppressed. However, I believe that researchers can be on the side of the oppressed without losing their independence. I cannot see how the interests of the oppressed can be served by a dogmatic acceptance of ideological stereotypes or a systematic avoidance of empirical evidence contrary to such stereotypes. If it is accepted that minority groups differ considerably in terms of their access to political and economic power, while police officers vary to a significant extent in their attitudes and orientations towards police work, then the possibility of establishing a clear boundary between the 'two sides' is much more doubtful. I also make no pretence that my work is more valid simply because I am female and belong to a visible minority group, even though it may be more politically acceptable in the current climate than similar work carried out by a white male researcher. My social and economic advantage as an academic precludes me from truly representing 'the voice of the oppressed'. My gender and ethnicity may have been a constraint in some situations but they can be a resource in others. I agree with Solomos that part of the research agenda must be 'a continual process of self-critical awareness that research can have both intended and unintended political consequences' (*ibid.*: 13).

Structure of the Book

The problem of police racism is examined in Chapter 1 within the context of Australia's history of colonisation and ethnocentrism. A review of the literature found evidence of prejudice, harassment and abuse by police against visible minorities. Aboriginal people and young people of non-English-speaking backgrounds were particularly vulnerable, while immigrants who did not have a good command of English were also disadvantaged by police officers' reluctance to use interpreters.

Chapter 2 examines different explanations for the existence and tolerance of police racism in society. It is suggested that police racism cannot be explained away by the commonsense view that police are merely reacting to the occurrence of crime, and hence if minority groups are over-policed or over-represented in criminal statistics, it is because these groups are more likely to commit offences. Neither is it satisfactory to view police racism as nothing more than a reflection of institutionalised racism in Australia. It is argued that the most useful explanations can be derived from a deeper understanding of the structural and cultural organisation of police work. Policing practice reflects the current priorities and values built into our laws and institutions. The type of crime considered worthy of police attention is often biased against minority groups. Every interaction with citizens involves a moral judgment of their social risk and the potential exercise of coercive force. Street-level policing is characterised by wide discretionary powers, low visibility and minimal supervision. These working conditions give rise to an 'occupational culture' of policing (Manning 1977), which consists of a range of informal assumptions, values, and accepted practices that tend to circumvent or defy legal rules and formal instructions. Thus, it is often argued that police racism is condoned, covered up and even rationalised by the occupational culture.

Chapter 3 turns to a review of the solutions or policy options for improving police–minorities relations and fighting police racism. Two broad approaches have been taken: the first is to tighten the rules and regulations that govern police actions in order to control discrimination and abuse, while the second aims to change police culture through improved selection and training and the introduction of community-based policing strategies. Each approach on its own has been found to be less than adequate. For example, rules and regulations imposed by those at the top of the organisation can be ignored or side-stepped by street-level officers, while anti-racism training often loses its relevance once officers are faced with the reality of police work. It is argued, however, that police reform is not a matter of choosing either one or the other of these approaches. Rather, it is the way police culture has been conceptualised that has caused a great deal of confusion. Several problems with current theories are identified: their inability to account for differences in culture, their neglect of the active role played by officers in the reproduction or transformation of culture, their failure to situate police culture within the political and social context of policing, and their silence about the scope and possibility for cultural change.

To address these theoretical weaknesses, an alternative framework for understanding police culture is constructed in Chapter 4, using Pierre Bourdieu's concepts of 'field' and 'habitus' to designate the structural conditions of policing and the learned dispositions of police culture respectively. In addition, the four dimensions of cultural knowledge proposed by Sackmann (1991) are adapted to provide a framework for a description of the habitus of policing. Central to this formulation is the active role of police actors. Officers working in a given 'field' develop and maintain a certain 'habitus' and make choices about their actions. The implication of this alternative framework is that it is futile to debate whether it is more effective to reform the police by tightening rules or by changing police culture. The relationships between structural conditions and cultural knowledge, and between cultural knowledge and actual practice, are neither deterministic nor uni-directional. This theoretical discussion is accompanied by a description of the habitus and the field of policing in New South Wales which sets the stage for the case study.

Chapter 5 provides a description of the nature and frequency of contact and the main areas of tension between the police and visible minorities in New South Wales. Chapter 6 outlines the recent history of the NSW police and describes the major organisational changes which have been implemented since 1984. These include a flattening and reorganisation of the rank structure, the introduction of merit-based promotion, and changes to recruitment and training, as well as the adoption of community-based policing strategies. The objectives of several community-based policing strategies and their initial implementation problems are then discussed.

The next two chapters present two case studies which highlight the limits and possibilities of change. Chapter 7 describes how an externally imposed reform, the Ethnic Affairs Policy Statement, became a meaningless paper exercise through the processes of inter-agency politics and internal bureaucratic resistance. Chapter 8 presents another externally driven reform: the formulation of a Police Aboriginal Policy Statement following adverse media coverage, including the documentary *Cop It Sweet*. The chapter highlights the power of media scandal as an instrument for change but warns of the potential consequences of a damage-control mentality within the organisation.

Chapter 9 makes use of diverse sources of information to evaluate the success of reforms as they relate to police–minorities relations. It scrutinises the processes by which policy is formulated and implemented, and examines the outcomes. The picture painted is not one of resounding success. While the rhetoric of change was strong at the top level of the organisation, and a great deal of structural change had been successfully implemented, the story was quite different as the focus moved away from the top. Uneven implementation, lack of quality control, and tokenistic attention to community consultation were some of the serious shortcomings noted. It would appear that rapid organisational change was effective in breaking up the old culture but it also left many, especially those in the middle ranks, disaffected and disillusioned. Even though top management maintained an optimistic view of reform, the organisation was still deeply divided in terms of its key ideology, community-based policing.

Chapter 10 draws together the case-study material and the theoretical discussion. It provides an analysis of the theoretical and practical implications of the New South Wales experience and discusses the prospects for cultural change. The book concludes that changing police culture requires changes not only in the cultural assumptions held by police officers but also in the political and organisational conditions of police work. In terms of improving police–minorities relations, this implies that strategies such as cross-cultural awareness training and community-based policing are ineffective on their own. They must be accompanied by appropriate structures of police accountability and legal regulation, as well as social reforms. However, change is difficult to achieve: it is traumatic and is therefore strongly resisted. Sustainable change can only be achieved through a combination of external pressure, organisational leadership and political commitment.

Notes

1 The fellowship, which amounted to a grant of $A50,000, was awarded competitively on the basis of proposals submitted by researchers. Applicants were free to select any research topic, although some general topics were offered as guidelines.

2 The fellowship allowed for a maximum of one year to complete the research project. The amount offered was not sufficient to cover the full costs of my salary for the year.

3 The original plan was not to survey police officers but to analyse the statistical data on police contacts with minorities. This plan was soon abandoned because the ethnicity or Aboriginality of citizens dealt with by the police was not routinely recorded, either on paper or electronically.

4 I have used the term 'visible minorities' to include both Aboriginal and NESB people.

5 Statistical information was available only for the 13,000 officers in the entire Police Service; it was not possible to compare the sample with the population of officers in the fifty-six targeted patrol areas.

CHAPTER 1

Policing in a Multicultural Society

Australia in the 1990s is a country of remarkable ethnic and cultural diversity, with more than 100 ethnic groups, speaking 80 immigrant languages and 150 Aboriginal languages (Castles *et al.* 1988: 25). More than one-quarter of its 17 million people were either born in non-English-speaking countries or the 'second generation' of those born in these countries (Jupp 1995). At the 1991 Census 265,459 people, or 1.6 per cent of the total population in Australia, identified themselves as being of Aboriginal or Torres Strait Islander origin (Australian Bureau of Statistics [ABS] 1994a: 5).[1]

Australia's ethnic diversity is, however, a relatively recent pheonomenon. At the time of European settlement in 1788, the continent had been inhabited by Aboriginal people for more than 50,000 years. After that the number of Australia's original inhabitants declined dramatically, from nearly one million to about 80,000 by the 1930s, largely as a result of 'disease, conflict and the disintegration of traditional society' (Human Rights and Equal Opportunity Commission [HREOC] 1991: 59). By the late 1940s, almost 90 per cent of Australia's population was of British descent. This was achieved through the White Australia Policy which discriminated against the immigration of non-Europeans and provided a system of assisted passage for British immigrants. Since the abandonment of discriminatory policies in the 1970s, however, Australia's population has become increasingly culturally diverse through immigration. By the late 1980s and early 1990s, only 18 per cent of immigrants to Australia were from the United Kingdom and Ireland, compared with 46 per cent in the early 1960s. During this period, the main sources of immigrants of non-English-speaking background shifted from European countries such as Italy and Greece to Asian countries such as Hong Kong, Vietnam, the Philippines, and Malaysia (ABS 1994a: 10).

Two hundred years of white settlement have turned Australia's indigenous people into the most marginalised and disadvantaged group in
society, constantly subject to harassment, discrimination, exclusion, and
even racist violence. It was estimated that 20,000 Aborigines were killed
in frontier conflict alone. Aborigines were randomly shot, massacred,
and even poisoned by white settlers for many years. Disgraceful treatment of Aborigines continued into the twentieth century, when Aborigines were segregated and detained in reserves and Aboriginal children
removed from their families and placed in institutions. It was not until
the 1960s that Australian governments recognised Aborigines as citizens
with full voting rights. Historical accounts also point to instances of
exploitation, abduction and segregation of Torres Strait Islanders since
the mid-1800s (HREOC 1991: 37–47). A national inquiry found widespread racist violence against Aboriginal and Islander people across
Australia, with the conduct of police officers cited as a major problem
(*ibid.*: 69–122).

The history of discrimination and oppression of people from non-
English-speaking countries is more recent but also alarming. Chinese
workers in the goldfields of Victoria were harassed, attacked and injured
by white miners in the 1850s. Melanesians forcibly taken from their
homelands to work in the sugar fields in Queensland were subject to
physical violence and racial prejudice. When the labour of these people
was no longer required, restrictions on non-European immigration were
enshrined in various State and federal laws for almost a century. A policy
of racial assimilation also found Southern and Eastern European immigrants subject to harassment and discrimination. The relaxation of
immigration restrictions and a policy shift to multiculturalism in the
1970s led to a steady increase in immigrants from non-English-speaking
countries. However, by the 1980s, concerns regarding the volume and
composition of immigrants became a recurring theme carried by the
Australian media through the so-called 'immigration debate', which
focused on the cultural, economic and, more recently, environmental
consequences of continuing and increasing levels of immigration. In
particular, some commentators saw the pace of Asian immigration as
detrimental to 'national cohesion'. While Australians remain divided on
the issue, the National Inquiry into Racist Violence found that among
reported cases of victimisation, Asian and Arab Australians were most
likely to be subjected to intimidation, harassment and violence (HREOC
1991: 172–5). Consultations with ethnic youth suggested that Asians,
particularly the Vietnamese, were increasingly the targets of racist
comments and discrimination in schools and workplaces (Cahill and
Ewen 1987; Office of Multicultural Affairs 1990).

Relations between police and minorities in Australia must be understood in the context of this history of colonisation, xenophobia and racism among white Australians. However, it should not be assumed that minority groups' experiences are homogeneous or static. For example, the depth and extent of discriminatory treatment suffered by Australia's indigenous people makes it inappropriate to lump their experiences with those of other Australians of non-English-speaking backgrounds (NESB). Certainly the legal system has, until recently, accommodated the dispossession of Aborigines of their own land, as it was impotent in stopping the murder of 20,000 Aborigines in the course of European occupation (Reynolds 1987: 1–5). Moreover, the historical role of the police in the suppression of Aboriginal resistance to European settlement and the 'protection' of Aborigines (Foley 1984) means that contemporary relations between police and Aborigines cannot be studied in isolation. Hence, even though the treatment of other ethnic minorities is in some ways an extension of Australia's treatment of Aborigines, there are undeniable differences between Aborigines and other ethnic minorities in their social conditions and experiences with the legal system. In fact, there may even be identifiable differences in experience between NESB groups. In Britain, for example, a survey by Jefferson and Walker (1992) in Leeds found that Asians (from the Indian sub-continent) reported fewer negative experiences and more favourable attitudes towards police than did Afro-Caribbeans. Though similar evidence is not available in Australia, the National Inquiry into Racist Violence reported that problems of racism and racist violence were far less significant among Southern European communities than those among the Asian, Jewish and Arabic communities (HREOC 1991: 140). Thus, although the following discussion focuses on some common experiences of police racism, it should not be assumed that all minority communities experience these problems to the same degree.

Police Racism

Many of the problems that exist between police and visible minority groups can be conveniently identified as aspects of 'police racism', although it is in fact an imprecise and emotive term which can at times confuse rather than clarify the nature of the problems. If we adopt the definition of racism given by Castles (1992a: 1), then 'police racism' refers to the process whereby police authorities stigmatise, harass, criminalise or otherwise discriminate against certain social groups 'on the basis of phenotypical or cultural markers, or national origin' through the use of their special powers. Like other forms of racism, police racism is not a static or simple phenomenon: 'it arises in differing situations, takes many forms and varies in intensity according to time and place' (*ibid.*). Manifestations of police racism can range from prejudicial attitudes and discriminatory law-enforcement practices, to the illegal use of violence against members of minority groups. 'Over-policing' of Aboriginal people is another aspect which has been the subject of a great number of research studies and inquiries in Australia. Among immigrants and Australians of non-English-speaking background, a major issue concerns police officers' reluctance to use professional language interpreters. For those with little or no facility in English, the presence of communication barriers amounts to a denial of equal access to justice, an obvious form of discrimination.

Insensitivity to Language and Cultural Differences

A major problem encountered by recent immigrants and refugees to Australia is their lack of ability or confidence to communicate in English. An unpublished NSW survey of community organisations (NSWEAC 1991) found widespread concern that police did not always use interpreters when needed and that unqualified or inappropriate persons were often used as interpreters. These allegations were supported by results of the survey by Chan (1992a) of NSW police officers (see Chapter 5) and the general findings of the Australian Law Reform Commission (ALRC):

> The Commission's consultations reveal that there is widespread concern about police reluctance to use interpreters when questioning suspects (or interviewing victims) with inadequate English skills. There is a perception that an interpreter is unlikely to be used for a relatively minor offence. This appears to be so even in jurisdictions where there is legislation requiring police to obtain interpreters before questioning a suspect. [ALRC 1992: 57]

A 1987 survey of sixty Vietnamese migrants in Victoria came to a similar conclusion about the low usage of interpreters by the Victorian police (Wilson and Storey 1991: 18). A general reluctance to use interpreters was also reported in the Northern Territory (O'Neill and Bathgate 1993: 142)

While administrative costs – both financial and in terms of delay – have often been cited as reasons for police not to use professional interpreters, a crucial issue concerns the extent to which police discretion is appropriately exercised in these situations. When dealing with ethnic youth, for example, there were complaints that police had a tendency not to accept that interpreters were needed – 'It was commonly presumed that the youth concerned went to school hence would understand English' (NSWEAC 1992: Section 2B4). The assumption that someone with a reasonable grasp of conversational English is competent to give legal evidence or answer questions in a police interrogation has already been challenged by linguistic specialists and lawyers (see Australia. Commonwealth Attorney-General's Department [CAGD] 1990: 42; Roberts-Smith 1989: 76). When interpreters are not used in criminal investigations, the disadvantages suffered by a person from non-English-speaking background may be compounded by their cultural fears and inhibitions:

> The intrinsic nature and potential consequences of criminal investigation make it perhaps the most stressful of all legal situations. This stress may be greatly increased by cultural and language difficulties. The relationship of citizens to police in their native country will be reflected in behaviour and attitudes shown by migrants to Australian police. Those migrants who come from a police state are likely to have a very different perception of the role and the function of police. Any encounter with the police, for whatever reason, may be a frightening experience. [CAGD 1990: 60]

The right to an interpreter has not been uniformly established in legislation throughout Australia – some States still rely on police and judicial discretion in establishing the need for an interpreter. The Australian Law Reform Commission's consultation shows, however, that statutory provisions requiring the use of interpreters may not in themselves be sufficient to remedy the problem.

Language barriers do not exist only in relation to immigrants and refugees from non-English-speaking countries. Some Aborigines also encounter difficulties in language communication. In some cases interpreters are not readily available for Aboriginal languages known by very few people (CAGD 1990: 113). The majority of Aboriginal people also speak dialects of English which may 'differ systematically from standard English in terms of sound system, grammar, vocabulary, meaning and appropriate use of language' (ibid.: 113–14). Foley (1984: 168–9) points out that non-standard grammatical usage of tense, gender, and number in Aboriginal English could lead to confusion and misunderstandings about time, number and gender in police interrogations. In Rv Anunga,[2] the Northern Territory Supreme Court set out nine guidelines which apply to the interrogation of Aborigines as suspects. These include the use of an interpreter where necessary, the presence of a 'friend' of the prisoner, the use of simple language in asking questions, the calling of legal assistance if sought, and other measures to lower the level of stress for the suspects. These guidelines are, however, not rules of law and non-compliance did not necessarily mean exclusion of the evidence.

Admittedly, the use of interpreters solves only part of the communication problems between police and minorities. Cultural barriers can be even more problematic because they may be less obvious than language barriers. Many Aboriginal and NESB people have difficulties with Anglo-Australian legal concepts and criminal justice processes, many of which have no equivalent in other languages. Bail, for example, is a common law concept which can easily be confused with a fine. Such a mistake can have extremely serious consequences for a defendant (ALRC 1992: 209). Police interrogation is another area fraught with problems for Aborigines and ethnic minorities:

> Confusion and misunderstanding may be caused by such things as double intent, coupled questions, tone of voice, loading of queries, leading questions, and the insinuation of things not verbalised, for example by gesture. It is quite common for authority figures to be told what the Aboriginal informant thinks they want to hear. [Foley 1984: 169]

The legal right to remain silent is another mystery to those not familiar with the British system. This was vividly illustrated by Coldrey (1987: 84–5) in the presentation of a 'classic piece of interrogation' where an accused Aboriginal couple answered 'yes' eighteen times without understanding the caution which the police officer had attempted to explain. Gibbon (1989) has criticised the language that police use in interrogations as an additional barrier to communication with ethnic minorities. The complex grammatical structure – with numerous clauses or phrases in one sentence – together with the use of abstract language and police jargon, makes it difficult for second-language speakers to understand. A question such as 'Do you agree that I also told you that at the conclusion of the interview you would be given the opportunity of reading through the interview?' would be considered comical if the consequences of misunderstanding it were not so serious for the respondent.

Prejudice and Stereotyping

Research studies in Britain and the United States have documented clear evidence of prejudicial attitudes and the regular use of racist language among police officers (Gordon 1983; Holdaway 1983; Smith and Gray 1983; Skolnick 1966; Bayley and Mendelsohn 1969). Similar complaints are found in Australia, although the evidence supporting these complaints is mainly based on community consultations rather than systematic observation. Police are often accused of forming stereotypical opinions about the criminality of certain ethnic groups. The consultations of the Australian Law Reform Commission, for example, identified concerns among community organisations and legal centres that 'whole communities [were] being put on trial and stigmatised for the real and imagined activities of some members of those groups' (ALRC 1992: 201). Besides problems such as Italian and Asian communities being typically associated with organised crime, the commission found that young people of particular ethnic backgrounds were type-cast as delinquents. An unpublished NSW Ethnic Affairs Commission survey of fifty-five community organisations also identifies stereotyping and harassment of NESB youth as a common complaint. The assumptions held by police were that NESB youth were 'trouble makers' and that they 'constitute themselves as gangs'(NSWEAC 1992: Section 2B4). Regular stereotyping by sections of the New South Wales population of Aborigines as a 'problem' has been documented by Cunneen and Robb (1987). Aboriginal people have been blamed for various forms of social disorder. It is therefore not surprising that police officers form similar associations between Aborigines and criminality. Some of this was evident from the the racist language and remarks used against Aborigines in *Cop It Sweet*.

Since police work is largely dictated by officers' perception of what constitutes suspicious activities and who is considered respectable, stereotyping and prejudice on the part of police officers can easily lead to harassment and community resentment. As law-enforcement officers, police can hardly claim professionalism and even-handedness if they allow racist attitudes to become an accepted part of their occupational milieu. Prejudicial attitudes are also obvious obstacles to gaining trust and cooperation from members of ethnic minority communities. British and American studies have found that blacks, in particular young blacks in inner cities, were more critical of police and more hostile towards police than other groups (Reiner 1985; Jefferson and Walker 1992). Less systematic evidence in Australia suggests that some minorities are afraid of police and do not trust them.

Over-policing: Unfair Targeting and Harassment of Minorities

While it is possible that police officers may put away their prejudices when performing their duties and make fair decisions, there is evidence that some ethnic minorities appear to be disproportionately represented in the criminal statistics. A review by Reiner (1985) of the British and American literature finds that young, low-income, ethnic males were more likely to be stopped and questioned by the police. Minorities were also more likely to be arrested, although there is some debate about whether this is due to situational factors such as suspects' disrespect towards police and the complainants' preferences. While American police used excessive force against white citizens twice as much as against blacks, the findings were reversed in cases of the use of deadly force by police.

One form of discriminatory policing practice is the unfair targeting and harassment of certain minority groups. At the policy level, this may be a resource allocation decision, so that more officers than normal are directed at the policing of some areas with a high concentration of certain minority groups. At the level of routine police work, this may reflect a strategy to single out certain minority group members regularly for questioning, or to selectively enforce laws so that certain minorities are more vulnerable to arrest and prosecution than the general population. The concept of over-policing encompasses both the *degree* (e.g. the number of officers stationed in areas with a high concentration of Aborigines) and the *nature* of police intervention. Examples of the latter are :

- the discriminatory use of particular legislation (for example, the use of public order offences);
- regular foot or vehicle patrols which create an atmosphere of surveillance and tension;
- spotlighting by police of houses in Aboriginal settlements;
- discriminatory policing of particular activities such as the stationing of police in front of hotels patronised by Aboriginal people. [HREOC 1991: 90–1]

Police harassment is a common complaint among juveniles (Alder *et al.* 1992; Youth Justice Coalition 1994). The same problem has been identified by NESB and Aboriginal youth in New South Wales, Victoria and the Northern Territory (Youth Justice Coalition 1990; 1994; NSWEAC 1992; O'Neill and Bathgate 1993: 141; Wilson and Storey 1991: 27–8). Consultations conducted by the National Inquiry into Racist Violence also found similar concerns among Aboriginal communities in Queensland, Western Australia and South Australia (HREOC 1991: 94–5). The problem is well illustrated by the Northern Territory report:

> young people of Vietnamese, Filipino and East Timorese background pointed to what they saw as evidence of discrimination ... In one consultation young men recounted that, with the exception of Aboriginal youth, police tended to focus on youth of Asian descent in public places, for instance at shopping centres or while walking along the street. One particular youth described the police tendency to 'spot-check' students walking after dark in public or cycling along the street. Another youth also alleged that at times the police shone lights in their face when questioning them ... [O'Neill and Bathgate 1993: 141]

It has been argued that over-policing is responsible for the gross over-representation of Aborigines in the criminal justice system. A study by Cunneen and Robb (1987: 70) of five north-western New South Wales towns found that Aborigines were over-represented by a factor of 3.2, i.e. Aborigines constituted 47.1 per cent of all those arrested in 1985–86, but Aborigines represented merely 14.6 per cent of the population in those towns. Once arrested, it would appear that Aborigines were also over-represented in police custody. A survey conducted in August 1988 found that Aborigines were placed in police cells at a rate of 27 times that of non-Aboriginal people, i.e. they were over-represented by a factor of 19.3. Aboriginal women were also disproportionately detained in police cells. In general, Aborigines were held in the cells for a longer period than non-Aborigines (McDonald and Biles 1991). The 1986 national prison census indicates that Aborigines were over-represented in the prison population by a factor of 9.7 (Walker and Biles 1987). Although statistical data in themselves do not automatically justify the conclusion that discriminatory police practices are occurring, they do provide a starting point for examining these problems. Whether or not police actually or routinely discriminate against minority groups, the *perception* of such discriminatory practices by minority groups must be taken seriously. Since fear and distrust of the police are common among some groups, any evidence of unfair treatment can only add to the distance between police and minorities. It is therefore not surprising that police often find that seeking cooperation from some members of minority communities can be a challenging task.

Abuse of Power and Excessive Use of Force

The National Inquiry into Racist Violence reported numerous incidents of police using 'intrusive and intimidatory practice', such as spotlighting, and conducting searches without a warrant, in their dealings with Aboriginal communities (HREOC 1991: 82–3). A survey of Aboriginal households in Adelaide found that 62 per cent of respondents had been visited by police during the previous two years, even though police had not been called. Twenty-four per cent of the households reported police entry of their households without invitation, without a warrant and without resulting in an arrest, while 19 per cent alleged that a member of the household had been physically abused by police (*ibid.* 1991: 83). Discriminatory and intimidatory policing practices in relation to Aborigines in public places as well as private functions were also reported to the inquiry (*ibid.* 1991: 85–8).

Most disturbing, however, was the 'overwhelming' evidence presented to the inquiry in relation to police violence against Aboriginal and Islander people, especially the shocking treatment of women and girls, which includes allegations of rape while in custody, sexual threats and abuse, in addition to verbal (sexist and racist) abuse and physical violence (HREOC 1991: 88–9). Similar treatment of juveniles was reported in a number of States. A survey by Cunneen (1990b) of 171 Aboriginal and Islander juveniles in State detention centres in Queensland, New South Wales and Western Australia found an alarming level of alleged police violence: 85 per cent reported that they had been hit, punched, kicked or slapped, and 63 per cent hit with objects, including police batons, telephone books, torches and other objects. These assaults took place on the street, during arrest and at police stations.

It was not only the frequency of violence, but also its nature, that was disturbing. Among the more sadistic police practices reported were the torture of a young Aborigine in Perth by assaulting him, then stripping and putting him in an air-conditioned room in mid-winter until he confessed to offences he had not committed; two police officers in Brisbane handcuffing a 15-year-old to a chair with rollers and then pushing him around the room and punching him; officers rolling a youth in a blanket in police cells before beating him; police kicking and punching a 16-year-old in New South Wales police cells after putting a blanket over his head; officers in Sydney smacking and punching a 16-year-old girl while she was ankle-cuffed to a table (HREOC 1991: 96–7).

With adult Aborigines in custody, practices such as brutal assault, hosing down detainees, denial of medical treatment, forcing detainees to drink water from toilet bowls, and other forms of abuse were reported to the inquiry (HREOC 1991: 105). Perhaps the most reprehensible of all was the finding that 'police officers had made suggestions of suicide or threatened to hang Aboriginal or Islander people when they were taken into custody' in order to control difficult prisoners or to intimidate suspects into making confessions (*ibid.*: 98).

The use of tactical response police against Aboriginal communities in Western Australia, the Northern Territory and New South Wales was another category of complaints received by the inquiry. The case of a pre-dawn raid on Redfern in 1990, conducted by 135 officers including members of the Tactical Response Group, was a high-profile example in New South Wales. Operation Sue involved the entry and search of ten dwellings on Eveleigh Street, Redfern. The justification of the raid was in terms of an abnormal increase in crime and the prevalence of a drug culture in the Aboriginal community (Landa Report 1991 Section 2.1). However, the Ombudsman's investigation concluded that:

> There is no dispute that there is crime in the area and that police have to do their job. The issues raised by Operation Sue concern the methods used to do that job. The arrests and charges arising out of Operation Sue were detailed for each target. There were nine arrests and the charges were minor. The operation was claimed to specifically target the drug problem – one marijuana plant was found ... Operation Sue was characterised by negligence and unprofessional policing in its most crucial area – intelligence gathering and planning. [*ibid.*: Sections 8.30–1]

The use of the Tactical Response Group was found by the Ombudsman to be 'not called for' for the majority of the targets. The Aboriginal Legal Service saw Operation Sue as an 'intimidatory offensive against the Redfern Aboriginal community' and 'a racist operation ... the same type of operations undoubtedly would not be considered by the New South Wales police force in a "white" high crime area such as Kings Cross, Darlinghurst, etc.' (Landa Report 1991 Section 8.22). Although police denied this intention, the Ombudsman observed that 'there was so little attention paid to the detail of the operation and the intelligence on which individuals were targeted ... that the evidence supports a strong inference that the police intention was to have a general impact' (*ibid.*, Section 8.22).

The Inquiry into Racist Violence did not receive many complaints about police abuse or violence against other ethnic minorities. However, the survey of community organisations conducted by the NSW Ethnic Affairs Commission did reveal concerns about 'occasional physical abuse by police, victimisation by police through the selective use of police powers, police brutality whilst youth are being detained or questioned by police' (NSWEAC 1992). In Victoria, similar allegations of police misconduct such as beatings in custody, property searches without warrants, harassment and abuse of individuals, were reported by the majority of community workers and some of the solicitors interviewed by Wilson and Storey (1991).

When presented with allegations of abuse and violence, police rarely took them seriously. Apart from a few police officers who gave evidence at the National Inquiry into Racist Violence to confirm the existence of police abuse and police violence against Aborigines, the reactions of police forces to these complaints have tended to be defensive. The fact that very few of these allegations were taken to formal complaint bodies or criminal courts does not imply that the victims were lying or exaggerating. It is more a reflection of the inaccessibility of the complaints process and the perceived futility of complaining against a powerful body such as the police. In fact, the difficulty of getting justice in cases alleging police misconduct adds another layer of injustice to the experience of minorities. The danger is that such behaviours may be accepted as part of the routine and what the victims 'deserve', as some young people in Australia have come to expect from the police (see Cunneen 1990b: 53).

Attitudes of Minority Groups towards Police

The attitudes of Aborigines towards police and the legal system are deeply affected by their memories of colonisation and oppression and the inability of European law to protect them. The role of the police in enforcing the *Aborigines Protection Act* 1909 in New South Wales, for example, turned police into a state agency responsible for issuing rations, removing 'neglected' children from parents, and controlling people's movement on Aboriginal reserves, as well as more traditional policing functions such as maintaining order. The Act remained in force until 1969 and had brought about 'widespread fear and dislike of the police' among Aborigines, even years later:

> The fear that the police were arriving to take the children meant that all the Aboriginal community treated any arrival by police with fear and suspicion. Indeed, some of the children forcibly removed by the police ... are now the adults being regularly arrested by police for the alleged commission of street offences. It is therefore not surprising that there are many levels of tension and conflict between the two groups ... [Ronalds *et al.* 1983: 177]

An inquiry conducted for the Northern Territory Police also found that some ethnic minority group members were fearful of the police:

> Fearful or anxious reactions were described by a number of people as their common response to police contact. Contact with police for routine offences or checks, for instance, traffic infringements and breathalyser tests and even police enquiries regarding a neighbour, could potentially be a source of fear and anxiety ... The desire for avoidance of contact with police was especially noticeable in the Vietnamese community where general interactions with police were viewed with great wariness ... This viewpoint is reflected in the Alice Springs consultations where Vietnamese-born people stated that they did not require the services of a police liaison person because they had done nothing wrong. [O'Neill and Bathgate 1993: 140]

Some immigrants' perception of the police is influenced by the experience they had of police in their country of origin. Where police forces in these countries have been associated with oppressive political regimes or arbitrary use of state powers, immigrants tend to avoid dealing with police or become hostile or anxious when questioned by police. Some even attempt to escape when confronted by police (Wilson and Storey 1991). Minorities' reluctance to report crime or cooperate with police investigations is partly a reflection of this distrust of police, and partly the fear of recrimination from offenders, especially those from the same ethnic community. Researchers in the Northern Territory also found evidence of this historical factor:

> The majority of people interviewed during this project described police operations in their country of origin in negative terms. The main reasons given were perceptions of bribery and corruption, over-policing and the tendency

to use violence. Filipino people commented frequently on individual instances of bribery, while Vietnamese people tended to view the police as part of one arm of an oppressive regime. [O'Neill and Bathgate 1993: 140]

The strained relations between some Aboriginal communities and the police might be expected to produce a similar problem of non-cooperation. However, very little has been written about it, perhaps because conflicts between Aborigines and police in some cases have gone beyond passive non-cooperation and have taken on confrontational features of 'riots' (see Foley 1984: 184; Cunneen and Robb 1987; Cunneen 1990a).

The problems outlined in this chapter are not new, but police–minorities relations in Australia were not subject to a great deal of public or academic scrutiny until the late 1960s and early 1970s (Lucas 1995). The 'very significant levels of police intervention in Aboriginal lives' during the nineteenth-century period of dispossession and the twentieth-century experience of 'protection' have largely escaped recording and accountability (Finnane 1994: 124–5). It is perhaps no coincidence that police racism emerged as a public issue in the 1970s, in a climate of growing political activism among Aboriginal people, wordwide movement towards civil rights and decolonisation, and declining police legitimacy amidst allegations of corruption (Lucas 1995). The discourse of government policies since the 1970s – which moved away from assimilationism towards multiculturalism, non-discrimination and reconciliation with Aboriginal people – also facilitated and encouraged closer scrutiny and documentation of discriminatory practices. Nevertheless, there is little to be gained by merely producing a catalogue of problems. Complaints of police racism, though disturbing in themselves, raise more fundamental questions about policing in a multicultural society. First, are complaints of police racism justified? If so, why does it exist and why is it tolerated in police forces? Is police racism simply part of the wider racist culture in Australian society, or is it peculiar to policing? Finally, if police racism is a problem, what can be done about it? The next two chapters will explore some of the answers to these questions.

Notes

1 The majority of Aboriginal people lived in New South Wales (26 per cent), Queensland (26 per cent), Western Australia (16 per cent) and the Northern Territory (15 per cent). However, indigenous people comprised 23 per cent of the population in the Northern Territory, compared with a maximum of 3 per cent in other States.
2 (1976) 11 ALR 412 (NT Sup Ct).

CHAPTER 2

Discrimination and Police Work

The problem of police racism is subject to varying interpretations. While many people would find the descriptions in the last chapter alarming, others are just as likely to dismiss them as exaggerated or isolated incidents. Whether police racism is perceived as a problem largely depends on how the nature and function of police work are understood. One popular view often advanced by police officers themselves, for example, is that police work is predominantly reactive: police officers mostly react to situations as they arise and as they are called to attend, and so it can be argued that certain minority groups are 'over-policed' precisely because they cause more trouble or commit offences more frequently. Thus, police racism does not really exist, or it can easily be explained away, and hence nothing needs to be done about it. In direct opposition to this view, however, is a belief that police are acting as agents of an essentially racist or oppressive system that criminalises behaviours among the powerless, including visible minorities. Hence racism is not simply an occasional feature, but an institutionalised component, of police function. Moreover, there is no simple solution to the problem: it requires the empowerment of minorities in their struggle for self-determination against the existing structures of domination and criminalisation.

There are, of course, other perspectives which take a less critical view of the policing function, but nevertheless do not see policing as strictly reacting to law-breaking activities. These explanations centre on the structural and cultural organisation of police work. For example, even though the criminal law may not be a crude instrument of the ruling classes, police work is often focused on the type of 'crime' that involves the poor and the powerless. Hence, minority groups in disadvantaged positions are likely to be over-policed compared with powerful members of the dominant culture. Alternatively, one can argue that discriminatory practices are tolerated because of the laxness of legal regulation and administrative control of police officers. Police racism is therefore the result of an inadequate system of accountability. Finally, it can be asserted that racism is embedded in and sustained by the informal occupational culture of police work. Thus, although discrimination is formally prohibited, the nature of street-level police operations is such that stereotyping, harassment, and even violence are routinely tolerated. The code of secrecy and solidarity among officers ensures that instances of discrimination are rarely discovered and, if so, are almost impossible to prove.

The purpose of this chapter is to unravel the assumptions and arguments behind these different ways of interpreting police racism. The three main perspectives which will be examined are abbreviated as reactive policing, institutionalised racism, and the organisation of policing. While each perspective highlights a particular aspect of the problem, it tends to obscure other, perhaps equally important, dimensions. It will be argued that the most useful theories are those that are capable of taking into account the complexity of the problem without distorting the lived experiences of the people involved – the visible minorities as well as the police officers.

Reactive Policing

The first perspective assumes that police forces are a natural, organised response to crime and disorder in society. They 'represent the successful achievement by the modern state as a means of social control in the absence of the norms and social bonds of traditional community life' (Finnane 1994: 10; also see Reiner 1992 and Brogden *et al.* 1988). Hence, a popular defence put up by police regarding allegations of over-representation and over-policing of minority groups is that police operations are reactive or demand-driven. It follows that police arrest more members of minority groups because they commit more crime; they deploy more officers in certain minority communities because demands for police service are greater in those communities. By extension of the same logic, police defend their targeting of minorities by referring to statistical evidence of minorities' past involvement in crime, and justify their use of excessive force on account of minorities' resistance to arrest. In other words, police are just 'doing their job', and usually doing it under very stressful circumstances. As suggested in the following discussion, there is some evidence in the literature to support the claim that what could be regarded as discriminatory outcomes of policing may be no more than the outcomes of normal policing. In general, however, these results are inconclusive.

Problems with Statistical Evidence

Walker's review of the statistical evidence from Britain illustrates the range of problems encountered in interpreting so-called race and crime statistics. Many of these problems are applicable in the Australian context. Walker points out at the very beginning that 'it would be unwise to draw conclusions regarding black *criminality* from official records', and she gives a number of well-known reasons:

> The black [Afro-Caribbean] and white populations differ in many respects, such as age, employment and social deprivation. Besides this, the statistics of arrests are the outcome of a series of events which depend on decisions made by the public (in reporting to the police) and the police (in arresting a suspect and deciding to prosecute), as well as the behaviour and visibility of the suspect. [Walker 1987: 39]

Using estimates of offence recording rates from the British Crime Survey (Hough and Mayhew 1983) and clear-up rates from the London police, Walker calculated the probability of arrest for burglary and robbery offences for black and white suspects, based on the hypothesis that the two groups offended proportionately to their numbers in the population. She found that if offending rates were the same for blacks and whites, the probability of black people being arrested for a burglary must be four and a half times that of white people; for robbery, it would have to be fourteen times greater. The author left it to the judgment of the reader whether such a degree of discrimination in police practice was plausible.

Since a large proportion of arrests (estimated at 20 to 57 per cent in London) come about as a result of police stopping people on the street, it is important to investigate whether the higher rate of arrest of black people is due to their higher rate of being stopped by the police. It has been well documented that young, unemployed males of minority groups are more likely to be stopped and arrested by the police (Smith 1983: 309). In combination, these factors create an 'overwhelming effect' on the likelihood of being stopped. Smith (1983: 309–10) found that for men aged between 15 and 24, the probability of being stopped was 63 per cent for West Indians, 44 per cent for whites and 18 per cent for Asians. Unemployed men were six times as likely to be stopped when on foot as those who have a job, while professional men were less likely to be stopped when on foot than men in other socio-economic groups.

Walker did not see these results necessarily as an indication of police discrimination, since black people might have been stopped more often because they were more likely to be unemployed, on the streets between 10 p.m. and 6 a.m., and unskilled manual workers. Her general conclusion is in the form of a plea for better data and more sophisticated analyses:

> Black people are over-represented in the Metropolitan Police District statistics of people arrested and of 'official' offenders and this may be due to a combination of factors. For example, the black community, as a whole, tends to be young, of low socio-economic status (having high proportions of unemployed and of manual workers) and 'socially deprived' and these are characteristics associated with offenders. In order to draw any valid conclusions regarding arrest and offender rates comparisons need to be made controlling for as many as possible of these characteristics. [Walker 1987: 54–5]

Other factors which Walker suggests should be 'controlled for' include the area of residence of the offender, the crime reporting rate, and the clear-up rate.

Controlling for Legal and Socio-demographic Factors

One of the most exhaustive investigations of the issue of over-representation of Aborigines in the Australian criminal justice system was carried out in relation to the arrest of Aboriginal youth in South Australia. Gale and Wundersitz (1987; see also Gale *et al.* 1990) examined the files of more than 7000 juvenile appearances before Children's Aid Panels and the Children's Court in Adelaide during a twelve-month period in 1983–84. As expected, Aboriginal youth were significantly more likely to be arrested (instead of being given a summons or notice) than non-Aboriginal youth (48 per cent compared with 17 per cent). The decision to arrest was then analysed in relation to 'legal' variables (such as the type of offence, the number of charges laid, the number of previous Court or Aid Panel appearances, and whether or not the juvenile was an absconder or under an existing order) and socio-demographic variables (such as· age, gender, residential address, family circumstances, and the employment status of the juvenile). Using logistic regression techniques, the researchers found 'no statistical evidence to indicate that, at the point of arrest, police overtly discriminate against Aborigines on racial grounds'(Gale and Wundersitz 1987: 92). Thus, they were able to 'explain away' the differential treatment of Aboriginal children by the fact that (a) young Aborigines were more likely to be charged with more serious offences and to have prior records of apprehension, and (b) young Aborigines were more likely to be unemployed and living in non-nuclear families.

These findings, of course, do not really answer the question of whether Aboriginal juveniles were arrested more often because of normal policing or discriminatory policing practices. Instead, they raise further questions which the researchers asked at the end of the paper: why should employment status make a difference, why were Aboriginal youth charged with more serious offences, why did they have more charges laid against them, and why were they more likely to have prior appearance records? Does it mean that the police were discriminating against the unemployed? Since the decision to arrest and the type and number of charges laid are subject to police discretion, did Aboriginal juveniles engage in more serious and more frequent offending behaviours or were they the victims of (cumulative) discriminatory police practices?

A later study examined similar data on juveniles in New South Wales for a twelve-month period in 1990 (Luke and Cunneen 1995). The sample consisted of 2165 police cautions and 16,100 finalised court appearances; about 15 per cent of these involved Aboriginal children. The data showed that Aboriginal children had a lower chance of receiving a formal caution and a higher chance of being charged and being refused bail compared with non-Aboriginal children. When only first offenders (with no prior court appearance or caution) were considered, the researchers found that Aboriginal juveniles were still being prosecuted at a higher rate than non-Aboriginal juveniles (87 per cent compared with 78 per cent). The difference was particularly large in rural New South Wales. When the type of offence was held constant by limiting the analysis to break-and-enter offences, the pattern remained, although the gap was narrower (91 per cent compared with 83 per cent), but there was virtually no difference in the Sydney area. Aboriginal first offenders were also more likely to be charged (instead of given an appearance notice or a summons) than non-Aboriginal first offenders. The authors conclude that:

> The study indicates that Aboriginal young people are more likely to receive harsher outcomes from police decisions to apprehend and prosecute, even when offence and criminal history differences are controlled for. It seems that young Aboriginal people have a 10–15% greater chance of going to court rather than receiving a formal police caution. While this difference is not large, the compounding effect over time may be very significant, particularly in relation to decisions concerning first offenders where the acquisition of a criminal record is likely to influence later discretionary decisions. [ibid.: v]

Since it was not possible to explain away the differential treatment of Aboriginal children by legal factors, the authors called for changes in police practice.

One aspect of the two studies worth further exploration is the apparent similarity of treatment between Aborigines and non-Aborigines in urban centres. Results of the NSW study regarding prosecution and those of the South Australian study regarding arrest were consistent in this regard: when young offenders from urban areas (Sydney and Adelaide, respectively) were considered alone, the NSW study found that the probability of first offenders being prosecuted for break-and-enter offences was virtually identical between Aborigines and non-Aborigines (85.4 versus 85.5 per cent), while the South Australian study found that the probability of arrest for first offenders charged with break and enter was also identical between the two groups (9.6 per cent). These findings are also consistent with the results of a survey in Manchester, England, where there was little difference between West Indians and white people in reported rates of police stop, search or arrest (Tuck and Southgate 1981). According to Walker (1987: 48), the difference between the Manchester results and the London results was explained by the fact that the Manchester data were derived from small homogeneous areas. In their 1987 study of arrest rates between blacks and whites in Leeds, England, Jefferson and Walker (1992) grouped the city into 'lighter' areas (those with less than 10 per cent non-white population) and 'darker' areas (those with more than 10 per cent non-white population). For males between 11 and 25 years of age, the researchers found that in the darker areas, which tended to be more socially disadvantaged with higher unemployment, whites had *higher* arrest rates than blacks, while the trend was reversed in lighter areas. This surprising result may be due to under-reporting by black victims of offences committed by black offenders, or under-recording of these offences by the police 'in the interests of improving race relations' (*ibid.*: 87).

Observational Studies

While statistical studies using official data have not offered conclusive explanations of differential policing practices, observational studies have produced equally inconclusive results. American studies have explained the higher arrest rates among blacks and minorities (even when the seriousness of the offence was taken into account) as the result not of overt discrimination, but of situational factors such as the lack of respect for police demonstrated by the suspects or the presence of complainants who demanded an arrest (Black 1971; Lundman *et al.* 1978; Sykes *et al.* 1976). An observational study by James (1979) of a special British crime squad to deal with black crimes in an urban police station concludes that police used the same techniques at every point of the arrest and questioning process regardless of whether they were dealing with black or white suspects. Thus the author suggests that it is normal policing, not racist policing, which is the problem.

The observational study by Smith and Gray (1983) of the police in

London is probably one of the most extensive and in-depth examinations of police practices in relation to ethnic minorities. Two male researchers studied a wide range of police work over a two-year period by observing police officers, conducting formal and informal interviews, and analysing internal documents. The researchers found that racist language and racial prejudice were 'prominent and pervasive' among police officers, and, on the whole, these are 'expected, accepted and even fashionable', and never discouraged or opposed by their peers or senior officers (*ibid.*: 109–10). Occasionally, 'Apart from these casually abusive references, there is a vein of deliberately hostile and bitter comment on black people by police officers' (*ibid.*: 113). Some of this hostility to black people is linked with 'racialist theories, right-wing politics, fear of violence and disorder caused by black people, a psychological need for retribution and the view that violent retribution is legitimate' (*ibid.*: 115). Although the police officers who expressed racist ideology or initiated racist talk were, in the judgment of the researchers, a minority, they were responsible for shaping the norms and setting the expectations of the group, to such an extent that officers who were not prejudiced had come to adopt the racist language in conformity to the group. In terms of actual practice, however, the researchers argued that it would be wrong to assume that discriminatory or hostile behaviour necessarily followed from the prevalence of racist talk among police officers. Indeed, one of the researchers witnessed an instance where an officer, having just used the term 'spades' to describe black people, showed remarkable professionalism in handling a case with a black victim (*ibid.*: 126).

The researchers described the encounters between police officers and black people as 'fairly relaxed' even in the six months before the 1981 Brixton riots broke out, although there was a higher level of tension for some time after the riots. They also did not observe police making racial remarks to the public, but conceded that their presence might have influenced police behaviour. Their conclusion was that there was 'no widespread tendency for black or Asian people to be given greatly inferior treatment by the police' (Smith and Gray 1983: 128). This conclusion is actually not as unequivocal as it appears, since the authors used words such as 'obvious' in terms of racial motivation, 'widespread' in terms of behaviour, and 'greatly inferior' in terms of treatment of minorities. As well, the conclusion was heavily qualified by the authors themselves. In their view, unequal treatment could come about as the result of various factors: police stereotyping ('police officers tend to make a crude equation between crime and black people ... [and] to justify stopping people in these terms'); assumptions about communities (police are reluctant to act over matters involving Asians because they feel that the Asians do not want police to intervene); fear of repercussions (police may tend to be careful with black people because of the repercussions of mishandling the matter); and situational hostilities (where police are confronted with large numbers of hostile minorities as in a riot). These factors operate in addition to actual racial prejudice (two such instances were given).

Social Disadvantage, Offending and Over-policing

A case study of crime and policing in the north-west region of New South Wales provides a combination of statistical, social and historical understanding of the over-representation of Aborigines in the criminal justice system (Cunneen and Robb 1987). The region studied has the highest proportion of Aboriginal population in the State. An analysis of the social and economic indicators showed that Aboriginal people had an extremely high rate of unemployment and suffered severe disadvantage in areas of housing, health, education and dependence on social security (*ibid*.: 35).

The authors dismissed a single cause of over-representation of Aborigines in the police statistics. They reasoned that it would be unlikely that the level of over-representation could be accounted for by police discrimination alone, since to achieve such outcomes statistically, the police would *either* have to ignore about 15,000 offences committed by non-Aborigines *or* invent over 2000 offences committed by Aborigines in one year. Thus, Aboriginal people might have a higher rate of offending as a result of poverty and social disadvantage, but they were also over-policed through a selective use of public order and drunkenness offences. The two aspects were not seen to be mutually exclusive:

> It might be noted that the over-commission of offences by Aboriginal people and over-policing are not necessarily two separate issues but indeed feed off one another as part of a continuum. In this sense the historical relationship of Aboriginal people to policing is important. A part of Aboriginal popular memory in the north-west is the history of large scale police intervention into everyday life. As a response to that history there is often aggressive hostility shown towards police in the public sphere. [Cunneen and Robb 1987: 222]

Two New South Wales studies have examined the relationship between social disadvantage and the rate of offending. The report *Kids in Justice* (Youth Justice Coalition 1990: Chapter 4) explored the relationship between juvenile offences and the socio-economic and demographic characteristics of six local government areas in New South Wales. The areas chosen were Willoughby, Campbelltown, Bourke,

Wagga, Shoalhaven, and South Sydney. The results, based on Children's Court data in 1988–89, were as follows. Bourke, a remote rural town which had the highest rate of youth unemployment (35.8 per cent) and the highest percentage of families receiving the supporting parent's benefit (16.9 per cent) also had the highest juvenile offence rate (94.8 per 1000 10–19-year-olds).[1] A breakdown of offences by category (*ibid.*: 127) shows that Bourke also had the highest proportion (35.3 per cent) of 'good order' offences. This was attributed to the 'over-zealous' use of public order offences against Aborigines by the police (*ibid.*: 139). At the other extreme, Willoughby, an affluent residential area on the north shore of Sydney, which had the lowest rate of youth unemployment (12.5 per cent), and the lowest percentage of families receiving the supporting parent's benefit (2.0 per cent), also had the lowest juvenile offence rate (12.2 per 1000). In addition to drawing attention to social and economic factors related to offending, the report also provides qualitative information about each of the areas, documenting the 'conflict involving competing views of the public space' between cultures and age groups in these communities. While limited in scope, this study has begun to explore the relationship between social disadvantage and juvenile offences at a geographical level.

The link between regional data on offending and socio-economic indicators was explored more thoroughly in relation to adult offences (Devery 1991). Using Local Court appearances data from 1987 and 1988, Devery calculated measures of offending for each of 176 Local Government Areas by counting the number of 'proven offenders' who reside in the given area. These data were then compared with population and socio-economic data derived from the 1986 Census. Offences not included were assaulting police and offensive behaviour, which are 'sensitive to variations in policing'. Using correlation and principal component analysis, Devery found that a higher level of socio-economic disadvantage (e.g. a high proportion of single parents, Aborigines, unemployed people and public renters) in a community significantly increases the risk of criminal offending in that community.

Devery disagrees with Cunneen's notion of 'over-policing' (but see Cunneen 1992 for a discussion of the usefulness of the concept). He explains the high level of police personnel in north-western towns such as Bourke, Brewarrina, Walgett and Wilcannia as reflecting the high crime rate and hence high demand for policing services in these areas. Instead, Devery uses his findings to suggest that the over-representation of Aborigines in arrest and court appearances in north-west New South Wales may be a result of 'multiple deprivation'. Citing the results of a study by Ross and Whiteford (1990), Devery notes that Aborigines 'are more likely to be unemployed, more likely to be in poverty and more likely to live in single-parent families' – factors which are associated with high conviction rates. Devery argues that variation in policing resources alone does not account for the differences in conviction rates. In fact, Devery's and Cunneen's positions are not irreconcilable:

> *This is not to say that policing is an insignificant factor, particularly when it comes to Aboriginal communities. However, it is possible to give too much weight to the role of policing in the production of high crime rates in some areas.* If we dismiss the link between Aboriginality and court conviction rates, arguing instead that the link can be explained by over-policing, then we make the assumption that the social and economic marginalization of Aborigines has no influence on their risk of committing crime ... [Devery 1991: 26, my emphasis]

Clearly, it is misleading to argue that the relationship between economic and social disadvantage and crime is consistent with only one interpretation: that is, *either* disadvantaged people commit more crime *or* disadvantaged people are more likely to be criminalised by the justice system. In fact, two recent US studies on juvenile crime found evidence to support all of the following interpretations:

- Economic deprivation is strongly associated with diminished regulatory capacity of a community, which in turn has the strongest direct effect on delinquency (Bursik and Grasmick 1993). This is consistent with the indirect effect of economic adversity implicit in 'social disorganisation' theory.[2]
- Economic deprivation also has a significant direct effect on delinquency (Bursik and Grasmick 1993). This is consistent with a perspective that suggests that crime is an alternative means of gaining sustenance.[3]
- Racial inequality and concentration of 'underclass' poverty influence the level of formal control exercised by the juvenile justice system (Sampson and Laub 1993). This is consistent with the hypothesis that underclass blacks are considered threatening by middle-class populations and thus subjected to increased control.

It should also be pointed out that if alternative sources of information on offending are used (e.g. self-report data), the issue of differential enforcement no longer arises. Fergusson *et al.* (1993), for example, made use of self-report and parental report data on offending to study a birth cohort of 1265 children born in an urban area of New Zealand. Their results showed that children of Maori or Pacific Island descent were between 1.45 and 2.25 times more likely to offend before the age of fourteen than children of Pakeha (European) ethnic status; but these differences were no longer statistically significant (except for one category, 'other offence') when social, economic and family factors were controlled for. Even before adjustment, the self-report offending differentials between the ethnic groups were much smaller than the differentials evident in official statistics. Some of the discrepancy may be explained by discriminatory enforcement practices, although self-report studies often pick up different types of offending behaviours.

In this section the claim that police racism is not responsible for the over-representation of minorities in the justice system has been investigated. Studies linking social and economic disadvantage to criminal convictions and proven Children's Court outcomes in New South Wales (Devery 1991; Youth Justice Coalition 1990) suggest that Aborigines may have higher offending rates as a result of social and economic disadvantage. However, there is also evidence that the over-representation of Aboriginal children in the juvenile justice system cannot be explained by socio-economic factors alone and discriminatory police practices cannot be ruled out (Gale *et al.* 1990). The cumulative effect of differential treatment at various stages of the justice process is also a cause for concern (Luke and Cunneen 1995).

Institutionalised Racism

Critical interpretations of police work assume that the essence of policing is to carry out a 'coercive, class-based "civilizing" function' (Jefferson 1991: 168; see also Brogden *et al.* 1988). Within this perspective police are 'inevitably, and usually wilfully, the agents of an oppressive state' (Finnane 1994: 10). Hence, police racism is seen as institutionalised oppression, given the historical and structural positions of minority groups, especially Aboriginal people, in Australian society. Inequality of power and opportunity is built into social and political institutions. Violence and abuses suffered by minorities have become a part of life. Thus, while individual police officers may or may not be racially prejudiced, they are inevitably part of the oppressive apparatus of the dominant classes of society. Examples of this type of interpretation can be found in the report of the National Inquiry into Racist Violence:

> The 'Redfern Raid' graphically illustrates the concept of institutionalised racism in action. The individual officers were not necessarily motivated by racism, they simply believed that this was an appropriate way to deal with the Aboriginal community. [HREOC 1991: 212]

The analysis by Gordon (1983) of police racism in Britain begins with the premise 'There can be no doubt that police officers are racist', but argues that individual prejudice does not constitute the main explanation for racist policing:

> The British state defined black people as a problem, both through immigration laws to keep them out, and through measures of 'integration' designed to manage the 'problem' already here. In this management of the 'black problem' the police have played a key role ... They have not acted as mere servants of the state, doing what was asked of them. They offered their own definition of black people as a policing problem, a definition which both reflected the institutionalised racism of the state and society at large and reinforced it. [*ibid.*: 73]

Gordon sees racism as linked to the political economy of black labour in Britain: where black workers were once sought for post-war economic reconstruction, they became a problem when their labour was no longer required (Gordon 1992).

Commenting also on the situation in Britain, Jefferson (1993: 10) claims that police racism is '*not* primarily about discriminating against young black males, but rather about the production of a criminal Other in which, currently, young black males figure prominently' (original emphasis). Because policing is bound up with the imputation of suspicion and criminality, the demarcation between the respectable and the disreputable, the exercise of coercive force and the maintenance of the dominant social order, discriminatory practices are often 'justified' by 'utilizing a discourse of criminality rooted in notions of differential crime proneness' (*ibid.*: 3). Racist policing constructs a 'reality' that certain groups are more disorderly, more deviant than others, and hence more deserving of police attention and police action, when, in fact, officers are afforded considerable discretion in relation to decisions to stop, search, arrest, and charge:

> what all this amounts to is that being the wrong age, sex and class, in the wrong place at the wrong time, displaying the wrong demeanour and attitude, spells 'trouble' to police, whatever the colour of your skin ... [*ibid.*: 19]

Reiner comes to a similar conclusion that the problem of police prejudice in Britain is not an individual attitudinal problem, but a structural problem: 'a reflection of the racism prevalent in British society and the social groups from which the police are drawn, as well as the situations in which many police–black encounters occur' (Reiner 1985: 161). There is, however, some doubt as to whether racist attitudes invariably lead to discriminatory or abusive police practices. Observational research by Smith and Gray (1983: 334–5) in London, mentioned earlier, finds that, in spite of their general hostility and racist attitude towards black people, the police often have 'friendly and relaxed relations with individual black people in specific circumstances'. It may be that using institutionalised racism as a general explanation of racial stereotyping and discriminatory police practices is at best simplistic in its conception of the state, and at worst an excuse for not recognising other important dimensions of the problem:

> this sort of characterisation of all police and all aspects of policing as equally and undistinguishably racist precludes any serious analysis of how and why policing changes, and of separating out potentially positive developments within police strategy and thinking. The state, and its coercive apparatus the police, are blanketed together as a monolithic reflex of the racist logic of capital. [Reiner 1985: 167]

There is no doubt that racist sentiments are present and perhaps even rampant in some sections of Australian society and among police officers, and that social and political institutions have not, by and large, ensured that marginal and disadvantaged groups, such as Aborigines and other visible minorities, are not further disadvantaged by the system. To recognise that there are other dimensions to the problem of police–minorities relations is not to deny the existence of institutionalised racism in Australia, but to begin to discover the concrete areas in which disadvantage and discrimination are built into the criminal justice system, so that appropriate countermeasures can be formulated and put in place.

Organisation of Policing

The third perspective being examined is in fact a combination of theories, all sharing the same assumption that the existence and toleration of police racism are related to the way in which police work is organised structurally and culturally. For example, while police may see themselves as merely reacting to crime, the type of 'crime' considered worthy of police attention is often biased against the poor and the powerless. Hence discriminatory practices are built into the legal framework and management strategies of police work. Another view is that police racism is inadequately controlled by the existing structure of police accountability: officers are given wide discretion with minimal supervision, but are rarely disciplined or punished for discriminatory practices. Finally, a powerful argument can be made that police officers have developed an occupational culture which informally tolerates and covers up such practices.

Legal and Management Focus of Police Work

Brogden *et al.* (1988) have argued that normal policing *is* discriminatory against certain categories of people, such as young, black, working-class, because discrimination permeates the nature and context of police work. Policing practice reflects the current priorities and values built into our laws and institutions. For example, the bulk of police work is not directed at white-collar or corporate offences, but at what are loosely referred to as 'street crimes' and other comparatively minor crimes against persons and property. The existence of legal discretion and the cost of tackling the crimes of the rich and powerful have meant that 'Any organization wanting to maximize outputs and minimize trouble for itself would take a similar line of least resistance'; that is, it would focus on the control and criminalisation of the poor and powerless, especially by means of highly discretionary legal powers in relation to public order offences (*ibid.*: 147). Similarly, because of the traditional association between poverty and crime, police services have been in greater demand, and hence police resources and activities have been concentrated in predominantly working-class areas, or areas where other social services have failed to meet the needs of their residents. Here, those who deviate from society's images of middle-class respectability and conformity are often considered by police as 'trouble'. Every interaction with citizens involves a moral judgment of their social risk and the potential exercise of coercive force. Young, working-class, unemployed, and non-white people who spend a great deal of their leisure time in public space are often easy targets for police harassment and questioning, a practice which would not find many opponents among the 'respectable' members of society. Thus, the authors argue, it does not require deviant police practices or illegal use of police powers to explain why the young, the poor, and ethnic minorities receive discriminatory treatment by the police:

> Given the nature of the criminal law, these groups find many of their routine activities on or close to the borders of illegality. Given the nature of police deployment the activities of such groups get more than their fair share of attention. Given the nature of police cultural stereotypes, the activities of such groups are more likely to be negatively evaluated. And given police discretion … such negative evaluations can be acted upon. Thus it is that the law, police deployment, cultural stereotyping and police discretion combine to produce a criminalized class … [*ibid.*: 149]

Control of Police

Another frequently advanced theory explains the toleration of discriminatory police practices in terms of the inadequacy of existing accountability and disciplinary mechanisms. The National Inquiry into Racist Violence found a widespread perception among Aboriginal people that 'police are not accountable for their actions' and that police violence is either ignored or not dealt with (HREOC 1991: 210). The inquiry was told that most people did nothing about police malpractice because they believed that it would be a waste of time. People were deterred by the fact that complaints were to be lodged with police and investigated by police. In general, complaints procedures are seen as inaccessible to members of minority groups. A survey conducted by the Commonwealth Ombudsman in 1992 found that 43 per cent of people of non-English-speaking background and only 30 per cent of Aborigines had heard of the office of the Ombudsman, compared with more than 60 per cent of the respondents from Australia or other English-speaking countries. Among those who were aware of the Ombudsman, there was a generally poor level of understanding of the process and a fair degree of distrust of the system. The NSW Ombudsman explains the low level of complaints from Aborigines as a consequence of the perception that the 'system is structured against them':

> Complaints have to be in writing and provide enough detail on which to pursue inquiries. Where literacy is not an insurmountable problem, letters often relate a litany of grievances against many authorities and the police role is bound up with more general matters. The scope of the Ombudsman's jurisdiction is often difficult to explain. Aboriginal Legal Services tend to advise against complaining because they have little confidence in the system and they fear the possibility of a complaint compromising their position in any related criminal charges. [NSW Ombudsman 1992: 44]

Again, the issue of police investigating themselves and the fear of future harassment were raised as real concerns among Aborigines.

The use of criminal law against police malpractice is a course fraught with difficulties. As an outspoken former Director of Public Prosecutions observed, because of their 'position, knowledge and experience', police officers are less likely to plead guilty and much more likely to be acquitted in a criminal trial than normal (Bongiorno 1994: 38). In general, police officers enjoy significant advantages over ordinary citizens in the criminal justice process: they are far more competent in handling themselves during investigative interviews and courtroom cross-examinations; they are more likely to be supplied with competent, experienced defence counsel by their unions; and their membership in the police force means that they are investigated by officers who are in some sense 'friendly' to them and backed up by witnesses who are generally sympathetic. The use of intimidatory tactics by friends of accused officers against witnesses is not unheard of (*ibid.*: 39). It is also not unusual for the defence to be in possession of confidential documents such as 'intelligence reports on witnesses, privileged legal opinions and analyses of evidence' from police sources (*ibid.*: 39).

Police Culture

Police culture refers to more than the cultural background of police officers. Of course, one factor which contributes to strained police–minorities relations may be that most police officers come from an Anglo-Australian background and have great difficulties coping with different cultures. Police in the Northern Territory, for example, have expressed concerns about the difficulty of working with Aboriginal communities (O'Neill and Bathgate 1993: 30). The National Inquiry into Racist Violence also received a suggestion that ignorance or misunderstanding of Aboriginal culture was often an underlying cause of conflict (HREOC 1991: 211). Ignorance of minority cultures, insensitivity to other traditions, or intolerance of cultural differences may have led to ethnic stereotyping and racial prejudice, as well as a reluctance to use professional interpreters if police assume that certain minority groups tend to lie about their lack of facility in English. What police researchers have called 'police culture', however, is one that is peculiarly tied to the occupation.

The concept of 'police culture' originally emerged from ethnographic studies of routine police work which uncovered a layer of informal occupational norms and values operating under the apparently rigid hierarchical structure of police organisations (Cain 1973; Manning 1977, 1989; Holdaway 1983). The meaning of police culture is loosely defined. Manning (1977: 143) refers to the 'core skills, cognitions, and affect' which define 'good police work'. It includes 'accepted practices, rules, and principles of conduct that are situationally applied, and generalized rationales and beliefs' (Manning 1989: 360). Reiner (1992: 109) equates it with the 'values, norms, perspectives and craft rules' which inform police conduct. Skolnick (1966) speaks of the 'working personality' of a police officer. Features of police culture are said to include: a sense of mission about police work, an orientation towards action, a cynical or pessimistic perspective regarding the social environment, an attitude of constant suspicion, an isolated social life coupled with a strong code of solidarity with other police officers, political conservatism, racial prejudice, sexism, and a clear categorisation of the public between the rough and the respectable (Reiner 1992: 111–29). Among these characteristics, the so-called 'siege mentality' and 'code of silence' have often been linked with the concealment and proliferation of police misconduct.

As Van Maanen (1978a: 116) points out, police are not unique in having developed a distinctive culture, since 'Workers in all occupations develop ways and means by which they manage certain structural strains, contradictions and anomalies of their prescribed role and task.' Most police researchers have concentrated their studies on the occupational culture of policing *at the street level*. Nevertheless, a well-recognised distinction has been made between the 'street cop culture', which yearned for the 'good old days' when 'the public valued and respected a cop, fellow officers could be counted on, and superior officers or "bosses" were an integral part of the police family', versus the 'management cop culture', which sought to clean up, professionalise and make the police more productive, efficient and responsive to the community (Reuss-Ianni and Ianni 1983).

Even though police forces are typically organised along the lines of a militaristic bureaucracy, police officers exercise extremely wide discretion at the street level. Decisions by street-level officers are usually made with little or no supervision:

> because police tasks at the lower levels are ill-defined, episodic, nonroutine, accomplished in regions of low visibility, and are dispatched in ways that most often bypass the formal chain of command in the organization, control over the work itself resides largely in the hands of those who perform the work (Banton, 1964; Cain 1973; Manning 1977). In this sense, police agencies resemble symbolic or mock bureaucracies where only the appearance of control, not the reality, is of managerial concern. [Van Maanen 1983: 277]

The reality of police work, then, allows a great deal of room for individual officers' discretion in decisions to stop, search or arrest suspects (Cain 1973; Manning 1977). Such discretion is often informed by stereotypes of what constitutes 'normality' or 'suspiciousness'. The occupational culture, therefore, condones various forms of stereotyping, harassment or even violence against those who are seen to be 'rough' or 'disreputable'. The code of secrecy and solidarity among officers, an integral part of this culture, ensures that deviant practices are either covered up or successfully rationalised.

Several assumptions are implicit in most discussions about the police occupational culture: that there is a close relationship between the demands of police work and the existence of the culture; that the culture is relatively stable and uniform over time and space; and that the culture has a negative influence on police practice.

Relationship with Demands of Police Work

The existence of a direct connection between the demands of police work and the development of the occupational culture has been suggested by a number of researchers. Skolnick (1966) sees the 'working personality' as a response to the danger of police work, the authority of the police constable, and the pressure to be productive and efficient. Reiner (1992) similarly suggests that the 'cop culture' develops as a way to help police cope with the pressure of police work. Van Maanen (1978a) points out that the nature of police work, the potential for danger, the shift work, the uniform, the sense of isolation, and the proliferation of rules and regulations within police departments all contribute towards the formation of this culture. For example, cynicism and 'hardness', qualities commonly attributed to police officers, are developed as ways of coping with the hostility and degradation often encountered in the course of 'doing society's dirty work' (*ibid.*: 120).

Police culture is therefore not primarily negative. It is seen to be functional to the survival of police officers in an occupation considered to be dangerous, unpredictable, and alienating. The bond of solidarity between officers 'offers its members reassurance that the other officers will "pull their weight" in police work, that they will defend, back up and assist their colleagues when confronted by external threats, and that they will maintain secrecy in the face of external investigations' (Goldsmith 1990: 93–4). The development, transmission and maintenance of this culture are assumed to be also related to the demands of police work (Reiner 1992: 109).

Stability over Time and Space

If aspects of the police culture are 'rooted in the recurrent problems and common experiences of police' and they 'arise as a way of coping with, and making sense of, a given environment' (Manning and Van Maanen 1978: 267), one would expect the occupational culture of policing to be fairly homogeneous among officers working under similar conditions. Indeed, referring to studies of police in the United States, in Europe and in Asia, Skolnick and Fyfe (1993: 92) observe that the 'fundamental culture of policing is everywhere similar ... since ... the same features of the police role – danger, authority, and the mandate to use coercive force – are everywhere present'. Manning and Van Maanen also comment on the culture's 'remarkable stability through time' and its persistence in spite of external efforts to change it:

> In the operational environment of the ... street level of policing, many old habits and traditions have survived largely intact despite the persistent efforts

of officialdom to introduce new ideas, tighter organizational controls, and sophisticated technologies into the daily affairs of patrolmen. Even the introduction of better educated and more highly trained recruits has provided precious little encouragement for those seeking to alter the police culture from the inside. This latter point is particularly crucial, for it suggests that there are powerful means available within the occupation that act to systematically discourage innovation while they encourage the status quo. [Manning and Van Maanen 1978: 267]

Negative Influence on Police Practice

Although police culture is seen as functional to the survival and sense of security among officers working under dangerous, unpredictable and alienating conditions, it is the negative, rather than the positive, influence that has become prominent in discussions about police culture. The Fitzgerald Report (1989: 200), for example, found that within the Queensland Police Force at the time, there was a culture of 'contempt for the criminal justice system, disdain for the law and rejection of its application to police, disregard for the truth, and abuse of authority'. Fitzgerald has emphasised that the 'unwritten police code' was a 'critical factor in the deterioration of the Police Force': the so-called 'police code' has helped police 'verballing' and corruption to flourish within the force while protecting wrong-doers from detection and prosecution. More recently, the Mollen Report (1994) made a similar link between police culture and police corruption in New York City.

    This type of explanation is an example of what is called 'subcultural' theories of criminality (see, generally, Downes and Rock 1982: Chapter 6). Originally used for explaining juvenile delinquency, subcultural theories postulate that delinquent groups conform to a subculture which condones deviant behaviour. When applied to police racism, subcultural theory views discriminatory practice as an integral part of the nature and condition of police work; it also explains why it is so difficult to detect and prevent such practice. Subcultural theories are attractive in that, by conceiving of deviance 'as a solution … to dilemmas' that police officers face (ibid.: 115), they explain the apparent rationality of deviant behaviour to those inside the subculture. They also help those outside the subculture to understand why it is usually difficult to 'correct' such behaviour. The main problem with subcultural theories is the way culture is conceptualised. Typically, it is conceived in 'functionalist' terms, which means that there is a kind of circularity in logic when the cause of deviant behaviour is equated with its beneficial consequence. For example, it may be true that a code of silence regarding deviant activities among police officers can lead to internal solidarity once such a code has been established. However, it would not be quite as believable to explain a conspiracy to cover up deviance as something promoted by police officers in order to bring about internal solidarity (see *ibid.*: 90–3 for a critique of functionalism). In any case it should be emphasised that subcultural theories are only one of many possible explanations of police misconduct. Other equally powerful theories include the lack of external control, the abundance of criminal opportunities, learning theory, and thrill-seeking explanations.

The theories canvassed in this section all locate explanations of police racism within the structural and cultural organisation of police work. The advantages of these theories over reactive policing and institutionalised racism are substantial. Without accepting the commonsense view that police officers are merely responding to crime or dismissing all policing efforts as part of an oppressive racist system, these theories are able to explain:

- the over-policing of certain minorities in terms of the legal framework and management strategies of policing;
- the stereotyping and harassment of certain minority groups in terms of the police cultural attitude of constant suspicion and the categorisation of people according to perceptions of respectability;
- the abuse of power and excessive use of force against certain minority groups in terms of the police culture of secrecy and solidarity, as well as the inadequacy of the accountability structure; and
- the tolerance of these practices within the organisation in terms of the positive function of police culture.

Of course, these explanations have disadvantages as well. In some ways they can be criticised for being too narrow in focus. By concentrating on the organisation of police work, these perspectives ignore social factors that may have led to differential offending patterns among social groups, which in turn may have affected the way these groups are being policed. These theories also lose sight of the way racism may have been historically embedded in the wider social and political institutions of Australian society. Nevertheless, theories based on the organisation of police work are useful for capturing the complexity of the problem of police racism and understanding why it is such an intractable and pervasive problem in policing. They are also more consistent with the lived experience of visible minorities (who find it difficult to accept that police harassment is simply 'reactive policing') and that of police officers (those who are sympathetic to anti-racist policies find it insulting to be treated as mere agents of a racist system). Not surprisingly, police reform strategies are predominantly guided by these theories. The next chapter provides an overview of these strategies.

Notes

1 Offence rates are based on total proven outcomes in Children's Court 1988–89 per 1000 population aged 10–19 years. There appears to be an inconsistency in the report between page 126 and page 133: the offence rate was based on 'per 1000 10–19 years old' in the former and 'per 1000 15–19 years old' in the latter. I assume that the latter was incorrect.

2 Note that studies based on aggregate rather than individual-level data (such as Devery 1991) are fairly limited in their ability to explain delinquent behaviour because of the 'ecological fallacy' (see Farrington et al. 1986), e.g. even if economic deprivation and delinquency rates are correlated over time or space, this does not necessarily mean that economically deprived youth are more likely to commit crime than other young people. It is possible that offenders choose to live in 'socially disorganised' areas.

3 A recent study of over 700 disadvantaged Australian youth (Daniel and Cornwall 1993: 16) reported that young people who were consulted

readily made the link between poverty and crime ('It's either steal, or starve') ... Virtually all stealing and dealing, they believed, started because of grinding poverty and the instinct to survive. After the initial try it became easier to continue. In every focus group participants stated that lack of money (income) forced some young people to resort to crime.

A study by Presdee (n.d.: 41) of young people in Adelaide also concluded that many were committing crime 'in order to subsist'.

CHAPTER 3

Strategies for Change

Reformers have advocated many strategies for improving relations between police and minorities over the years. While some of these strategies are specifically directed at the so-called 'race relations' aspects of policing, there is increasing recognition among police reformers that problems of police–minorities relations require more than piecemeal or localised changes. Rather, poor relations between police and minority groups are a reflection of more general deficiencies in either police training or police management. In order to achieve fundamental change, these deficiencies need to be dealt with, not as isolated problems, but systematically. Evidence of a willingness to change can be found in virtually all Australian police forces. At a national conference in 1990, senior police from all States and Territories of Australia, New Zealand and Fiji, community leaders, government representatives and researchers met to examine the trends and issues of police service delivery to multicultural communities (Australian Bicentennial Multicultural Foundation [ABMF] 1990). An impressive array of initiatives undertaken by Australian police forces was presented at the conference. In some instances, there have been substantial changes to the police organisation, including recruitment, training, philosophy and style of policing. In others, innovative experimental programs are being trialled. Where traditional policing emphasises arrests and charges, fast cars and random patrol, the new vision of policing is one of being accountable to the community and establishing a partnership with the community in policing. It recognises the ineffectiveness of traditional policing methods as well as the resourcefulness of the community in matters of crime prevention and social control. Following the conference, a National Police Ethnic Advisory Bureau was set up as a joint initiative of all Australian police commissioners, the Australian Bicentennial Multicultural

49

Foundation and the Department of Immigration and Ethnic Affairs. The bureau was to act as a national agency to provide advice and to assist police to develop appropriate policies and programs to deliver service to multicultural communities (see Etter 1993).

This willingness to change coincided with a worldwide disillusionment with the paramilitary model of traditional policing and a national move to professionalise the policing occupation in Australia (Etter 1992). In 1992, Australian police commissioners identified seven key and critical issues of the future of policing: the role of the police, the environment, police professionalism, police accountability, police and other agencies, technological advancements, and the change process. The 'increasingly multicultural nature of the Australian community' was one of the environmental considerations. The 'blueprint for the future' of policing was not one of piecemeal tinkering with police practices or the police image, but a dramatic departure from traditional policing:

> Police, in order to be competitive and to attract the resources necessary to fulfil their role of the future, must become outward-looking, increasingly sensitive to developments and trends in their environment, responsive and resilient to change, innovative and creative in their approach to problem solving and idea generation, and more open and accountable to the community and Government. [Northern Territory Police 1991: 32]

Thus the strategies of policing in a multicultural society are not an augmentation of traditional policing; they are part of a totally new approach to policing, which emphasises innovation, change, problem-solving, openness and accountability.

The purpose of this chapter is to examine critically the strategies that are typically advocated or introduced to improve police–minorities relations and to combat police racism. These strategies are largely based on the assumption that change must be directed at the structural or cultural organisation of policing. In effect, they do not subscribe to the notion that police work is purely demand-driven so that discriminatory practices can be justified by differential offending patterns among minority groups. Nor do they consider the perspective that policing takes place in a context where racism has been institutionalised in every form of social and political life (see Chapter 2). A convenient way of describing these reform strategies is to adopt the typology used by Brogden et al. (1988). They distinguish between two main approaches to achieve police accountability: the first advocates tightening of rules as a means of controlling police discretion, while the second aims at changing the informal culture of police organisations. In the following sections, these two approaches will be described in relation to initiatives taken in Australia.

The relative merits of tightening rules compared with cultural change strategies will also be discussed with reference to the available literature. It will be seen that the majority of initiatives taken by Australian police forces to improve relations with minority groups are directed at changing police culture.

Tightening Rules

Rules may be tightened by means of a range of measures, including changes to legislation, administrative rules, codes of practice, accountability procedures or policy guidelines. This approach is found, for example, in many of the recommendations of the National Inquiry into Racist Violence:

- That the Federal Government accept ultimate responsibility for ensuring, through national leadership and *legislative* action, that no person in Australia is subject to violence, intimidation or harassment on the basis of race ...
- That *statutory codes of practice* be developed for police in relation to Aborigines and Torres Strait Islanders and people of non-English-speaking background to ensure better protection of the rights of those people and clearer accountability of police.
- That police operations reflect the *principles* of equity and equality towards people of Aboriginal and non-English-speaking backgrounds and ensure that particular communities are not targeted for extraordinary policing measures.
- That racist violence, intimidation and harassment by members of the police forces be considered a serious *breach of duty* and attract severe *penalties*, including dismissal from the force. [HREOC 1991: 270, 332, my emphasis]

In the wake of the Brixton riots in Britain, Lord Scarman made similar recommendations that prejudiced and discriminatory behaviour be included 'as a specific offence in the Police Discipline code' and that the normal penalty for breaching this code be dismissal (Scarman Report 1981: 201). Scarman also recommended that the law regarding police power to stop and search should be rationalised and additional safeguards introduced; that lay visitors to police stations should make random checks on interrogation and detention of suspects; and that independent investigation of complaints against police be introduced (*ibid.*: 207–8).

In general, rule-tightening involves the making or changing of internal or external rules (Brogden and Shearing 1993: 107–22). Internal rule-making includes the setting of 'professional' standards, codes of practice, as well as various paper or technological (voice or video) record-keeping requirements to increase the 'transparency' of police practice. External rule-tightening includes legislative reform, independent appraisal of police effectiveness through victim surveys, reform of complaints systems, and the establishment of monitoring schemes such as lay visitors or other more interventionist auditing functions (*ibid.*: 120–2). Two examples of such strategies in Australia are the formulation of policy statements on ethnic or Aboriginal affairs and the legislation of rights to interpreters.

Policy of Access and Equity

The Commonwealth government has maintained a policy of access and equity as part of its National Agenda for a Multicultural Australia (Office of Multicultural Affairs 1989). Virtually all Australian police forces have made commitments to provide accessible and equitable service to ethnic minorities. In some forces this principle is implicit in their general policy, while in others it is explicit in a formal statement.

For example, in New South Wales, all government departments and statutory authorities were requested by the Premier to prepare an Ethnic Affairs Policy Statement (EAPS) and submit an annual report to the Ethnic Affairs Commission regarding their progress in achieving previously set objectives. The 1988 NSW Police Service policy statement 'commits all portions of the Police Service to provision of services that are both accessible, ethical and appropriate to all members of ethnic minority groups, in accordance with the statement of values' (NSWPS 1988a: 18). This was updated in the *Ethnic Affairs Policy Statement Strategic Plan 1992–1995* to link the EAPS with the NSW Police Service's Corporate Plan (see NSWPS 1992). The EAPS structure was replaced in 1993 by a New South Wales Charter of Principles for a Culturally Diverse Society (see Chapter 7 for details of the EAPS program in New South Wales).

Similarly, the Victoria Police's Statement of Principle contains a commitment to 'providing professional and equitable service on a 24-hour basis to the community of Victoria, irrespective of race, colour, descent or national or ethnic origin, gender, social standing or religion'. The force is 'opposed to any forms of racism and will not tolerate any expression of racially motivated conduct by its members'. The goals are to 'provide services responsive to the needs of the community', to establish 'long-lasting harmonious relations with the ethnic communities', and to 'eliminate barriers that may now exist' (see Victoria Police, n.d.: i).

The utility of such formal statements lies principally in the exercise of setting goals, designing performance indicators, establishing schedules and anticipating obstacles – an exercise that each police organisation normally undertakes as part of its strategic planning. Annual reporting, where required, is then supposed to oblige the organisation or an external agency to monitor and assess its achievements. The recognition of cultural diversity in the community and the commitment to provide equal and accessible services to all people are, of course, an important step forward. However, as will be explored in the New South Wales case in Chapter 7, these broad statements of policy do not provide adequate guidance in terms of everyday police work and, unless gross levels of discrimination against ethnic minorities can be proved, such statements have minimal effect on police practices. In other words, these policy statements need to be backed up by relevant programs, adequate resources, appropriate administrative support, rigorous monitoring, and an effective accountability structure.

Statutory Right to Interpreters

A major component of providing accessible and equitable police services to ethnic minorities is overcoming the language barriers. In Australia, both federal and State governments provide professional interpreter services which police forces can make use of on a user-pays basis (see Chapter 5). Police forces have different rules regarding the use of professional interpreters, and a great deal of discretion is exercised by individual police officers in judging whether a person has adequate English-language skills (CAGD 1990).

Except in Victoria, South Australia and the federal jurisdiction, however, there is no statutory right for citizens to have access to interpreters when dealing with the legal system. In Victoria, the *Crimes (Custody and Investigation) Act* 1988 requires that a person arrested by the police be given the right to an interpreter if he or she 'does not have a knowledge of the English language that is sufficient to enable the person to understand the question'. A specialised Legal Interpreting Service was established within the Victorian Ethnic Affairs Commission. The service provides interpreters 24 hours a day and seven days a week to designated public agencies. Police are required to contact the service 'in the first instance, where an interpreter is required' (ABMF 1990: 45). Its training officers also train police officers in the use of interpreters (CAGD 1990).

The reluctance of some police officers to use qualified interpreters when dealing with ethnic minorities has been regarded as a reform issue, even in jurisdictions where the right to interpreters is provided by legislation (see Chapter 1; NSW EAC 1992; ALRC 1992: 57; Wilson and Storey 1991: 18; O'Neill and Bathgate 1993: 142). Financial cost and delay are the usual justifications for police reluctance to use interpreters.

The technical and ethical standards of some interpreters are also the subject of complaints by users of interpreting services.

It would appear, however, that the use of qualified interpreters is also guided by external considerations. Police tend to use professional interpreters when preparing cases for prosecution, in order to prevent having their evidence disputed in court. The introduction of electronic recording of police interrogation in some jurisdictions has also meant that the usage of qualified interpreters is virtually mandatory for indictable offences. Petty offences and casual inquiries, on the other hand, are often dealt with using friends and relatives, local business people, ethnic liaison officers, or police officers who speak the language (see Chapter 5). Some police forces encourage those officers who have linguistic skills in community languages to assist in appropriate circumstances.

The decision to use or not to use professional interpreters is obviously not always a straightforward one for police officers. Statutory requirements do not take away the need for officers to make judgments regarding the English facility of the person in custody. As well, budgetary and organisational considerations often come into play. Reformers bent on limiting discretion could go on to add layer upon layer of rules. For example, discretion could be further restricted by detailed instructions and guidelines; practices could be monitored internally or externally for abuse; or courts could rule inadmissible evidence obtained without a professional interpreter; and so on.

Weaknesses of Rule-tightening

The rule-tightening approach assumes that police organisations are bureaucratic and mechanical (see Morgan 1986: Chapter 2; Colebatch and Larmour 1993), so that changes in practice can be brought about by changes in rules imposed from the top or from an external body. Studies of police organisations have discovered, however, that police bureaucracies are an embodiment of contradictions. Police organisations assume the appearance of a quasi-military, hierarchical structure which is based on rules and oriented towards commands. Yet control of police management over subordinate officers is extremely limited because of the nature of police work (Van Maanen 1983: 277). As in other complex organisations, researchers have found that with police officers, 'it is the immediate work or peer group and not the larger organization that motivates and controls the individual's behaviour' (Reuss-Ianni and Ianni 1983: 251).

Thus, attempts to impose change from above have rarely succeeded. In the New York City Police Department, where the 'management cop culture' and the 'street cop culture' confront each other, resistance to change was strong at the bottom:

> The street cops who are still into the old ways of doing things are confused and often enraged at the apparent change of the 'rules' of the system. So they fight back in the only way they have at their disposal: foot dragging, absenteeism, and a host of similar coping mechanisms and self-defending techniques. [*ibid.*: 270]

A familiar scenario in police organisations is one in which police executives are enthusiastic and optimistic about change, but for patrol officers at the 'coalface', it is business as usual. Yet, it is precisely on the streets that the police interact with citizens, especially victims of crime and suspected offenders. Change, if it has any meaning at all, has to be demonstrated when police officers stop a motorist, interview a victim, question a juvenile, carry out an investigation, and arrest a suspect. The difficulty of effecting change from the top down implies that changes imposed from outside the organisation are even more likely to be circumvented (see Chapter 7). Despite the weaknesses of the 'sociologically impoverished' conception of organisations as machines (Brogden *et al.* 1988: 164), however, rule-tightening remains a popular option among police reformers. Failures of rule-tightening measures are often met with further calls for rule-tightening.

Changing Police Culture

Disillusionment with rule-tightening as a way of reforming the police leads to a growing interest in the second approach: changing the police culture. Brogden and Shearing have observed that when rules are not congruent with practice, police often find ways of 'ingeniously' getting around the rules. They argue that rule-making must be complemented by strategies 'to change the culture from inside' (Brogden and Shearing 1993: 97). In their evaluation of the British law reforms in the 1980s, McConville *et al.* (1991: 193) similarly question the utility of law reform as a method of changing police practice, given the occupational culture's resistance to change, although they concede that changes in laws did have some impact on behaviour and that wider impact could be achieved through further fine-tuning of the rules. The authors suggest that to change police practices, an 'attack upon police occupational culture' would be necessary. This is to be achieved by redefining the police mandate and instituting new forms of accountability. The uneven impact of law reform on police practices was also observed by Reiner, who concludes that legal regulation is of limited effectiveness: 'key changes must be in the informal culture of the police, their practical working rules' (Reiner 1992: 232).

Brogden and Shearing (1993) mention two ways in which 'orthodox' solutions seek to change police culture: first, by 'taking the police to the community', and second, by 'bringing the community to the police'. In Australia, the first approach includes various recruitment and training strategies, while the second typically involves 'community policing' strategies. These will be discussed briefly.

Recruitment and Training

The idea of this approach is to attract a different category of recruit and provide better police training so that police become more responsive to community needs. A number of recommendations by the National Inquiry into Racist Violence relate to issues of training and recruitment:

- That police training include appropriate education in cultural issues and community relations and provide for supervised placements in areas with significant numbers of persons of Aboriginal and non-English-speaking backgrounds.
- That the elimination of racist attitudes and practices be accorded an essential place in the recruitment and training of police, and that such attitudes and practices not be condoned in policing operations.
- That Federal and State police forces promote the recruitment of persons of Aboriginal and non-English-speaking backgrounds, and provide special training programs to ensure that persons of those backgrounds are able to meet recruitment standards and prerequisites. [HREOC 1991: 333]

The Royal Commission into Aboriginal Deaths in Custody (Johnston 1991) also recommended that Aboriginal people be actively recruited into police forces and that an understanding of Aboriginal history and the history of police–Aborigines relations be made a substantial part of police training. In Britain, Lord Scarman also recommended the recruitment of more black people into the police, and the improvement of police training to give more attention to 'training in the prevention, as well as the handling, of disorder, and in an understanding of the cultural backgrounds and the attitudes to be found in our ethnically diverse society' (Scarman Report 1981: 200).

In recent years, with the push for professionalisation of police in Australia, police education and training have boomed. Many police forces have made substantial revisions to their training curriculum; there is a move away from a focus on operations towards a wider educational base, emphasising 'effective skills training in the areas of communication, negotiation, conflict resolution, cross-cultural awareness and the proper use of police discretion' (Etter 1992; NSW Police Recruit Education Programme 1991).

Cross-cultural training is reportedly carried out in virtually every police force in Australia. The Western Australia Police, for example, provides cross-cultural awareness training within its cadet traineeships, its recruit training and, until 1992, as part of all in-service training. In October 1992, a federally funded scheme was introduced to provide two-day workshops on cross-cultural training for all police officers (MacGregor n.d.). The Queensland Police Service made use of a Mobile Cross-Cultural Awareness Training Unit to conduct about 380 hour-long workshops throughout the State (Queensland. Criminal Justice Commission [QCJC] 1993: 51). In the Northern Territory, cross-cultural awareness issues are covered in the Aboriginal Affairs and Ethnic Affairs modules of recruit training, which consists of 20 hours of material presented over ten weeks.

While the intentions of these training initiatives are laudable, there is evidence to suggest that the effect of training recruits is often undermined by the reality of police work and the 'commonsense' of the police occupational culture (Brogden *et al.* 1988: 32–3; Centre for Applied Research in Education [CARE] 1990). Cross-cultural awareness training, in particular, must be conducted with great care, or it can confirm existing prejudices rather than lead to greater tolerance of minority cultures (Southgate 1984). In general, training and education must be seen to be relevant to police operations and pitched at a practical rather than an abstract level. Training must also be reinforced and supported by peer groups and senior officers if it is to have any long-term influence on behaviour. A review of the Northern Territory program in 1993 found that it lacked police-specific information and immediate relevance:

> Police were concerned that training needed to reflect north/south distinctions in Aboriginal cultures; that it should be specific to the locality; that training should occur closer to their transfer to the specific locality rather than at the end of recruit training; that it should be more concerned with contemporary issues rather than 'dreamtime' and history. [O'Neill and Bathgate 1993: 155]

The employment of Aborigines in Australian police forces has become an important issue following the Royal Commission into Aboriginal Deaths in Custody. Given the low number of Aboriginal police officers in the police forces,[1] the federal Labor government provided funds through the Department of Employment, Education and Training for the implementation of the Royal Commission's recommendations. The Queensland Police Service, for example, has implemented an Aboriginal and Torres Strait Islander (ATSI) Pilot Program which involves the design and accreditation of a bridging course for Aborigines who are interested in joining the police but who do not have the educational qualification to gain entry. Students who have completed the six-month certificate course are eligible to compete for recruitment. The Queensland Police also appointed a consultant to develop strategies for ATSI recruitment and career development (QCJC 1993: 30). Similar bridging courses exist in New South Wales (see Chapter 6) and in Western Australia.

Aboriginal police aides are employed in the Northern Territory, Western Australia and South Australia. In the Northern Territory, police aides perform two main functions: as law-enforcement agents with limited police powers, and as liaison officers in their communities. Suitable candidates are nominated by the Aboriginal community, although police reserve the right to decide on appointment from the nominees. A review of the police aide scheme found support for it among police, police aides and the communities. However, there were problems relating to coordination and supervision, morale, training, career, and working conditions (O'Neill and Bathgate 1993: Chapter 2).

Difficulty in attracting suitably qualified minority members to join the police appears to be a common problem in the United States, Canada and Britain (Thomas-Peter 1993). In Australia, there is a similar reluctance among certain ethnic communities to join the police, and those who do join sometimes find themselves in a difficult position with respect to their own communities. Once inside the police force, minority officers face a number of difficulties, including name-calling and racist prejudice within the police ranks, while also being resented by white members of the public (Wilson et al. 1984). Police management has begun to recognise that minority officers must be given the same career opportunities as other officers and not have these opportunities limited because they are 'needed' in their own community.

Community Policing

The second method of changing police culture typically involves the building of direct links between the police and the community. This includes many of the initiatives under the umbrella of 'community-based policing', such as community consultative committees, Neighbourhood Watch, and other community crime-prevention programs. The theory is that 'if the police culture is subject to continuing encounters with community sensibilities, it is liable to undergo a positive modification' (Brogden and Shearing 1993: 103). Accountability to the local community is also supposed to influence the occupational culture by providing 'an alternative reference group, away from the immediate work-group influence of police peers' (*ibid.*: 104).

The adoption of community-based and problem-solving policing strategies (see Alderson 1983; Weatheritt 1987; Bayley 1989; Goldstein 1979) is by far the most significant ideological shift in recent years in Australian policing (Moir and Moir 1992). This approach emphasises the importance of involving the community in a partnership relationship in policing, and de-emphasises the traditional police preoccupation with random patrol, fast car response, and retrospective criminal investigation. A partnership with the community is manifested in various community liaison activities, the appointment of liaison officers, the establishment of crime-prevention measures such as Neighbourhood Watch and Safety House, an increased use of foot patrols, and the encouragement of grass-roots feedback through community consultative committees.

The benefit of a community-based policing strategy for multicultural communities is that when police work is geared to a local level of accountability, the provision of quality service to ethnic minorities is no longer a marginal issue for police commanders whose jurisdictions have a sizeable minority population. In some cases, information pamphlets and phrase books are printed in community languages, multilingual liaison officers are employed, and language-specific community consultative groups are set up. Most of the efforts are directed at reducing the distance between police and ethnic minorities, instilling confidence and building support among ethnic minorities.

The rhetoric of community policing is found in almost all Australian police forces. In Queensland, for example, the traditional, reactive style of policing used by the Queensland Police was severely criticised by the Fitzgerald inquiry. The inquiry recommended that community policing be adopted as the 'primary policing strategy', so that the force could move 'towards mobilising the community and its police to prevent crime, maintain order and deliver services dictated by the needs of the community' (Fitzgerald Report 1989: 381). The corporate plan of the Queensland Police Service now reflects a strong emphasis on community policing, which consists of four 'programmatic elements': (a) the organisation of community-based crime prevention, including community consultative committees and various community watch schemes; (b) a reorientation of patrol activities towards visibility, awareness of community concerns, and order maintenance; (c) increased accountability to local communities and (d) decentralisation of command.

A 1994 review of the implementation of reform in the Queensland Police Service found 'a significant expansion of Neighbourhood Watch...', Safety House and Adopt-a-Cop programs', 'improved liaison with the ATSI community, and, to a lesser extent, other minority groups'. In addition, other projects had been established, such as the Women's Safety Project, the Beat Policing Pilot Project in Toowoomba and the Police–Community Network in Inala (QCJC 1994: 67). In terms of police–minorities relations, the review reported the establishment of a small Cross-cultural Support Unit with cross-cultural officers appointed at each of the metropolitan regional offices, the appointment of forty-five ATSI liaison officers to deal with drug and alcohol abuse issues, and the formation of liaison groups such as an ATSI Police Advisory Committee and an Ethnic Advisory Group.

In general, however, the review did not think that the Queensland Police Service had achieved its goal of putting the philosophy of community policing into practice:

- Steps to improve police–community liaison have concentrated on generic programs without sufficient regard to the needs of individual communities.
- Problem-solving is not yet a standard police response ...
- Apart from two high-profile projects, there has been little change to police patrol practices, and little increase in the numbers of police 'walking the beat'. [QCJC 1994: 68]

The review found that the concept of community policing was not 'widely understood or accepted' within the Queensland Police Service. It was 'associated with "soft", public relations-oriented, activities which are peripheral to the "real" business of policing' (*ibid.*: 70).

This result is not surprising (see also the experience of New South Wales in Chapters 5 to 10). In spite of its attractive rhetoric, community policing is more often talked about than practised. The review by Bayley (1989) of community policing in Australia suggests a widespread confusion of community policing with public relations, a common perception of the former as a soft option, a failure by its proponents to make a convincing case for its adoption, and a tendency to view community policing as a marginal or add-on specialty rather than an integral part of all policing activities. The concept of community-based policing is often interpreted in a tokenistic and superficial way, so that there is no real equality in partnership between the police and the minorities. Consultation of the community tends to involve respectable and established members of the community rather than those seen to be marginal or troublesome by the police, and police rarely see operational issues as an appropriate matter for consultation with the community. While Bayley is optimistic about community policing expanding and being more widely implemented in Australia in the future, there appears to be a clear need for police forces to evaluate their present efforts and to develop a more comprehensive and comprehensible model of what community policing consists of in all aspects of mainstream police activities.

Weaknesses of Cultural Change

The cultural change approach to police reform is based on a model of organisation which is the opposite of the machine metaphor. Rather, police organisations are seen as havens of subcultural practices which may bear little relationship to official policies. In effect, policies are made by the 'street-level bureaucrats' (Lipsky 1980), who exercise considerable discretion in their work, rather than by ministers or top-ranking officials.

However, if deviant cultural practices are developed by street-level officers to cope with the demand and uncertainty in their work, changing the workforce (through recruitment or training) is unlikely to have any impact on such practices. Brogden and Shearing (1993) suggest that policing style is unlikely to change as a result of changes in recruitment policy. For example, women recruited into male-dominated police forces adapt either by embracing the male police culture, and thus becoming 'defeminised' into *police*-women; or by taking on a more traditional, service-oriented role, and thus becoming 'deprofessionalised' into police-*women* (see Martin 1980; Sutton 1992; Heidensohn 1992; Young 1991).[2] Similarly, there is evidence that black officers recruited into predominantly white police forces in the United States become committed to the *status quo* and take on the 'working personality' of white officers (Cashmore 1991). In Britain, research has shown that police officers recruited from minority ethnic groups tend to accept racist jokes and banter as inevitable and part of the occupational environment (Holdaway 1991; 1995).

Improved police training is likewise ineffective in changing deviant cultural practices unless the nature and structure of police work are substantially transformed:

> In the case of racism, the evidence suggests that the culture is too resilient to be significantly modified in this way. Any initial impact of anti-racist training is lost soon after the trainee officer is placed 'on the street' as the culture, with its immediate relevance, resumes as the key practical teaching guide. In South Africa, such changes to date have been essentially cosmetic, *ad hoc*, and ignore the racism embedded in the institutions of training themselves (Rauch 1992), [Brogden and Shearing 1993: 102]

The building of direct links between the police and the community also has its problems. In Britain, where community consultative committees were set up to satisfy the requirement of the *Police and Criminal Evidence Act* 1984, there was a divergence of views about the purpose of these committees: whether they were to be an instrument of democratic local control over police policy, or a forum of consultation 'without power and formal political accountability' (Morgan 1987: 32). The composition of the British committees illustrates the problems inherent in this strategy:

> Committee members are seldom under 30 years of age and typically are active 'respectable' members of the community ... They are not generally people who have been in conflict with the police or have adverse personal experience of them. Groups hostile to the police typically dismiss consultative committees as a meaningless charade on the grounds that they lack power and are merely for public relations; such groups often refuse to be involved. [*ibid.*: 33]

Community consultative committees were originally intended to involve members of the community in the planning of police operational strategies. However, according to Morgan (1987: 39), operational policy was rarely a topic for discussion in the British committees, partly because most committee members preferred to leave operational matters to the police, and partly because of the sensitivity of such matters when police discretion was exercised. Members who sought information on operational policy tended to be marginalised and labelled as troublemakers.

The problem, as Smith (1987: 63) points out, is that there is not going to be a consensus about the kind of policing the community wants. There is not one public, but many, and policing is about dealing with conflicts, often between some of these publics (see also Moir and Moir 1992): 'The idea of community cannot be successfully applied to policing if it is used to avoid finding the forms and institutions needed to strike a balance between conflicting demands' (Smith 1987: 63–4).

I have argued in Chapter 2 that the most useful theories for understanding the existence and tolerance of police racism are those which take into account the structural and cultural organisation of police work. Police racism exists and is tolerated because it is in some ways *embedded* in the nature of police work, in the structure of police accountability, and in the informal police culture. It therefore makes sense that anti-racist strategies should follow the two general approaches outlined in this chapter, that is, tightening the regulation and control of police practice or changing the police culture. Yet it is clear from the literature that both approaches have serious flaws: regulation from without and control exercised from the top are often ignored or subverted, while strategies aimed at changing culture mostly produce the appearance rather than the reality of change. Brogden *et al.* (1988: 167) have argued that the crucial issue is not 'whether formal rules should be tightened *or* the cop culture co-opted', but the *relationship* between formal rules and subcultural values. They suggest that deviant cultural practices are allowed to thrive in police organisations because formal rules and structures are too 'permissive'; therefore the tightening of formal rules should be seen as the primary concern in the change process:

> the key lies with the formal rules, on the grounds that it is the permissiveness of the external structure (the uncontrolled discretion), and the concomitant internal permissiveness (an inevitable consequence of a system of legal accountability which renders operational policy redundant) which creates the *space* for occupational culture to flourish. Controlling the (external) discretion would leave the (internal) culture with few spaces to flourish. At *that* stage, with the rules tightened, co-optive work on the cop culture ... would be important – but as a subordinate not superordinate factor in the process of change. [*ibid.*: 170, original emphasis]

While this argument seems plausible at first sight, it is both practically and conceptually misleading. In practice, externally imposed rules are not always successful in narrowing discretion. If regulation is not always effective, it makes little sense to talk about it as a *primary* factor of change. At the conceptual level, it is misleading to suggest that police culture can thrive only in the space created by discretion. While it is true that a *different* culture may be created when rules are tightened, there is no guarantee that it is a 'better' culture. The relationship between formal rules and informal culture is rarely quite so straightforward. In fact, it can be argued that the debate about how police reform should be achieved has been *based on a faulty conception of police culture*: that the culture is uniform, unchanging, powerful, and somehow separate from formal structures. The notion that police officers all become 'socialised' into this all-encompassing and unchanging police culture, and that it dictates their values and their actions, seems as believable as that of the monolithic racist state apparatus which takes over every aspect of social life. This notion of police culture explains everything and it explains nothing.

Is it time, then, to discard this tired, old concept? I think not. I argue that it is important to retain a conception of the informal, and often invisible, aspects of social life, and to explore their relationship with social practice. Empirical research on police work has uncovered something which could be vital to our understanding of how and why police racism is tolerated in police organisations, as well as why reforms seem to make little difference to policing practice. Rather than discarding the notion of police culture because of inadequate theorising, I argue that the theories need to be reconsidered. This is what I shall attempt to do in the next chapter.

Notes

1 Froyland and Skeffington (1993) reported that there were at least 20 Aboriginal police officers in the Northern Territory out of a force of 700; 163 in New South Wales out of 16,000; 3 or 4 in South Australia out of 4000.
2 In fact these are not the only two responses but two ends of a continuum. As Heidensohn (1992: 86) points out, 21 of the 28 female officers observed by Martin (1980) were in between these two extremes.

CHAPTER 4

Re-examining Police Culture

It was argued in the last chapter that the debate about how police should be reformed – whether through law reform or cultural change – has been stymied by an inadequately theorised notion of police culture. The purpose of this chapter is to identify the weaknesses of the current theories and demonstrate a more fruitful approach. I will begin with a general critique of the traditional formulation of the concept, and then go on to discuss how police culture can be reconceptualised to provide more useful answers to questions such as why reforms often make little difference to police practice. The reconstructed framework makes use of a cognitive model of culture, while adopting Pierre Bourdieu's concepts of 'field' and 'habitus' to represent the structural conditions of policing and the learned dispositions of police culture respectively. Central to this formulation is the active role played by police actors, who develop a certain 'practical consciousness' (Giddens 1984) in relation to a given set of working conditions. The final section of this chapter explains how this framework applies to the relations between police and visible minorities in Australia and discusses its implications.

Problems with Current Theories

There are four major criticisms of the way police culture has been con-ceptualised. In spite of Reiner's acknowledgement that the 'cop culture' is not 'monolithic, universal nor unchanging' (Reiner 1992: 109), police culture is often described as though it is. Indeed, the first criticism con-cerns the failure of existing definitions of police culture to account for internal differentiation and jurisdictional differences. What is often described as the police occupational culture in fact refers to the 'street cop culture', rather than the 'management cop culture' (Reuss-Ianni and Ianni 1983). Manning observes that police organisations are structurally and culturally diversified:

> The police as an organization do not possess a 'common culture' when viewed from the *inside*. Instead, there is an elaborate hierarchical rank structure which replicates the social distribution of secret knowledge. Police organizations are segmented, specialized and covert to a striking degree. Social relationships among policemen are based to an unknown extent upon *differential information* and ignorance, a structural fact that maintains organizational stratification ... [Manning 1978b: 244, original emphasis]

Manning (1993) has suggested that there are 'three subcultures of policing': command, middle-management, and lower participants. My research in New South Wales finds that officers in middle-management positions held a distinctively negative view of the organisation. Differences were also detected between officers holding different functional responsibilities (see Chapter 9). Thus, a theory of police culture should account for the existence of multiple cultures within a police force and variation in cultures among police forces.

The second criticism relates to the implicit passivity of police officers in the acculturation process. Reiner (1992: 109) suggested that officers are not 'passive or manipulated learners', but did not elaborate on the nature of the 'socialisation' process. Fielding's research in Britain demonstrated that the individual officer is the 'final arbiter or mediator' of the structural and cultural influences of the occupation (Fielding 1988: 10). While the culture may be powerful, it is nevertheless up to individuals to accommodate or resist its influence:

> One cannot read the recruit as a cipher for the occupational culture. The occupational culture has to make its pitch for support, just as the agencies of the formal organization exert their influence through control of resources. The stock stories of the occupational culture may be effective as a means of ordering perception which maximizes desirable outcomes. If they contradict the recruit's gathering experience they are likely to be dismissed. [*ibid.*: 135]

Similarly, the salience of work demands and occupational pressures is mediated by individual experiences. For example, a focus on risk and uncertainty is part of the enacted environment (Weick 1979) of police work, since the perception of danger 'is constructed and sustained by officers in the course of their routine work' (Holdaway 1983: 19; also see Manning 1989, Fielding 1988). Thus, a sound theory of police culture should recognise the interpretive and active role of officers in structuring their understanding of the organisation and its environment.

The third criticism of police culture as currently formulated is its apparent insularity from the social, political, legal and organisational context of policing. Some have argued that police corruption and misconduct could not exist without the tacit approval of the community (Sparrow *et al.* 1990: 133–4). There is evidence that the secrecy and solidarity of the culture sometimes break down under the strain of external investigations. Punch (1985) has documented the internal conflict and divisions caused by a corruption scandal in a Dutch police force, although he was pessimistic about its eventual impact on corrupt practices. The NSW case study shows that top police management was not insulated from public scandals but was constantly in damage-control mode (see Chapter 8). A theory of police culture must, therefore, situate culture in the political and social context of policing.

The final criticism is related to the first three: an all-powerful, homogeneous and deterministic conception of the police culture insulated from the external environment leaves little scope for a cultural change. As Manning (1993: 14) suggests, 'the tensions apparent in the occupational culture generally and between the organization and the environment are the dialectic source of change in policing'. A satisfactory formulation of police culture should allow for the possibility of change as well as resistance to change.

In the following sections, I shall outline an alternative theoretical framework for understanding police culture. The framework will have to address the criticisms raised in this section: it must account for the existence of multiple cultures, recognise the interpretive and creative aspects of culture, situate cultural practice in the political context of policing, and provide a theory of change.

A Reconceptualisation

Several useful ways of theorising about culture can be found in the literature. In particular, Schein's and Sackmann's cognitive perspective of culture provides for the existence of multiple cultures within a police organisation. Shearing and Ericson's phenomenological treatment of culture recognises the active and creative role played by members of the police force. Finally, Bourdieu's relational theory, which explains cultural practice as the result of interaction between cultural dispositions (habitus) and structural positions (field), situates culture in the social and political context of police work. All three perspectives provide for some theorising of change. Each of these perspectives will be discussed in turn.

Culture as Knowledge

Organisational theorists provide a useful framework for conceptualising police culture. For Schein (1985: 57), culture is the property of a stable social unit which has a shared history. Culture is a 'learned product of group experience'. Although Schein distinguishes between three levels of culture, namely artifacts, values, and basic assumptions, he stresses that the term culture should be 'reserved for the deeper level of *basic assumptions* and *beliefs* that are shared by members of an organization' (*ibid.*: 6). His definition of organisational culture is particularly appropriate when applied to police organisations:

[Culture is] *a pattern of basic assumptions – invented, discovered, or developed by a given group as it learns to cope with its problems of external adaptation and internal integration – that has worked well enough to be considered valid and, therefore, to be taught to new members as the correct way to perceive, think, and feel in relation to those problems* [*ibid.*: 9, emphasis in the original]

Sackmann, adopting Schein's definition, describes the essence of culture as 'the collective construction of social reality'. Her model of culture encompasses all forms of shared organised knowledge: 'the form of things that people have in their minds; their models for perceiving, integrating, and interpreting them; the ideas or theories that they use collectively to make sense of their social and physical reality' (Sackmann 1991: 21). She classifies cultural knowledge in organisation into four dimensions: (a) *dictionary knowledge*, which provides definitions and labels of things and events within an organisation; (b) *directory knowledge*, which contains descriptions about 'how things are done' generally in the organisation; (c) *recipe knowledge*, which prescribes what should or should not be done in specific situations; and (d) *axiomatic knowledge*, which represents the fundamental assumptions about 'why things are done the way they are' in an organisation. Axiomatic knowledge, often held by top management, constitutes the foundation for the shape and future of the organisation. It may be adjusted or revised from time to time as a result of critical evaluations or growing experience.

Like Schein, Sackmann sees cultural cognitions as being held by groups rather than individuals. These cognitions are socially constructed, and may be changed or perpetuated by organisational processes through repeated applications. In time, these cognitions are imbued with emotions and acquire degrees of importance; they also become 'habits' of thoughts that translate into habitual actions.

The significance of this formulation of culture as knowledge lies in its ability to account for multiple cultures. Schein (1985) suggests that whether an organisation has a single culture or multiple subcultures is an empirical question. Much depends on the existence of stable groups with shared experiences:

> One may well find that there are several cultures operating within the larger social unit called the company or the organization: a managerial culture, various occupationally based cultures in functional units, group cultures based on geographical proximity, worker cultures based on shared hierarchical experiences, and so on. The organization as a whole may be found to have an overall culture if that whole organization has a significant shared history, but we cannot assume the existence of such a culture ahead of time. [*ibid.*: 7–8]

While top management may have imposed or negotiated a consensus about the rationale of the organisation (axiomatic knowledge), there is no reason to assume that the other dimensions of knowledge are invariant throughout the organisation. Sackmann's own case study found that both dictionary and recipe knowledge varied according to members' responsibilities and positions in the hierarchy.

This cognitive model of culture, however, leaves a number of questions unanswered. For example, how does knowledge lead to action, and under what conditions does it happen? Sackmann postulates that axiomatic knowledge is held by top management who may initiate change as a result of internal or external threats. However, it is possible that lower-level members of the organisation may hold rather different views about 'why things are done the way they are'. Punch (1983b) has suggested that police culture has its primary allegiance not to the organisation but to the job and the peer groups. If axiomatic knowledge is not shared between top management and the lower-ranking members, what, then, would be the implications for the other dimensions of knowledge? There is also little discussion in Sackmann about how the various dimensions of knowledge connect with the power relations external to the organisation, and those between organisational members and their environment.

Culture as Construction

Not all formulations of police culture treat officers as passive objects moulded by the almighty culture. Using the ethnomethodological critique of a rule-based conception of culture, Shearing and Ericson (1991) have argued that rather than being socialised into, and guided by, the police culture in their work activities, police officers are active in constructing and making references to the culture as guiding their actions. For police officers, the police culture is a 'tool-kit 'used in the production of a sense of order, and the constant 'telling' of the culture accomplishes for the officers a 'factual' or 'objective' existence of this culture. The transmission of this culture is not by a process of socialisation and internalisation of rules, but through a collection of stories and aphorisms which instruct officers on how to see the world and act in it. Stories prepare officers for police work by providing a 'vehicle for analogous thinking', creating a 'vocabulary of precedents' (Ericson *et al.* 1987). Stories create a way of seeing and being through the narratives and the silences that surround the stories.

This way of interpreting police culture removes the deterministic framework of a rule-based theory of action and provides for variations in the application of police cultural knowledge:

> It recognizes that police stories provide officers with tools they can use to get them through the business of police work without minimizing the fact that this still requires individual initiative and daring. It also recognizes that officers differ in their competence in using this cultural tool-kit ... Finally, it recognizes that what they do will be retrospectively constituted as ordered via the reflexive methods that are part of this doing. [Shearing and Ericson 1991: 506]

Thus, cultural knowledge in the form of police stories presents officers with ready-made schemas and scripts which assist individual officers in particular situations to limit their search for information, to organise information in terms of established categories, and to constitute a sensibility out of which a range of actions can flow, and which provide officers with a repertoire of reasonable accounts to legitimate their actions. This model of police culture, however, is silent about the social and political context of police work, even though police stories undoubtedly contain implicit or explicit expressions of power relations within police organisations.

Culture as Relations

Instead of viewing culture as informal influences which seek to undermine or subvert the formal goals or rules of organisations, researchers are increasingly looking to sources of irrationality in the formal structure itself (see Powell and DiMaggio 1991: 13). Ericson (1981), for example, found that departures from due-process protection of the accused were not 'extra-legal' rules at all, they were decisions legitimated by the criminal law itself. The question remains: how do formal structures influence cultural practice?

A useful approach to understanding the formation of cultural practice is found in the social theory of Pierre Bourdieu. Two key concepts of relevance here are those of the *field* and the *habitus*:

A field consists of a set of objective, historical relations between positions anchored in certain forms of power (or capital), while habitus consists of a set of historical relations 'deposited' within individual bodies in the form of mental and corporeal schemata of perception, appreciation and action. [Wacquant 1992: 16]

For Bourdieu, society is constituted by an ensemble of relatively autonomous fields. A field is a social space of conflict and competition, where participants struggle to establish control over specific power and authority, and, in the course of the struggle, modify the structure of the field itself. Thus a field 'presents itself as a structure of probabilities – of rewards, gains, profits, or sanctions – but always implies a measure of indeterminacy' (Bourdieu, quoted in *ibid.*: 18). In terms of police work on the streets, for example, the field may consist of the historical relations between certain social groups and the police, anchored in the legal powers and discretion that police are authorised to exercise and the distribution of power and material resources within the community.

Habitus, on the other hand, is closer to what has earlier been described as cultural knowledge. It is a system of 'dispositions' which integrate past experience and enable individuals to cope with a diversity of unforeseen situations (Wacquant 1992: 18). Instead of seeing culture as a 'thing' – a set of values, rules, or an informal structure operating on actors in an organisation – Bourdieu argues for the primacy of *relations*, so that habitus and field function fully only in relation to each other. Habitus generates strategies which are coherent and systematic, but they are also 'ad hoc because they are "triggered" by the encounter with a particular field' (*ibid.*: 19). Like the police stories discussed earlier, habitus allows for creation and innovation within the field of police work. It is a 'feel for the game'; it enables an infinite number of 'moves' to be made in an infinite number of situations. It embodies what police officers often refer to as 'commonsense' (see Manning 1977) and what are commonly known as 'policing skills' (see Brogden *et al.* 1988).

Police practices have the appearance of rationality, but the 'cop code' is more the result of 'codification' by researchers and police officers than a set of rules which generate practice. Bourdieu has argued that rationality rarely plays a part in practical action:

The conditions of rational calculation are practically never given in practice: time is limited, information is restricted, etc. And yet agents *do* do, much more often than if they were behaving randomly, 'the only thing to do'. This is because, following the intuitions of a 'logic of practice' which is the product of a lasting exposure to conditions similar to those in which they are placed, they anticipate the necessity immanent in the way of the world. [Bourdieu 1990: 11]

Thus, Bourdieu's theory is successful in relating policing 'dispositions' or cultural knowledge to the social and political context of policing. It also allows for the existence of multiple cultures, since officers in different organisational positions operate under different sets of field and habitus. The main weakness of this framework, however, is that it over-emphasises the positional and dispositional aspects of policing 'at the expense of the interactive-situational' dimension (Mouzelis 1995). The fact that police practices can be the result of *conscious* decisions and strategies cannot be ignored. The role of police actors in interpreting their positions and making creative and conscious decisions must therefore be an essential component of the reconceptualised understanding of police culture.

Cultural Change

The three perspectives outlined all allow some scope for cultural change. Shearing and Ericson (1991) have the least to say about change but their model provides for human action that is both 'guided and improvisational'. For Bourdieu, cultural change is possible through changes in the field or in the habitus, although no explicit theory of change is outlined. Habitus, according to Bourdieu, is 'an *open system of dispositions* that is constantly subjected to experiences, and therefore constantly affected by them in a way that either reinforces or modifies its structures' (Bourdieu and Wacquant 1992: 133). Thus, changes in the field affect the habitus, because the field 'structures the habitus' (*ibid.*: 127).

Sackmann's work offers the most explicit theorising about the processes of change. Sackmann suggests that cultural cognitions are 'socially created, maintained, changed, and perpetuated'; they 'emerge in the process of joint problem-solving in which meanings are negotiated' (Sackmann 1991: 41). These 'solutions' to perceived tasks or problems, when adopted by others repeatedly, become associated with emotions and different degrees of importance. Aspects of cultural knowledge are then communicated to new members who acquire and reinforce this cultural knowledge by learning, but may also import different cultural knowledge into the organisation. According to Schein (1985: 24–7), culture in organisation is learned either through 'anxiety and pain reduction' (to make life more predictable) or through 'positive reward and reinforcement' (to repeat whatever worked). Cultural knowledge, Sackmann observed, acts as a link between strategy and organisational processes. Thus changes in organisational culture occur when axiomatic knowledge is changed; this in turn sets off other changes:

existing cultural knowledge, strategy and organizational processes began to be questioned when top management group perceived threats in the internal and external environments of the firm. As a first step they debated and negotiated axiomatic knowledge. Once in place this axiomatic knowledge defined the firm's purpose, its strategic intention, its design, and characteristics of preferred members ... In the process of negotiating axiomatic knowledge, existing dictionary and directory knowledge was altered. This knowledge then guided the thoughts, attention, and actions of organizational members both in terms of organizational processes and in terms of strategic concerns and their implementation. Their actions, and the outcomes of their actions, in turn, maintained, reinforced, and further adjusted directory, dictionary and axiomatic knowledge ... [Sackmann 1991: 156]

Field, Habitus and Police Practice

The implications of the new conception of police culture can now be spelt out. The close relationship between police cultural knowledge (habitus) and the structural conditions of police work (field) has long been recognised in the literature, since culture is said to have been developed as a way of coping with the danger and unpredictability of police work. The link between cultural knowledge and police practice is also commonly assumed, although not clearly established. The danger of not exploring the links between structural conditions, cultural knowledge and police practice is that a simple-minded model of linear causality is often implied (see Figure 4.1).[1] Such a model neglects the centrality of the police officers as active participants in the construction and reproduction of cultural knowledge and institutional practice. It also gives a misleading impression that it is possible to change cultural knowledge and police practice simply by changing structural conditions.

In the revised model of police culture, the *active role* of 'police actors' (which include all members of the police organisation) forms a crucial link between these elements. This link is often missing in discussions of police culture and institutional practice. The main point being made here is that structural conditions do not completely determine cultural knowledge, and cultural knowledge does not totally dictate practice. Working within the structural conditions of policing, members have an active role to play in developing, reinforcing, resisting or transforming cultural knowledge. They are not passive carriers of police culture. In a

STRUCTURAL   CULTURAL
CONDITIONS ⟶ KNOWLEDGE ⟶ POLICE
(The Field)   (Habitus)   PRACTICE

Figure 4.1 A linear model of the production of police practice.

similar way, to borrow the game analogy used by Bourdieu (1990), officers who have learned 'a feel for the game' (cultural knowledge) are not
restricted to a limited number of 'moves' (modes of practice). Hence
any changes to structural conditions are taken into account by officers in
their practice. Whether a structural change results in any change in
cultural knowledge or institutional practice depends on the nature of
the change and the capacity of officers to adapt to the change. The
relationships between the elements are neither uni-directional nor
deterministic (see Figure 4.2).

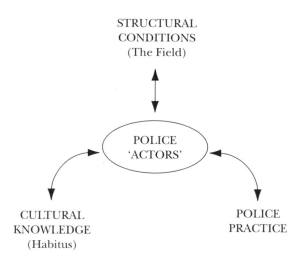

STRUCTURAL
CONDITIONS
(The Field)

POLICE
'ACTORS'

CULTURAL
KNOWLEDGE
(Habitus)

POLICE
PRACTICE

Figure 4.2 An interactive model of the production of police practice.

This perspective of organisational culture and institutional practice is
increasingly being recognised by organisational theorists (see Powell
and DiMaggio 1991). Instead of viewing institutional behaviour as the
product of the internalisation of values and attitudes, theorists are finding other types of models more useful and more powerful. For example,
instead of explaining racist police practice in terms of the inculcation of
racist values among officers through a vaguely understood process of
socialisation, we can view officers as active decision-makers who are nevertheless guided by the assumptions they learn and the possibilities they
are aware of. Their acquiring of cultural knowledge creates schemas and
categories which both help them to organise information and lead them

to resist evidence contrary to these schemas. Their awareness of structural possibilities provides 'menus of legitimate accounts' (*ibid.*: 15) or a 'vocabulary of precedents' (Ericson *et al.* 1987) which they can use to justify their actions. Hence, institutional practice is partly the product of a 'practical consciousness' (Giddens 1984) or a 'logic of practice' (Bourdieu 1990: 11) which is based not on rational calculations but on learned 'commonsense' and skills. However, practice is also partly guided by the actor's awareness of how an action can be retrospectively justified rationally, that is, what types of justification are organisationally permitted.

This type of analysis can be extended to the group or organisational level. It is a well-recognised perspective in organisational theory that organisations do not simply react to their environments; they *enact* them (Weick 1979). This means that organisations—or, more precisely, *people* within organisations—are not passive entities; they take an active part in the construction of their environments. When applied to policing, this has significant implications for understanding how structural conditions impact on organisational practice. The analysis by Smith (1994) of the Queensland police bureaucracy prior to the Fitzgerald inquiry, for example, illustrates how a police organisation could enact its political environments to ensure its own survival. For many years, the Queensland Police Force succeeded in exerting major influence on law-enforcement policies, obstructing the implementation of reforms, and using propaganda to promote a favourable public image, in spite of the presence of entrenched corrupt practices.

Recognising the active role played by police actors (and groups of actors) is an important antidote to the simplistic view that deviant institutional practice is *caused* by a deviant police culture, which is in turn a necessary product of the structural conditions of police work. Constructing better theories is not a pointless academic exercise. Better theories provide a way out of the blind alleys of traditional ways of thinking about culture; they uncover possibilities and useful alternatives for reform.

In summary, it has been argued in this section that Bourdieu's concepts of field and habitus, when combined with an explicit recognition of the active role played by police actors, provide a useful framework for conceptualising police culture. In addition, Sackmann's dimensions of organisational knowledge can be a fruitful way of filling out the habitus of police work. This way of thinking about police culture overcomes most of the weaknesses in existing theories. In the following sections, the relevance of this framework for understanding the relations between police and minorities will be discussed. I will begin by describing elements of the habitus and the field which constitute the culture of policing. The discussion of the habitus draws on a range of findings from the literature, while the description of the field is based mainly on Australian and New South Wales sources.

The Habitus of Policing

Many aspects of police racism can be analysed in terms of the relation between the field and the habitus of police work. The following discussion of habitus makes use of what the research literature has informed us about the four dimensions of cultural knowledge in street-level police work: axiomatic knowledge (which constitutes the basic rationale of policing), dictionary knowledge (which sets up categories about people whom police come into contact with), directory knowledge (which informs officers on how to go about getting their work done), and recipe knowledge (which prescribes the menu of acceptable and unacceptable practices in specific situations).

Axiomatic Knowledge: The Police Mandate

This refers to the fundamental assumptions about 'why things are done the way they are' in an organisation. Police traditionally see their work in terms of waging a 'war against crime', maintaining order, and protecting people's lives and property. Reiner (1992: 112) points out that officers often regard their work with a sense of mission: 'their sense of themselves as "the thin blue line", performing an essential role in safeguarding social order, which would lead to disastrous consequences if their authority was threatened'. Manning (1978a: 8) observes that 'Based on their legal monopoly of violence, [police] have staked out a mandate that claims to include the efficient, apolitical, and professional enforcement of the law.' Manning calls this the 'impossible mandate' which is driven by public expectations rather than the reality of police work. The heroic public image of the police as 'crook-catchers' and 'crime-fighters' is encouraged by officers themselves. The public in turn demands 'more dramatic crook-catching and crime prevention'. These demands are then converted by police organisations into 'distorted criteria for promotion, success and security' (ibid.: 13).

As a result of the acceptance of this 'impossible' mandate, police often make a distinction between 'real police work' and the work they routinely perform. 'Real police work', for the young American officers observed by Van Maanen, is about exercising their special occupational expertise: 'to make an arrest, save a life, quell a dispute, prevent a robbery, catch a felon, stop a suspicious person, disarm a suspect, and so on'. Yet, very little of these officers' time on the street is spent on what they consider to be their 'primary function'. 'Real' police work, then, becomes both 'a source of satisfaction and frustration' (Van Maanen 1978a: 121–2).

Dictionary Knowledge: Police Categories

Research studies have suggested that 'police work requires officers to summarise complex and ambiguous situations in a short period of time and to take some action' (Holdaway 1995). Hence officers develop routine ways of categorising their environment and the people they encounter in the community. American researchers found that police officers develop notions of normal and abnormal appearances in relation to the public places they patrol. These notions of normality and abnormality depend on context:

> Among the Americans, the police are occupational specialists on inferring the probability of criminality from the appearances persons present in public places ... What is normal for a place is normal for the place at a time. The meaning of an event to the policeman at a place depends on the time it occurs. [Sacks 1978: 190, 194]

In a study of a suburban Canadian police force, Ericson (1982: 86) notes a similar tendency for patrol officers to develop indicators of abnormality: these include '1) individuals out of place, 2) individuals in particular places, 3) individuals of particular types regardless of place, and 4) unusual circumstances regarding property'.

Reiner (1992: 117–18) has also commented on the distinction police make with regard to the general public, between 'the rough and respectable elements, those who challenge or those who accept the middle-class values of decency which most police revere'. Muir (1977: 156–7) describes a similar 'separation of people into the governables and the rebels ... those who might revolt against police authority from those who would not'.

As pointed out in Chapter 1, police in Australia have been accused of forming stereotypical opinions about the criminality of certain ethnic groups (ALRC 1992: 201) and regularly linking Aboriginal people with crime and social disorder (Cunneen and Robb 1987). Ericson's study in Canada found similar typifications by police of racial and ethnic minorities and young people with disorderly appearance and conduct who were considered 'the scum of the earth' (Ericson 1982: 66–7). Ethnic stereotyping works to reinforce police discernment of respectability, and is 'a stable feature of the occupational culture' (Holdaway 1995).

Directory Knowledge: Police Methods

Directory knowledge informs police officers how operational work is routinely carried out. To a certain extent these operational methods follow from the definitions and categories designated by dictionary knowledge. For example, in proactive policing, officers are 'chronically suspicious' and are forced 'to make snap decisions about the appropriateness of what people are doing' (Bayley and Mendelsohn, 1969: 93). Having developed indicators of normality and abnormality, roughness and respectability, police officers tend to target the unusual and the disreputable. Following these 'cues' may be routine police work, but the effect may be serious for minorities (*ibid.*). In Redfern, Sydney, for example, an individual 'out of place' is an Aborigine driving a red Laser (as mentioned in the television documentary *Cop It Sweet*). Young people congregating in parks, shopping malls and pinball parlours are also obvious targets for proactive stops.

An important feature of police work is the capacity and authority to use coercive force if necessary. Bittner considers this capacity to use force as 'the core of the police role':

> every conceivable police intervention projects the message that force may be, and may have to be, used to achieve a desired objective ... It is very likely ... that the actual use of physical coercion and restraint is rare ... What matters is that police procedure is defined by the feature that it may not be opposed in its course, and that force can be used if it is opposed. [Bittner 1978: 36]

This capacity to use force by the police is 'essentially unrestricted': apart from the use of deadly force and the obvious restriction that force must not be used maliciously, there are very few guidelines regarding when 'forceful intervention was necessary, desirable or proper' (*ibid.*: 33). This lack of regulation and guidance means that the concept 'lawful use of force' by the police is 'practically meaningless' (*ibid.*).

The use of force or the threat of force by police is often seen as a legitimate means of taking charge of situations: to maintain authority, to control suspects, and to obtain information. A study by Westley (1970) of an American police force found that the use of violence for the purpose of maintaining respect for the police was not seen as illegitimate by almost 40 per cent of the seventy-four policemen surveyed. A study by Baldwin and Kinsey (1982) of a British police force found that police would often use the threat of violence to obtain information or confession, but reserve actual violence for those who 'cut up rough'. Van Maanen (1978b: 224) suggests that people placed into the 'assholes' category by American police are vulnerable to so-called 'street justice – a physical attack designed to rectify what police take as personal insult'.

The use of force is, of course, only one of many ways of taking charge of situations efficiently. A Canadian researcher has commented on the tacit condoning of 'shortcuts' by officers, since legal procedures are seen as impediments to justice:

> Taking charge efficiently may seem to call for minor and sometimes major shortcuts in legal niceties. The officer may bluff or bully, mislead or lie, verbally abuse or physically 'rough up' the alleged offender. Senior officers are not concerned to eliminate such shortcuts, but merely to manage them, so as to keep citizens' complaints ... at a minimum while getting the day's work done. [Lee 1981: 51]

In general, the research by Manning (1978c: 73–4) suggests that police officers see their work as uncertain and unclear ('You never know what to expect next') and hence decisions are based on experience, commonsense and discretion, rather than 'an abstract theory of policing, the law, or police regulations'. Decisions can only be justified situationally ('You can't police by the book'). The centrality of experience as the foundation of policing is taken for granted and seen as essential in the definition of occupational competence.

Recipe Knowledge: Police Values

This refers to the normative dimension of cultural knowledge. It suggests what should or should not be done in specific situations. It provides recommendations and strategies for coping with police work. Van Maanen's research into an American police force provides some significant observations. For example, officers learn to 'stay out of trouble' by doing the minimum amount of work required; 'gung-ho' officers are regularly ridiculed by their peers (Van Maanen 1978a: 125). Officers also develop a sceptical attitude towards police supervisors and managers, and learn not to expect much from the organisation; their rewards come in the form of camaraderie and 'small favours' granted by sergeants (*ibid.*: 127). In addition, officers learn to 'cover their ass' to avoid disciplinary actions. Consequently, written records of events are often manipulated by officers to protect themselves against possible reviews by supervisors (Manning 1977: 191).

Another well-documented aspect of police recipe knowledge is the apparent 'code of silence' and solidarity among police officers when faced with allegations of misconduct. The American study by Westley (1970) found that, if faced with a partner's misconduct, eleven out of sixteen officers would not be willing to report this misconduct, while ten would be prepared to perjure themselves in court to protect their partner. Reiner (1992: 116) sees solidarity as a response to the working conditions of policing, 'a product not only of isolation, but also of the need to be able to rely on colleagues in a tight spot, and a protective armour shielding the force as a whole from public knowledge of infractions'. Skolnick and Fyfe observe that, following the notorious beating of Rodney King by members of the Los Angeles Police, one of the indicted officers called for the resignation of the Police Chief Daryl Gates because Gates had betrayed 'the code' which 'decrees that cops protect other cops, no matter what, and that cops of higher rank back up working street cops – no matter what' (Skolnick and Fyfe 1993: 7). The code, according to Skolnick and Fyfe, is typically enforced 'by the threat of shunning, by fear that *informing* will lead to exposure of one's own derelictions, and by fear that colleagues' assistance may be withheld in emergencies' rather than by violent means (*ibid.*: 110, original emphasis).

One documented case in New South Wales shows the hazards faced by whistle-blowers within the force. When a relatively inexperienced police officer reported that his supervising sergeant assaulted a person in custody, he was given the 'cold-shoulder treatment' by senior officers and others who sided with the sergeant. The same sergeant was seen by a probationary constable two months later assaulting another offender. The probationary constable reported the matter to his senior officers. The sergeant was subsequently recommended for dismissal by the Police Tribunal. Both constables who had complained against the sergeant had since resigned from the Police Service. The lack of support from senior officers during the investigation and court proceedings was considered the main reason for the first officer's decision to resign (NSW Ombudsman 1991: 130–2).

The Field of Police–Minority Interactions

Bourdieu's definition of the field emphasises the historical, structural relations between positions of power. To understand the relations between the police and visible minority communities in Australia, it is important to provide a brief overview of six elements of the field: the political context of policing; the social and economic status of visible minorities; government policies towards minorities and Aboriginal people; discretionary powers of the police; legal protection against police abuse; and the internal organisation of the police force.

Political Context

In spite of the apparently apolitical nature of police organisations, policing is inherently political, since it is an institution 'created and sustained by political processes to enforce dominant conceptions of public order'

(Skolnick 1972: 41; quoted in Reiner 1992: 2). As Manning (1978a: 18–19) points out, the law is itself a political entity, being the 'product of what is right and proper from the perspective of different politically powerful segments within the community'.

The historical account by Finnane (1994) of policing in Australia is replete with examples of the political nature of police work, both in its more explicit form of controlling political dissent and in the routine tasks of maintaining social order. In Queensland, for example, the police were used in the 1970s and 1980s by the conservative State government 'as front-line troops in a tactical battle with street demonstrators', 'as means of surveillance of troublesome politicians and other opponents of the ruling regime', and 'generally, ideologically, as points of resistance to the government's social and political enemies' (Finnane 1990: 164). There is little doubt that the police culture condemned by the Fitzgerald Report (1989) was partly the product of the political condition at the time.

The analysis by Henry (1994) of police corruption in New York City also suggests that the political environment can foster or impede corrupt practice. He found that between 1972 and 1992 there was a general decline in media and academic attention to issues of police corruption. This period coincided with a gradual 'collapse' of the Police Department's corruption control system (Mollen Report 1994). Henry hypothesises that this easing of external pressure allowed police administrators to shift their attention and priority away from corruption controls.

Other commentators also suggest that police deviance can thrive only in a climate of public tolerance. Sparrow et al. (1990) described the experience of a new police commissioner in Philadelphia, Kevin Tucker, who commissioned a survey of public opinion regarding the police. In spite of a major bungle and a serious corruption scandal in the police department, 70 per cent of the respondents rated the police as good or excellent overall, with only 5 per cent saying that they were doing a poor job. This high rating was given even though half of the respondents thought the police were rude, 49 per cent thought the police took bribes, and 66 per cent thought that the police used excessive force. These results suggest that there was an implicit 'deal' between the police and the public that 'if the police did a good job of fighting crime and responding to calls for service, they could be indulged a little in other ways' (ibid.: 133).

Morton's analysis of police corruption in Britain found that police often justified irregular practices by referring to this public tolerance: 'the public does not much care about procedure provided results are achieved and provided that lapses in principle do not become scandals' (Morton 1993: 343). Skolnick and Fyfe made a similar point about public support for aggressive policing in spite of the revelation of the beating of Rodney King:

> Today, permanently changing police organizational norms that tolerate and encourage brutality requires change in the public expectations to which those norms are responsive. However repulsed viewers may have been by the graphic display of brutality shown in the King tape – and by the fury of the riotous response to it – there is considerable support among the public for an aggressive, kick-ass style of policing. [Skolnick and Fyfe 1993: 189]

The absence of public concern and political pressure to scrutinise the standards of police conduct means that there is little political risk for police organisations that ignore or pay only notional attention to police deviance. The experience of the *Cop It Sweet* scandal in New South Wales suggests that well-targeted media and public pressure could create political conditions which made it impossible for police misconduct to be tolerated or ignored (see Chapter 8).

Social and Economic Status of Minorities

Historically, the relations between police and Australia's indigenous people have been conflictual and tense. The history of colonisation and dispossession of Aboriginal people has already been referred to in Chapter 1. For a hundred years from the mid-nineteenth century police acted as agents of the state to effect 'protection' of Aboriginal people. This special role meant that police were not merely in the business of detecting crime and keeping order, but undertook 'interventions in family life, surveillance of itinerant Aborigines, management of Aboriginal money, inspection of work arrangements, handing out of blankets and rations, and other duties' (Finnane 1994: 112). Such interventions were not only destructive, as in the large-scale removal of Aboriginal children from their parents in New South Wales, but they were instruments for criminalising Aborigines and opportunities for police abuse. Wootten (1989) has criticised the policy of assimilation operating at the time as a form of genocide.

With the decline of protection, the relations between Aborigines and police became more conflictual (Finnane 1994). I have already noted in previous chapters the disproportionately high rate of Aborigines represented at various stages of the criminal justice system and the frequency and intensity of policing experienced by Aboriginal communities. Social and economic conditions among the indigenous population continue to be poor in the 1990s. For example, indigenous children had generally low school retention rates, with 42 per cent leaving school by age 15, according to data from the 1991 Census. The unemployment rate of

Aboriginal and Torres Strait Islander people in New South Wales was 36 per cent, compared with 11 per cent for all other NSW people.[2] The majority of indigenous people aged 15 years and over (63 per cent) had an annual income of $16,000 or less. The estimated life expectancy for Aboriginal women in western NSW was fourteen years less than that for the female population of NSW, while for men the life expectancy was nineteen years less than the total male population. The Aboriginal infant mortality rate was estimated as two or three times that of the total NSW population (NSW Office on Social Policy 1994). Hence Aboriginal people remain socially disadvantaged, politically powerless and easy targets for law-and-order campaigns in Australian society.

Social and economic conditions vary considerably among NESB people in Australia. For example, official unemployment rates[3] from the 1991 Census show that people born in Vietnam had the highest unemployment rate: 45.9 per cent for men and 44.8 per cent for women, compared with 11.5 per cent and 9.5 per cent for Australian-born men and women respectively (Collins 1996). Other groups with extremely high unemployment rates were those born in Lebanon (33.7 per cent for men and 32.9 per cent for women), Turkey (29.7 per cent for men and 34.0 per cent for women), and Taiwan (27.5 per cent for men and 27.8 per cent for women). Unemployment rates among people born in English-speaking countries such as the United Kingdom, Canada and the United States were similar to or below those of Australian-born men and women. However, three NESB groups also had lower unemployment rates than the Australian-born: the Italians (10.0 per cent for men and 7.6 per cent for women), the Dutch (11.0 per cent for men and 7.9 per cent for women), and the Japanese (4.9 per cent for men and 8.6 per cent for women). The economic positions of NESB people in Australia seem to range from better than average to extremely poor.

Collins (1996) suggests that with economic restructuring and changes to Australia's immigration policy in the 1980s and 1990s, the traditional patterns of labour market segmentation have changed somewhat. It was true twenty years ago that workers born in Australia or English-speaking countries tended to be employed in the 'primary labour market' with high-status and well-paid jobs, while NESB workers were concentrated in the 'secondary labour market' with semi-skilled or unskilled jobs. The situation in the 1990s is much more complex. As a result of changes to the immigration policy, most NESB immigrants admitted to Australia in the last ten years were highly skilled and qualified professionals. The introduction of the 'business migration' category also led to an increase of affluent business immigrants, mainly from Asian countries. A bifurcated pattern of labour market segmentation has now emerged among the NESB immigrants:

30 per cent of Japanese and Taiwanese-born men were managers or administrators in 1991, compared with 16 per cent of the Australian-born. Those born
in Hong Kong, Korea and Malaysia tend to cluster in the finance and business
sectors of the economy while the Chinese, Japanese and Thai-born are concentrated in the personal and recreational services, including the restaurant
and tourist industries. In contrast, Indochinese men and women – particularly
those from Vietnam who arrived as refugees – are concentrated in low-skilled
jobs in the declining manufacturing industry ..., with Vietnamese women
overrepresented at eight to twelve times the rate of Australian-born women in
the declining clothing industry ... [*ibid.*]

In terms of social mobility, there is evidence that children of NESB
immigrants perform well in the education system and attain higher occupational status than their parents. However, given the downward mobility experienced by many immigrants when they moved to a new country,
upward mobility of their children is hardly surprising (Castles *et al.*
1988). Moreover, the stereotype of the high-achieving Asian-Australian
students and the 'ethnic work ethic' is often used as a justification for
leaving the problems of social and economic inequality to individuals
and market forces, and for ignoring the structural disadvantages
suffered by those who did not fit the stereotype.

Although the plight of other ethnic minorities is substantially better
than that of the Aboriginal people, those who are poor, uneducated and
lacking in English facility are still relatively powerless. I have already
highlighted the findings of the National Inquiry into Racist Violence and
other bodies that particular ethnic communities are more likely to be
victims of discrimination, intimidation and harassment in the school or
workplace. Negative experiences with police in their native countries
have made some immigrants fearful and distrustful of the police. Conflict between police and ethnic groups tends to be higher in relation to
young people, especially homeless, unemployed or otherwise marginal
groups (Chan 1994). Communities whose members are more educated
and affluent are generally more able to mobilise community and legal
resources to assert their rights.

Government Policies

In response to the changing ethnic profile of the Australian population,
the federal government has, since the 1970s, pursued a policy of multiculturalism which attempts to redress the disadvantages and barriers
faced by NESB immigrants and their communities. More recently,
following the High Court decision in *Mabo*, the Keating federal government enacted the *Native Title Act* 1993 (Cth) to recognise and protect
native land title and pave the way for reconciliation with the indigenous
people.

Multiculturalism

Multiculturalism is a relatively new policy and has remained controversial among Australians.[4] Ethnic diversity was never the intention of the post-war immigration policy, which initially promised that 'there would be ten British immigrants for every "foreigner"' (Castles 1992b: 8). It was the shortage of British, and later other European, immigrants which led to the relaxation and eventual abolition of the White Australia Policy. The objectives of the immigration program were predominantly economic and strategic, although humanitarian and family-union migration categories grew in importance during subsequent years. The government's original response to the growing numbers of non-Anglo immigrants was to pursue an assimilationist policy, which encouraged immigrants to identify and integrate with the dominant culture. When it became obvious that assimilationism led to labour market segmentation and social disadvantage among immigrants, multiculturalism was put forward as an alternative.

Australian multiculturalism has gone through a number of different phases (Castles 1992a; Vasta 1993). During the early 1970s, multiculturalism concentrated on social reforms to redress the disadvantages suffered by immigrants. Following the election of the Liberal coalition government in 1975, multiculturalism was redefined to recognise cultural pluralism while emphasising the primacy of the dominant culture and institutions. In 1982 the federal government felt the need to respond to the growing complaints by Anglo-Australians that multiculturalism had led to their being disadvantaged while welfare programs for immigrants were being overfunded. A White Paper, *Multiculturalism for all Australians*, tried to convince Anglo-Australians that multiculturalism was relevant and important for national cohesion. However, multiculturalism was soon under attack during the 'immigration debate' of 1984 which coincided with an economic recession and growing concerns among Australians regarding the benefits of immigration and multiculturalism. The call for the restriction of immigration from Asia 'quickly took on racist overtones, reminiscent of the "yellow peril" slogan of the past' (Castles 1992b: 14). The Labor government attempted to appease critics by cutting back on multicultural programs, but was soon forced to reverse these cuts when marginal Labor seats in Sydney and Melbourne were threatened by ethnic protests. The current policy of multiculturalism emphasises its economic benefits as Australia becomes increasingly involved in international trade and communication and as the government sees Asia rather than Europe as crucial to Australia's future.

The *National Agenda for a Multicultural Australia* (Office of Multicultural Affairs 1989) identifies three dimensions of the new policy: 'the right of all Australians, within carefully defined limits, to express and share their individual cultural heritage, including their language and religion' (cultural identity); 'the right of all Australians to equality of treatment and opportunity, and the removal of barriers of race, ethnicity, culture, religion, language, gender or place of birth' (social justice); and 'the need to maintain, develop and use effectively the skills and talents of all Australians, regardless of background' (economic efficiency). The limits are also carefully spelt out. They include 'an overriding and unifying commitment to Australia, to its interests and future, first and foremost'; the acceptance of the 'basic structures and principles of Australian society – the Constitution and the rule of law, tolerance and equality, Parliamentary democracy, freedom of speech and religion, English as the national language and equality of the sexes'; and the 'responsibility to accept the right of others to express their views and values'. The current model of multiculturalism has reinforced the principles of 'access and equity' which recognise that public service should be equally accessible and available to all citizens. In New South Wales, access and equity principles were reflected in the Ethnic Affairs Policy Statement program which made individual public service providers responsible for ensuring that mainstream programs were properly designed and effectively delivered (see Chapter 7).

Even in its current form, multiculturalism is not without contradictions. As Vasta points out, multiculturalism, as a strategy to manage cultural differences, is full of ambivalence:

> it is simultaneously a discourse of pacification and emancipation; of control and participation; of legitimation of the existing order and of innovation. Multiculturalism is part of a strategy of domination over minorities by the majority, but also points beyond this, to the possibility of new forms of social and cultural relations. [Vasta 1996]

It is this Janus-faced nature of multiculturalism which must be appreciated in any study of racism and anti-racist policy. The critics of multiculturalism, then, as Vasta correctly suggests, are not all racists. For example, Aboriginal people are not interested in, and have a deep mistrust of, such state-sponsored policies. Aborigines are the original inhabitants of this continent, not one ethnic group among others. Their living conditions, health status, life expectancy and education are still of Third World standards, in contrast to the majority of ethnic communities. Other criticisms of multiculturalism came from diverse sources: classical humanists who fear the policy's concentration on differences instead of commonalities may lead to conflicts and social disintegration; Anglo-Australians who 'feel a sense of loss of community, of traditions and of a way of life previously seen as homogeneous and comforting'; and immigrants who are not benefiting from multicultural policies because of the wide gap between official policies and actual practice, and the fact that multiculturalism preserves power relations within traditional cultures (*ibid.*). The recognition that multiculturalism is not a panacea for racism but is still a valuable source of anti-racist strategies is an important one which has implications for police reforms.

Reconciliation

The term 'reconciliation' is used here loosely to denote a policy to redress the disadvantage and dispossession suffered by Aborigines and Torres Strait Islanders since white settlement.[5] Early government policies towards Aboriginal people were aimed at segregation and regulation. So-called 'protection' legislation was passed in every State and remained in force for the first half of the twentieth century. After World War II, an assimilationist policy was adopted by governments, although segregation of Aboriginal people and restriction of their access to certain institutions and activities remained for decades. In 1967 a national referendum gave the Commonwealth (federal) government the power to make laws in relation to Aboriginal people. The short-lived Labor government elected in 1972 introduced a policy of 'self-determination' which aimed to involve Aboriginal people in the administration of Aboriginal affairs and remove their structural disadvantages. This was soon replaced with 'self-management' and 'self-sufficiency' in 1975 by the newly elected Liberal coalition government.

During the late 1970s and early 1980s, land rights legislation was passed in all States except Western Australia and Tasmania. Such laws were aimed at returning culturally significant land to the Aboriginal people, compensating communities for dispossession and loss of land, and assisting communities to purchase land for economic development. However, lands owned privately or needed by governments are not available for claim. Land ownership also does not imply sovereignty or law-making power on the land.

In 1991 a Council for Aboriginal Reconciliation was established by the federal government, with bipartisan support, to promote reconciliation between the Aboriginal and non-Aboriginal people and to develop strategies for reconciliation. The council's definition of reconciliation was 'about improving relations between Aboriginal and Torres Strait Islander people and other Australians' (1993, quoted in Cunneen and Libesman 1995: 202). The functions of the council appear to be primarily related to education, consultation, planning and advising the Minister; its powers are also restricted to inviting submissions, holding inquiries, organising conferences, undertaking research and public education. For indigenous Australians, the council clearly does not go far enough. The concept of reconciliation advanced by the council was criticised for 'its vagueness and the lack of emphasis on land rights and sovereignty' (Kelly 1993, quoted in Cunneen and Libesman 1995: 204). It was in danger of becoming a 'talk-fest' and 'merely a process to find a process'. While the council aims to build compassion and change attitudes among non-indigenous Australians, what Aborigines demand is justice (Kelly 1993).

The High Court's decision in *Mabo* in 1992, however, opened up real possibilities for reconciliation through the recognition of prior ownership of land by indigenous people. Prior to *Mabo*, the traditional view was that before 1788 Australia was *terra nullius*, 'a land belonging to no-one' (Reynolds 1987: 12). The High Court rejected this notion and affirmed that indigenous inhabitants had legal rights to their traditional land. Following the *Mabo* decision, Prime Minister Paul Keating announced a process of consultation to develop a national response. The *Native Title Act* 1993 (Cth) was passed by parliament to recognise and protect native title, and a National Native Title Tribunal was established in 1994 to process claims. As part of the recognition of native title, the federal government planned to establish a land fund and a new agency to acquire and manage land for indigenous people. Finally, the government promised to implement a 'Social Justice Package' to address the disadvantages suffered by the Aboriginal and Torres Strait Islander people. Pearson (quoted in Cunneen and Libesman 1995: 212) saw *Mabo* as an opportunity 'for a new partnership to be forged where a direct relationship between Aboriginal people and the Federal Government is established, unencumbered by State and local interference, and where the fullest self-determination is acknowledged as inhering in the country's original people'.

Opposition to land rights and native title legislation has been vocal from some mining interests, farmers and politicians. It is too early to tell whether the *Native Title Act* 1993 and its 'Social Justice Package' can be effective in mending relations between Aboriginal and non-Aboriginal Australians and establishing self-determination for Aboriginal people.

Discretionary Powers of the Police

Police have wide discretionary powers to stop, question, arrest, search and detain suspects. It does not matter that the laws governing some of these powers are often 'an amalgam of common law decisions, scattered statutory provisions, and de facto practice', nor that they have been 'left in a state which is so informal, so uncertain and so inconsistent for so long' (New South Wales Law Reform Commission [NSWLRC] 1990: 4, 18). As many commentators have pointed out, the ideology of the rule of law and the rhetoric of 'rights' are not always reflected in law or in practice (Dixon 1993; McBarnet 1979; Ericson 1982). One example of how difficult it is to make a distinction between consent and coercion is in the practice of 'voluntary attendance' at police stations in Australia. The voluntariness of such an appearance, given the potential consequences of non-cooperation, is highly questionable, yet it provides police with powers to detain suspects for questioning without any of the safeguards available to an arrested person (NSWLRC 1990: 66–7; Dixon 1993).

Thus, what some members of minority groups might describe as unfair targeting or harassment is well within the powers available to the police for order maintenance. Other problem areas of police powers affecting police–minority relations, such as the use of special task forces, the disproportionate deployment of resources, the frequency and intrusiveness of patrol operations, are mostly outside legal regulation. Finally, there are no statutory requirements in some Australian jurisdictions for the use of professional interpreters during police questioning of suspects with inadequate language skills. Guidelines such as the *Anunga* rules (Chapter 1) are not legally binding.

Legal Protection Against Police Abuse

Although various anti-discrimination laws operate at the federal and State levels in Australia, they are quite limited in effectiveness for dealing with police abuse. State laws provide civil remedies and apply to specific areas such as employment, accommodation and access to goods and services. The federal *Racial Discrimination Act* 1975 prohibits a wide range of discriminatory acts which contravene basic human rights and freedoms. The applicability of these laws and existing criminal laws to protect minorities against police abuse is not clear (HREOC 1991: 27–32). Similarly, police instructions and guidelines for police handling of minorities do not have the force of law (*ibid.*: 27–32, 319). The adequacy of the present system of police accountability has been questioned by the National Inquiry into Racist Violence. As mentioned previously, minority groups generally do not understand or trust the existing complaints system. They are fearful of future reprisals in a system where police are responsible for investigating themselves. The formal procedures are intimidating as well as prohibitive for those without literacy or English skills. In New South Wales, for example, the complaints procedures were said to be 'far too formalised, legalistic, cumbersome and time-consuming' (Tink Report 1992: 15). The large volume of minor complaints consumed a great deal of resources and led to long delays in processing. Ironically, while an Aboriginal liaison officer was available for assisting with complaints from Aborigines, the Ombudsman's office did not have a budget for professional interpreting services.

Internal Organisation

Most police forces are still organised on the military model, with uniforms, a chain of command, progression through the ranks, strong disciplinary rules, and formal training. This model of organisation seems fitting for an institution which sees its mission as the legitimate use of coercive force in the 'war against crime'. The military metaphor usually translates into a disciplinary regime that insists on the proliferation of rules and regulations: 'What sorts of rules and regulations exist in such a setting are in some ways less important than that there be plenty of them and the personnel be continually aware that they can be harshly called to account for disobeying them' (Bittner 1978: 42).

In contrast to this seemingly hierarchical model of organisation, much police work at the operational level calls for individual judgment, localised responses, and discretionary decisions. Far from being rule-driven, policing is characterised by 'situationally justified actions' (Manning 1977): that is, actions are taken as the situations demand, and then rationalised afterwards in terms of the available rules. Hence, police organisations are considered a form of 'symbolic bureaucracy ... which maintain an image of complete adherence to bureaucratic rules when internally they conform to such rules little or not at all' (Manning and Van Maanen 1978: 4).

Schein (1985: 224–5) has suggested that the most powerful primary mechanisms in which leaders of organisations typically embed and reinforce organisational culture are: '(1) what leaders pay attention to, measure, and control; (2) leader reactions to critical incidents and organizational crises; (3) deliberate role modeling, teaching, and coaching by leaders; (4) criteria for allocation of rewards and status; (5) criteria for recruitment, selection, promotion, retirement and excommunication'. Other mechanisms, such as organisational structure, systems and procedures, design of physical space, stories and legends, and formal statements of organisational philosophy, are seen as secondary. They work to reinforce culture only if they are consistent with the primary mechanisms.

The research literature provides some indication of what leaders of police organisations typically pay attention to. Accountability in police organisations traditionally takes the form of explicitly and continually paying attention to internal discipline, such as dress code, departmental procedures, and so on, rather than auditing how officers make decisions and deal with citizens. Rewards are typically given for staying out of trouble and for 'good pinches' (Bittner 1978: 46). The military metaphor breaks down even further where the police supervisors, far from leading their officers into battle, are perceived as no more than disciplinarians. Bittner describes the typical relationship which emerges between police officers and their superiors as one in which 'supervisory personnel are often viewed by the line personnel with distrust and even contempt', yet to secure loyalty from their subordinates, supervisors often resort to 'whitewashing bad practices involving relatively unregulated conduct' or covering officers' mistakes (*ibid*.: 48). Van Maanen (1983: 280) similarly noted a 'high degree of mutual dependence and reciprocity' between officers and their sergeants. Because officers mostly work out of their supervisor's sight, the emphasis is on *results* (arrests, for example) rather than means. This lack of supervision of police work, coupled with power and discretion, creates ample opportunities for irregular practice and corruption (Morton 1993: 342). At the same time, to stay out of trouble, officers develop anxiety-avoidance mechanisms rather than problem-solving strategies.

The Mollen Commission Report provides useful case-study data on how leaders of a police department contributed to the culture of corruption through their reactions to organisational crises. The commission found that the New York City Police Department had become 'paranoid over bad press'; they were more concerned with the damage brought about by negative publicity than with the problem of corruption. As a result, anti-corruption efforts were all but abandoned (Mollen Report 1994: 3). Lower-level officers were justifiably sceptical about their leaders' public display of commitment to fighting corruption. The Mollen inquiry found widespread disenchantment with and cynicism about the department. This fostered an even stronger bond of loyalty and solidarity with fellow officers (*ibid*.: 63–4). It would appear that leaders of police organisations, through the types of activities they pay attention to and reward officers for, are primarily responsible for contributing to the development and reinforcement of negative aspects of police culture.

By relating these aspects of the field with the habitus of policing discussed earlier, we can see how police practices of the kind being complained about by ethnic minorities can result. Thus, stereotyping, harassment, abuse of power, and violence occur in a policing field characterised by public apathy, disadvantaged minority groups, unfettered police powers, and inadequate mechanisms for accountability.

New Meaning of Cultural Change

This reconceptualisation of police culture sheds new light on the debate about the most effective way of reforming the police: whether the rules should be tightened or the police culture changed (see Chapter 3). Changing police culture now has a new meaning: cultural change is no longer restricted to efforts such as improving police training or the adoption of community policing; it can encompass changing the field, that is, the social, economic, legal and political sites in which policing takes place. I have argued that police culture should not be understood as some internalised rules or values independent of the conditions of policing. Bourdieu's conceptions of field and habitus assist our understanding of the relationship between the formal structural context of policing and police cultural practice. Changes in the field (e.g. in the formal rules and structures governing policing) inevitably alter the way policing is carried out, since habitus interacts with the field, but the resulting practice may or may not be substantially or even discernibly changed. Once again, the analogy of sports may be useful. If the rules of a game or the physical markings on the field have been changed, experienced players may be able to adjust quickly to the new rules and hence show no sign of changing their performance. Conversely, changes to habitus (e.g. in the objectives of policing) also affect practice, but unless the field is changed in a way that reinforces the new habitus, habitus itself may revert to its old dispositions. It is therefore unproductive to debate whether it is more important to tighten rules or to change culture. It may be that it is easier to tighten the law (at least as it is 'in the books') than to change police culture, but the results of both can be unpredictable. Moreover, changing the field can be just as difficult as changing habitus when the distribution of power and resources is the target of change.

To summarise, the concept of police culture as currently theorised in the literature suffers from many problems. I have drawn on Bourdieu's theory of practice and Sackmann's dimensions of cultural knowledge to establish a more satisfactory framework for understanding police culture. The new framework explains police cultural practice in terms of the interaction between the social and political context of police work (the field) and the institutionalised perceptions, values, strategies and schemas (the habitus). The advantage of this framework is its ability to account for the existence of multiple cultures and its capacity to theorise about cultural change. Police officers are not cast as passive 'cultural dopes' (Garfinkel 1967) who play no part in the reproduction or transformation of the culture. The field, which consists of structural relations between police and minority groups, is normally neglected in the theorising of police culture. In Bourdieu's formulation, it is the social space in which cultural practice is produced. Change in cultural practice can occur by changing elements of the field or by changing the habitus, but the 'success' of reforms cannot be guaranteed. This chapter suggests that a better-developed model of police culture can help us understand more readily why police reforms appear to make little difference to racist police practice.

The utility of this framework will now be discussed in the following chapters in relation to the experience of reform in New South Wales. Such a case study is extremely valuable, because, apart from a few isolated evaluation studies of particular programs, there has been a paucity of detailed empirical research on police reform in any Australian jurisdiction. As pointed out in the introduction to the book, the New South Wales experience is unique and historically significant. A close scrutiny of this experiment in police reform is an instructive exercise.

Notes

An earlier version of this chapter was published as part of Chan (1996).
1 Mouzelis (1995) came to a similar conclusion about the importance of not ignoring any one of the three dimensions of 'social games': social positions, dispositions, and interactive situations.
2 A national survey of Aboriginal and Torres Strait Islander people (ABS 1994b) conducted in 1994 found that the overall unemployment rate was 38 per cent, with young people the most affected (50 per cent in the 15 to 19 age group and 46 per cent in the 20 to 24 age group).
3 Official unemployment rates tend to underestimate the extent of unemployment, since people who have given up looking for jobs are not counted.
4 This discussion of multiculturalism is largely based on a working paper by Castles (1992b).
5 The discussion in this section is largely based on Cunneen and Libesman (1995).

CHAPTER 5

Police and Minorities in New South Wales

New South Wales is the oldest and most populous of the Australian States, situated on the south-east coast of the continent (see map). Although its area is more than three times the size of the United Kingdom, New South Wales has a population of only about 6 million, just over one-third of the total population of Australia. Post-war immigration has substantially altered the ethnic mix of the State's population, which was predominantly Anglo-Celtic until recent decades. According to the 1991 Census, 23 per cent of the population in New South Wales were born in foreign countries. The majority of overseas-born came from Europe and the former USSR (53 per cent), the rest came from Asia (23 per cent), and other countries. Among the Australian-born NSW residents, almost one-quarter had at least one foreign-born parent. Close to one million people (aged five or over) in the State spoke a language other than English at home; this represents about 17 per cent of the State's population aged five or more (NSW Office on Social Policy 1994). Chinese (Cantonese or Mandarin) was the most common non-English language, spoken by about 2.3 per cent of the population aged five or over. Italian and Arabic were spoken by about the same proportion of the population. Other common languages include Greek, Spanish, Vietnamese, German and Filipino. Since the majority of immigrants settle in capital cities, in some areas of Sydney over half of the population speak a non-English language at home (Jupp 1995). About 26 per cent of Australia's indigenous population live in New South Wales, where there were approximately 70,000 Aboriginal and Torres Strait Islander people in 1991, representing just over 1 per cent of the State's population.

The cultural diversity of the New South Wales population is rapidly changing the social environment of policing. In this chapter, the overall

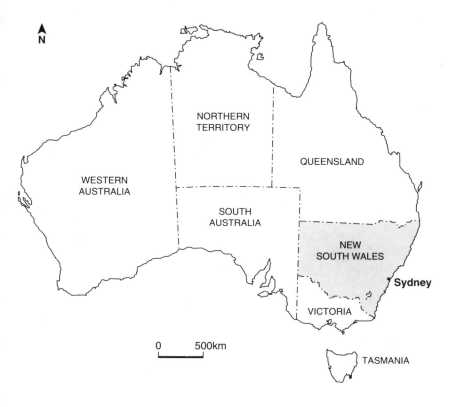

impact of this changing environment on policing is described in terms of the nature and frequency of contact that police have with visible minorities, the types of problems that have arisen, and how officers and members of minority groups perceive these problems.

Police Contact with Minorities

As a result of the changing social environment, police officers in every jurisdiction are being put in situations where they are in frequent contact with people from non-English-speaking backgrounds. In my 1991 survey of NSW officers who work in areas with at least 15 per cent NESB population (Chan 1992a), the majority (nearly 70 per cent) of officers reported that they were in contact with NESB people many times a week, or even several times a day.[1] Their contacts with Aboriginal people were much less frequent, usually less than once a month for the majority of the officers (see Table 5.1).

According to the survey respondents, a substantial proportion of the officers had occasional or frequent contact with more than twenty different ethnic groups. The five minority groups most frequently encountered in New South Wales were the Lebanese, the Vietnamese, the Italians, the Chinese and the Greeks (Table 5.2), and indeed their languages were reported to be the most frequently encountered non-English languages (Table 5.3). These results are consistent with the 1991 Census finding that the most commonly used languages in New South Wales were Chinese (Cantonese or Mandarin), Italian, Arabic and Greek, each spoken by 1 to 2 per cent of the State's population (NSW Office on Social Policy 1994).

Table 5.1 Frequency of police contact with Aborigines and people of NESB

Q: In the past twelve months how often have you come into contact with Aborigines and people of NESB in the course of your work?

	Percentage of respondents in contact with:	
Frequency	Aborigines	People of NESB
Several times a day	8	36
Many times a week	7	33
Once or twice a week	13	18
Once or twice a month	19	5
Occasionally, less than once a month	39	7
Never	15	0

Note: Total number of respondents = 332.

Table 5.2   Minority groups most frequently encountered by police

Q: Which particular groups do you usually encounter in the course of your duties?

| Group | Percentage of respondents who encountered these groups: | | | | |
	Never 0	Occasionally 1	Quite often 2	Very often 3	Average score
Aborigines	19	59	12	10	1.144
Chinese	13	44	26	17	1.460
Dutch	74	26	1	0	0.274
Egyptians	59	34	6	2	0.497
Filipinos	35	52	10	4	0.826
Germans	57	38	5	0	0.485
Greeks	15	45	28	12	1.375
Hungarians	61	34	5	1	0.451
Italians	14	37	32	17	1.535
Indians	32	50	16	3	0.893
Japanese	42	31	17	10	0.948
Koreans	40	35	17	8	0.921
Lebanese	12	30	26	33	1.799
Maltese	43	35	17	6	0.851
Poles	58	35	6	1	0.497
Romanians	55	32	10	4	0.628
Russians	64	31	4	1	0.418
South Americans	46	40	11	3	0.704
Spaniards	55	36	6	2	0.555
Turks	41	36	15	8	0.893
Vietnamese	16	27	28	29	1.692
Yugoslavs	25	41	22	13	1.220

Notes:
Other major groups include Pacific Islanders, Tongans, Samoans, Fijians (mentioned by about 12% of respondents) and Maoris (mentioned by 5%). Total number of respondents = 332.

Unlike the United States and Britain, there are very few 'ethnic ghettos' in Australia. The description by Jupp (1995) of the historical patterns of Australian immigrant settlement suggests that ethnic concentration in geographical areas tended to be temporary. The normal settlement patterns for NESB immigrants follow three phases: 'firstly, settlement in inner-city areas or near migrant hostels; secondly, movement outwards along public transport routes; and thirdly, dispersal into more middle-class areas particularly for the younger generation' (*ibid.*: 136). Hence the most recently arrived groups such as the Vietnamese still tend to concentrate in a few suburbs close to their commercial and community centres, but most other ethnic groups are widely dispersed in residential suburbs. As a result of this general lack of ethnic concentration, police in some areas have to deal with a large variety of language and cultural groups. For example, in Cabramatta, an outer suburb of Sydney, there are more than 100 language groups in one police patrol area.

Police officers interact with minority groups under a variety of circumstances. In the 1991 NSW survey, the five most frequently mentioned situations in which police had contacts with NESB people were: traffic violations or accidents, domestic violence, minor disputes, minor property offences, and minor offences against the person. The NESB people that police were in contact with were either victims or complainants of these offences, or they were suspected of having committed these offences. Although the majority of police–NESB contacts appeared to be related to minor disputes or offences, 24 to 50 per cent of officers

Table 5.3   Non-English languages most frequently encountered by police

Q: Which non-English languages do you usually encounter in the course of your duties?

| Language | Percentage of respondents who encountered these languages: | | | | |
	Never 0	Occasionally 1	Quite often 2	Very often 3	Average score
Arabic/Lebanese	21	34	21	24	1.479
Chinese	21	39	24	16	1.351
Croatian	47	35	14	3	0.741
German	71	27	2	0	0.343
Greek	31	40	19	10	1.073
Indonesian/Malay	56	33	10	2	0.585
Italian	25	40	25	11	1.210
Japanese	44	32	16	8	0.887
Korean	48	31	13	8	0.805
Macedonian	62	26	10	2	0.515
Polish	66	29	4	1	0.391
Russian	73	24	2	1	0.306
Serbian	57	30	10	2	0.581
Spanish	60	32	6	2	0.489
Vietnamese	21	30	22	27	1.549

Note: Total number of respondents = 332.

reported frequent ('quite often' or 'very often') contact with NESB people with respect to serious property and interpersonal offences, as well as serious drug offences (Table 5.4).[2]

The most frequently mentioned situations of police contacts with Aborigines were similar to those for people of NESB, except for contacts relating to traffic and drug offences, which occurred very rarely with Aboriginal people.[3] Although the frequency of police contact with Aborigines was generally lower, the 'moral context' of police interactions with Aborigines appeared to be quite different. Police interactions with NESB people were as likely to be in a situation of providing assistance (where NESB people were victims or complainants) as in the context of law enforcement (where NESB people were suspects or

Table 5.4   Type of contact police had with minorities

Q: What are the usual circumstances under which you come into contact with Aborigines and people of NESB?

Circumstances	Percentage of respondents who had these contacts 'quite often' or 'very often' with:	
	Aborigines	People of NESB
Minorities as victims or complainants		
Serious property offences	9	30
Minor property offences	11	41
Domestic violence	17	45
Other serious offences against the person	17	32
Minor offences against the person	15	35
Serious drug offences	3	24
Minor drug offences	4	25
Traffic violations, accidents	6	58
Minor disputes	18	48
Minorities as suspects or offenders		
Serious property offences	22	34
Minor property offences	25	40
Domestic violence	19	50
Other serious offences against the person	25	36
Minor offences against the person	23	40
Serious drug offences	7	29
Minor drug offences	10	32
Traffic violations, accidents	9	58
Minor disputes	19	44

Note: Total number of respondents = 332.

offenders), but their interactions with Aboriginal people were much more likely to be in the latter context. For example, only 9 per cent of police officers in the survey reported having frequent ('quite often' or 'very often') contacts with Aborigines as victims of serious property offences, but 22 per cent reported having frequent contacts with Aborigines as suspects or offenders of these offences. A similar pattern is evident with other offences, except for domestic violence and minor disputes (see Table 5.4).

What are some of the problems created by this culturally diverse policing environment? Certainly Australian police forces, still predominantly staffed by male Anglo-Australians,[4] are ill equipped to deal with the language and cultural differences they find in the community. Traditional policing methods and practices take little account of the wishes of the people being policed, let alone make adjustments for varying needs and cultural values. The powerlessness of some of the minority groups makes them easy targets for aggressive policing methods, often justified on the basis of maintaining order and controlling crime. In the next two sections, some of the major problems encountered by officers and complaints raised by minority groups are discussed in detail.

Overcoming the Language Barrier

From the police officers' point of view, the language barrier was one of the most significant problems they encountered in their work with visible minorities. Officers in the 1991 survey estimated that they had encountered language problems an average of fifty-two times in the past twelve months. This amounted to about once a week. Note, however, that there was extremely wide variation in this estimate. The median value was twenty times in the past twelve months, but this varied considerably by rank. Officers at senior sergeant rank or higher tended to have a much lower rate of encountering language problems, mainly because they had less frequent direct contact with citizens. As expected, officers working in patrols with higher percentages of non-English-speaking population tended to have more frequent experience with language problems (see Table 5.5).

Use of Interpreters

There is no statutory obligation in New South Wales for police to use professional interpreters when dealing with people who have an inadequate command of the English language. Police were instructed to use interpreters 'where necessary', to ensure that all ethnic groups have equal access to police service.

Table 5.5   Frequency of police encounter with language problems

Q: In the past twelve months, how often have you encountered language problems in your interactions with members of minority groups?

Rank	Median	Mean	Standard deviation
All ranks	20	52.1	87.8
Probationary constable	20	77.9	123.2
Constable	30	58.4	90.9
Constable first class	10	36.4	69.8
Senior constable	20	30.6	40.6
Sergeant	20	48.7	75.4
Senior sergeant	5	10.6	15.7
Inspector or above	2	35.0	86.9

Density of NESB	Unweighted mean	Standard deviation
All patrols	47.9	85.1
15–19%	20.2	52.9
20–24%	17.4	17.4
25–29%	44.0	71.1
30–39%	38.7	59.9
40%+	115.3	138.1

Notes:
All estimates above 365 have been excluded (about 8 cases) because these extreme values distorted the means. Information on NESB density of patrol was missing in some cases.
Total number of respondents = 332.

Accredited interpreters are available from the NSW Ethnic Affairs Commission in more than sixty-five community languages. The Commonwealth Department of Immigration, Local Government and Ethnic Affairs operates a Telephone Interpreter Service which provides both telephone and on-site interpreters. Since October 1991, callers to the '000' emergency number requesting police assistance have been able to access the Telephone Interpreter Service directly through dedicated telephone lines. The Drug Enforcement Agency makes use of its own translators for telephone intercepts and other intelligence activities.

In 1989, the NSW government introduced a user-pays system. The Telephone Interpreter Service also introduced cost recovery in 1991. Charges for on-site interpreter service in 1991 varied from $30 an hour (with an $80 minimum charge for up to two hours) during office hours to $75 an hour ($150 minimum) for Sundays and public holidays.

Telephone Interpreter Service charged $10 minimum for the first ten minutes and $5 for each subsequent five minutes during office hours, rising to $16 and $8 respectively after hours.

Community workers interviewed for this study told the researcher that 'non-use of interpreters' by the police was a 'burning issue'. Their complaint was that police did not always use professional interpreters except for criminal charges. Instead, they tended to use friends, relatives, bilingual police officers or ethnic liaison officers as interpreters. Allegations that the violent husband or the eight-year-old child was used to interpret in domestic violence situations were made by the workers.

According to an internal police document (dated March 1991), a number of concerns were raised both by the community and by officers within the Police Service regarding the use of interpreters:

- Complaints have been received from representatives of government organisations, community organisations and individuals regarding police denial of interpreters to people with poor or inadequate English-language skills.
- Operational police have also reported that they have been discouraged by patrol commanders from using qualified interpreters because of the substantial costs incurred.
- Examples of incidents are:
  1. A Detective Senior Constable rang the Ethnic Group Client Consultant to ask if there was any way an Indonesian interpreter could be accessed free of charge since her Patrol Commander had refused to approve the $80.00 required for an Ethnic Affairs Commission interpreter. The Detective in question was concerned about a client who was distressed and in fear for her life.
  2. The Immigrant Women's Resource Centre frequently complains of domestic violence victims being denied interpreters by police. Police they have dealt with have informed the Centre that patrol commanders would not approve expenditure for interpreters.
  3. The Duty Operations Inspector in one instance is reported to have discouraged a police caller from calling an interpreter because of the cost involved.

Concerns were expressed that the current practice would discourage NESB victims from reporting crime to police, 'and more seriously, reinforces negative stereotyping of police'. It might also 'expose police to charges of neglect of duty or misconduct' (*ibid.*).

The survey results appeared to support the complaint that professional interpreters were not used very frequently by the police. Although acknowledging that they encountered language problems almost once a week on average, officers in the survey reported that they very rarely made use of the professional interpreting services available. The most popular method of interpreting appeared to be using friends or relatives of the non-English-speaking person as interpreters (on average 7.5 times

Table 5.6   Police use of language interpreting resources

Q: How many times in the past twelve months have you made use of the following for interpreting languages?

Resource	Weighted mean	Standard deviation
Telephone interpreter service	3.6	6.9
On-site interpreters	2.6	7.1
Department of Immigration interpreters	0.8	2.4
Health Commission interpreters	0.1	0.7
Police with knowledge of language	2.8	6.4
Local citizens, business people, etc.	3.1	7.3
Local services, banks, etc.	0.2	1.5
Police ethnic liaison officer	0.7	4.0
Bilingual civilian ethnic liaison officer	0.5	3.6
Friend or relative of minority member	7.5	12.0

Note: Total number of respondents = 332.

Table 5.7   Police use of language interpreters

Q: Under what circumstances have you used an interpreter?

Circumstances	Percentage who used telephone interpreters:				Percentage who used on-site interpreters:			
	Never	Occas-ionally	Quite often	Very often	Never	Occas-ionally	Quite often	Very often
General inquiries	55	33	11	2	64	23	10	3
Interviewing victim	51	32	13	4	58	28	11	2
Interviewing complainant	55	32	11	2	63	24	11	2
Interrogation of suspect	63	21	11	5	63	23	9	5
Taking statement from suspect	67	20	11	3	65	21	10	5
Questioning of witness	62	27	9	2	67	21	9	4
Bail application	83	12	5	1	84	12	3	1
Court hearing	—	—	—	—	70	19	8	4

Note: Total number of respondents = 332.

in the past year). The Telephone Interpreter Service was used (3.6 times in the past year) more often than on-site interpreters (2.6 times). Local citizens and business people, etc., as well as police officers with knowledge of the language, were often used instead (see Table 5.6). Both telephone and on-site interpreters were used most frequently for interviewing victims (Table 5.7).

Further analysis of the data shows that 19 per cent of the respondents had never used professional interpreters. This finding varied considerably by rank and duty. While more than 40 per cent of probationary constables had never used professional interpreters, this percentage decreased substantially to about 10 per cent at the higher ranks. In terms of areas of duty, 100 per cent of the detectives reported having used professional interpreters, compared with 81 per cent of general-duty and 85 per cent of beat officers. Detectives had been virtually obliged to use professional interpreters for interviewing suspects for indictable offences since the introduction of the requirement to record such interviews on video and audio tapes.

When interpreters were not used, officers reported that they would often cope with the language difficulties by contacting English-speaking relatives or friends of the non-English-speaker to help out. A fair percentage of officers dealt with the situation by speaking slowly and making use of other ways of communicating. Some would delay the matter and others would call an interpreter in any case (Table 5.8).

Problems with the Use of Interpreters

One reason why professional interpreters were not used as often as they should be was the fact that with the user-pays system operating in New

Table 5.8   Methods of communication without interpreters

Q: What did you do if an interpreter was not called but there was a problem with language communication?

Method	Percentage of respondents who mentioned
Spoke slowly, tried to be patient, improvised	18
Used sign language, drawings	6
Contacted English-speaking friends/relatives	43
'No problem'	15
Interpreters called regardless	8
Tried speaking slowly, then contacted friends/relatives	6
Delayed matter	7

Note: Total number of respondents = 332. Multiple responses are allowed.

South Wales, police saw the use of professional interpreters as an unnecessary expense for certain types of contact with minority groups. Another reason was the delay and other problems connected with the use of professional interpreters. A federal government report has documented many of the existing problems with the access to interpreters in the Australian legal system (see Australia, CAGD 1990). Similar problems were raised in my NSW survey of police officers.

Among the 270 respondents who had used interpreters, about 36 per cent reported having experienced problems. The most common problems encountered were: the lack of availability (mentioned by 63 per

Table 5.9   Problems with use of interpreters, by duty

Q: (If you have encountered problems in relation to the use of interpreters) what types of problems have you encountered?

	Percentage of respondents who mentioned			
Problem	General duty	Beat police	Detective	Total
Lack of availability	69	92	53	63
Interpretation not truthful	13	8	42	20
Inadequate knowledge	27	0	11	19
Embarrassment	0	0	5	3
	(n = 48)	(n = 13)	(n = 19)	(n = 97)

Note: Multiple responses allowed. Percentages based on respondents who answered 'Yes' in the previous question, i.e. they have encountered problems in relation to the use of interpreters.

Table 5.10   Police budget and expenditure for use of interpreters and translators, 1991–92

Unit	Nominal allocation $	Allocation* $	Actual expenditure* $
State Command	38,000	1,960	2,547
North Region	35,000	3,213	4,220
North-west Region	35,000	10,819	9,790
South-west Region	35,000	25,016	15,641
South Region	35,000	17,713	14,580
Drug Enforcement Agency	75,000	35,000	11,860

* By 31 December 1991.
Source: NSW Police Service internal document dated January 1992.

cent of those who encountered problems), that the interpretation was not truthful (mentioned by 20 per cent), and inadequate knowledge on the part of the interpreter (mentioned by 19 per cent). Beat police were more likely to cite the lack of availability as a problem, while detectives were more likely to complain that the interpretation was not truthful. (Table 5.9).

Budget for the Use of Interpreters

If budgetary constraints had been a reason for police officers' reluctance to use professional interpreters, it would have been understandable, though not justifiable as a policy. Evidence which emerged from this study, however, showed otherwise. An amount of $260,000 was allocated by the NSW Police Service for interpreters and translators for the financial year 1991–92. This sum was distributed in the following way: $35,000 for each region, $38,000 to the State Command, $75,000 to the Drug Enforcement Agency, and $7000 to others. The even distribution of the budget to the four regions failed to take into account the variation in the concentration of non-English-speaking background population among the regions. Moreover, there was evidence that individual Commands had not necessarily allocated the full amounts towards the use of interpreting or translating services. An internal police document indicated that by the end of December 1991, only a small fraction of the money had been spent (Table 5.10). A memo from the Finance Branch of the Police Service indicated that 'the budget and responsibility for [Interpreter Services] was held by the Regions and Commands', who also 'hold the authority to decide whether the service is used or not'. In fact, the Commands 'have flexibility to use savings in this item to cover overruns elsewhere' (NSW Police Service, internal document, 11 March 1991).

Although there was no direct evidence that the budget for interpreters' service was being used for other purposes, one of the non-police sources I interviewed mentioned that a patrol commander had actually indicated that intention:

> What he actually said when we spoke to him was – this is a quote – he said, 'Well, if I have a budget to use interpreters and don't use them, then at the end of the year I can buy a typewriter.' Then he said, 'I'm shocking you, aren't I?'

Perhaps anticipating that kind of thinking, the Ethnic Client Consultant warned in an internal memo (dated January 1992) that 'the Police Service leaves itself open to criticism from the EAC if the allocation of $260,000 is spent on items other than translating and interpreting', since 'this sum is frequently quoted as a demonstration of the Police Service's commitment to providing equal access to ethnic minorities'. A discussion paper put out by the Ombudsman's office in 1994 also addressed this issue. Their finding updates my original research:

> Although the Police Service has demonstrated that the funding allocation for professional translators is being more fully spent since the Chan study, the service has not demonstrated that the allocation is adequate or that the number of instances in which police officers proceed without interpreters has been reduced. [NSW Ombudsman 1994: 11]

The inadequacy of the budget is not difficult to demonstrate: if the total budget ($260,000) was divided by the average cost of using interpreters per incident (about $200), there would have been funds for using interpreters about 1300 times per year, or only about twenty-five times a week for the entire State.

Other Initiatives

The Police Service makes regular use of printed aids such as Language ID cards (which allow a non-English-speaker to identify the language he or she speaks, so that an appropriate interpreter can be obtained), Multilingual Phrase Guides (which translate phrases commonly used by police officers into seventeen community languages), and Vietnamese Phrase Guides (which include a greater range of phrases used in a variety of situations). These guides were developed to facilitate communication between police and non-English-speaking members of the community. They were not meant to replace the use of interpreters. Contact with the ethnic media, both print and radio, is also a popular method of reaching members of NESB communities.

Some police officers have undertaken language courses to equip themselves with the basic vocabulary of a community language, but it is not an easy way to break down barriers. A Patrol Commander reported that one of his officers had taken a language and culture course and was 'equipped with a vocabulary of some 300 words in Vietnamese'. But when this officer tried using the language in the community, he found that the Vietnamese immigrants preferred to speak to him in English. His difficulty was also compounded by the presence of different local Vietnamese dialects and the fact that many Vietnamese were ethnic Chinese. The officer felt that what he learnt from the cultural studies was nevertheless valuable.

There are, of course, officers within the Police Service who are fluent in a variety of community languages because of their personal background. There was some attempt to develop a systematic register of information on bilingual officers, but the system was not kept up-to-date and information on the level of language proficiency was not recorded.

Other Difficulties with Visible Minorities

Apart from language problems, respondents in the survey were asked to nominate, with the help of a pre-coded list, other problems they had in their interactions with visible minority groups. The most frequently nominated problems were: ignorance of the law (indicated by 85 per cent of the sample), distrust of police (76 per cent), unwillingness to report crime (71 per cent), uncooperative attitude (70 per cent), hostility towards police (64 per cent), unwillingness to testify in court (61 per cent), and unwillingness to give statement (59 per cent).[5] Other difficulties mentioned by one or two respondents in each case include: hatred of police and arrogant belief in racial 'cause', lack of respect, fear of police, ignorance of police function, disrespect for law, use of language and cultural barriers as excuses to evade repercussions, unwillingness to cooperate with female officers, lack of confidence, and initiation of their own form of justice. These results suggest that officers themselves saw the lack of trust and cooperation from minority groups as a significant problem.

One officer provided a graphic illustration of the problem police had with the reporting of domestic violence in an ethnic community:

> We have had a lot of problems with domestics over the years, where people have been suffering dreadful domestic violence, and they have been ashamed to involve the police in their family problems, and as a result, I did one job where the whole family was murdered by a boyfriend, and there was seven of them killed, shot to death, and he then shot himself. And one of the survivors told me that they had thought about ringing the police, but they weren't sure if they should, and that was within a few hours of them all being killed.

Another serious instance of non-reporting was in relation to extortion in an Asian community:

> I think that's probably the crime of the decade ... it's the silent crime. Extortion of shopkeepers up here has gone virtually unreported. And we have made efforts in the past to try and get information from them, but even when we have had positive identification on a person doing things, we have reluctance to prosecute. It's a problem we keep confronting.

When questioned about the reasons for these difficulties, officers in the survey had a tendency to locate the problem within minority communities rather than within the police force. Cultural traditions (mentioned by 80 per cent of the respondents), previous experience with police in country of origin (71 per cent), fear of reprisals (59 per cent), community attitudes (42 per cent), and apathy of the community (38 per cent) were the most popular answers. Although 42 per cent mentioned historical reasons, and 35 per cent blamed the problem on the lack of communication between police and community, only 25 per cent thought that police attitudes were a factor and only 10 per cent saw ineffectiveness of the police as a reason for the difficulties. Other reasons, mentioned by one or two respondents in each case, also identified community attitudes as the locus of the problem: belief that all police are out to persecute them, inability to adapt to Australian way of life, lack of respect for authority, fear of police, dislike of police and authority, lack of knowledge about police and the law, apathy towards their communities, do not want to be involved, and manipulation of language difficulties to avoid penalty. Only a few mentioned government support, media image of police, lack of support from superior, and lack of effective training of police as reasons for the difficulties. A beat officer's interpretation is illustrative:

> I felt that they didn't trust us. There's a lack of trust, especially by the Asian population, of anyone in authority, in a uniform … They have, perhaps, an overbearing fear that one day there'll be retaliation when reporting [crime] … And in some instances I feel that a lot of Asian people have an underdeveloped sense of community … they may see something but they wouldn't be prepared to go to court to give evidence. That also intertwines with the retaliation aspect. … It's especially hard for people coming from Vietnam and Cambodia and Laos to associate us as the good guys after the horror stories we hear about their home countries. So they think of the police as agents of communist or military regimes and they're just tools or pawns of the government and in that sense used in their dirty work.

Drug crime investigators found it difficult to obtain information from the Asian community except through anonymous sources:

> With the Chinese traditionally they have a mistrust of authority and government and it's difficult to enlist these people, certainly on an upfront basis where they'll deal directly with you. At times, what you need to do is to really provide a means for them to be able to make contact with you anonymously and past experience has shown that if you can provide that means, that you can tap into quite a wealth of information, albeit anonymous … And a lot of times it's proved to be extremely reliable.

Persuading witnesses to give evidence or supply information was generally difficult. An investigating officer gave an example where the police succeeded in solving a sensational case:

It was a gangland killing by a Vietnamese gang against another one. A Melbourne gang came up to take over the street crime up here and they shot one of the gang leaders ... We arrested everybody, and there was co-operation from the Vietnamese community eventually. It was funny on the night there was probably thirty people in the restaurant, and everyone was in the toilet when the shooting happened. No one saw a thing. But over the next week or two we filtered through the witnesses and through interpreters we explained to them how serious it was, and if these men went free, then they would never be safe, that they were now part of Australia, and that they should cooperate. And they did, and they were really very good witnesses. They were terrific.

This officer described the sensitive police work that must be performed in that case to gain the trust of the community:

Well, what you've got to do is try and get the community to trust you, and when we initially take statements off them, we don't leave them go at that. See, it might be six months before the court case is coming up, and I know for a fact that some of the witnesses go through absolute misery, through being taunted by other people, and so we remain in contact with them. I'll give them a ring from time to time and say it's [name of officer] from the Detectives Office, how are you, Mrs [name of witness]? Everything all right? She will say, I am very frightened, I don't want to go to court. Even to the stage where I've been in the morning of the court case to pick all of the witnesses up and bring them to court. And you have them in a backroom so they don't have to face the people in the foyer while they are waiting to go to court, so you make them as comfortable and as protected as you can.

Unfortunately, such careful and sensitive police practice is either not common or not commonly recognised. Instead, conflict and confrontation have characterised relations between police and minorities in some areas of New South Wales. Problems between police and Aboriginal people in New South Wales have already been referred to in previous chapters. Detailed accounts of the problems can also be found in Cunneen (1990a; 1990b; 1994) and Cunneen and Robb (1987). The following case study focuses on the problems between police and Indo-Chinese youth, one of the most problematic aspects of relations between police and NESB people in New South Wales.

Harassment of Ethnic Youth

Community Complaints

One common complaint from workers in ethnic communities has been that police form stereotypical images of particular ethnic groups and have a tendency to harass members of these groups, especially the young people (see Chapter 1). Community workers consulted in the course of this project raised similar concerns about unfair targeting of young people from certain ethnic groups, verbal or physical abuse during police interrogation or in police custody, and active or passive condoning of racial conflicts by the police. Workers cited incidents of harassment and brutality against young people. One involved a group of nine or ten plain-clothes policemen descending on a group of twenty-five to thirty young Indo-Chinese boys who congregated in a flat one afternoon. The police recorded the names and took photographs of each of the boys, some as young as 14 years old. The reason given for this intrusion was that 'nowadays young people in that age group run away from home so often so they have to take the photos so they can easily identify them'.[6] Another incident related to police harassment of a group of Indo-Chinese youth who rented a house in the area. Police visited them 'at least three times a day, actually three times in one night', conducted searches without warrants and harassed the young people until they moved out of the area. Ethnic young people were also constantly 'being stopped by police and strip-searched'.

Besides complaints of police abuse of stop-and-search powers, community workers also supplied me with documented instances of police violence against young people of Vietnamese origin. In one case a young Vietnamese was found driving a stolen car. Even though he did not try to resist arrest, he was 'grabbed on the head' by a police officer and had his face slammed against a fence twice. He was then told to lie down, and when he did, the officer grabbed his hair and slammed his head on the ground three times before the youth was handcuffed and taken to the police station. At the station the young man saw an Asian police officer and called out to him to ring his mother. He was told to 'fucking shut up' by a young police officer who threatened to blow the fire extinguisher on his face. When the Vietnamese youth called out to the Asian officer a few more times, the young officer carried out his threat and blew the fire extinguisher on the youth's head and face. In another incident, an Indo-Chinese youth stopped by police was even more violently dealt with:

P. was then pushed violently forward. He fell down, twisted his ankle. The officer then grabbed him by the collar and pulled him up, then hit him under the chin with the other arm. The officer's watch hit P., the watch face broke under such force. P. fell backwards. The police officer grabbed P.'s head, dragged him and slammed it against the brick wall outside the block of flats there. Blood spurted out of the wound thus sustained on his head, at the right eyebrow. He was then elbowed on the back and kneed in the chest a few times. Then he was handcuffed with the hands to the back. He could not walk, his right ankle was hurting so much. The officer then dragged him by the collar and shoved him into the backseat of the police car.

The youth was then taken back to the station and interrogated even though he was bleeding profusely. He was subsequently taken to a hospital where he received five stitches to the wound. Back at the station, he was interrogated in English without an interpreter and without any effort to explain to him what was going on. He was later charged and then released.

Community workers in a western Sydney suburb also got together a group of about ten young people from the area to talk to me. The group, mostly homeless youth of Asian descent, told me other instances of being unfairly targeted, harassed, strip-searched, detained and assaulted by police. They felt that they were being picked on because they were Asian. However, they all agreed that one Asian police officer was a 'good cop' because, as one of the youth workers pointed out, he 'doesn't harass them and always tries to talk to them in a nice way, like ask them not to do stupid things and not to be involved in criminal things'. When asked why they didn't complain about the treatment they received from the police, the reply was they had to go to the police to complain against the police: 'they hit us there – how can we go there [to complain], come on!'

At the time of my fieldwork, relations between the police and the community workers were very tense. One youth worker had all but given up on the cooperative approach:

> We've got an intimidation campaign – if a young person is identified now as speaking out against police behaviour you can bet that that person's life is going to be made fairly difficult on the streets. There are also cases that I know of, and that I'm aware of, where workers have been harassed, phone calls made, followed by police officers, pulled over and charged with various things. I mean, the reality is, who's keeping an eye on the people keeping an eye on us? And the answer is, no-one, and they have to be held accountable. They cannot break the law. They have to enforce the law and that's a difficult job, I agree, but when they go around using the draconian tactics they're using with young people in this area, I'm not going to sit still and let it happen, and I don't think any of the other workers here are. We've tried the let's-talk-about-it approach, we've tried the let's-work-cooperatively-together, and they're not prepared to accept those offers of help ... Now I believe that workers in the community have a lot to offer the police department and we should be able to work constructively with them around issues of law enforcement.

Police Reactions

Police reactions to these complaints were typically defensive. They also tended to discredit the accusers. When questioned about some of these complaints, the senior officer could only remember one case, which had been conciliated and the police officer counselled for his action. In that situation, the senior officer was sympathetic to his subordinate: 'It's very easy to sit back in hindsight in an armchair and say you should have done this, you should have done that; it's not always that easy on the street.' He noted, however, that one of the youth workers had 'collided head-on with some of the police here because of his attitude':

> They see him as a trouble-maker. They see him as someone who wants to march in and bump tables and do things counter to what they want to achieve. No doubt their aims are different. The youth worker will try and do his thing and the police obviously have an enforcement role and the police role is traditionally adversary. The whole criminal justice system is an adversary situation so the youth worker may not understand fully either ... But on the other hand, police see government-employed social workers as not highly committed. They see themselves as having jobs, that is their primary concern, they don't see them as highly committed as, say, people like the Salvation Army or other volunteer organisations.

When the youth workers went to the press about some of the incidents, the comment from the police was that the youth workers were creating publicity to justify their existence because it was time for renewal of funding for the community centre. There was no recognition that police might have abused their powers or used excessive force on any occasion.

Police did not consider stereotyping a problem; it was seen as something that came naturally with dealing with 'bad' people from ethnic groups. One police officer explained that stereotyping may be the result of police experience with particular groups:

> I think it's the bad experiences a lot of police have had in dealing with the Vietnamese, that they become insular. If you are dealing with bad Vietnamese all the time, then they are all bad. Instead of keeping an open mind to these sorts of things, but I suppose if you are getting bashed with it everyday, I suppose you must get coloured a little bit.

Stereotyping was also considered justified, given what some officers saw as the reality of criminality among some Asian youth:

> It is organised gangs[7] of young, unemployed Asian youths ... supported by an uncle or an aunty or something, so they come out here by themselves and they've really got no parental control over them. And they find themselves unemployed in these pinball parlours and they'll be approached by an older man, who will recruit them and they'll have nice clothes to wear, and they'll have a car to drive, ... and for that they'll have to perform certain criminal acts like gold chain robberies ... They generally all hang together. They wear the same clothing. They're all in a group. A lot of them live ten or twelve in one unit.

In fact, this officer saw a real difference between some of the Asian criminals they deal with and offenders from other ethnic groups. While claiming that he was 'not being prejudiced at all', this officer asserted that unlike 'Aussies'[8] and other ethnic groups who were prepared to admit guilt when caught with evidence of wrongdoing, 'with Vietnamese and Cambodians, they basically ... won't admit to breathing ... they will come up with some fantastic story even in front of the judge, right to the last minute, they'll fight it to the death'.[9] This officer felt that 'there's an absolute contempt for the police and the authority by these groups'.

Police also saw stopping and questioning young people as part of their job. One officer defended this practice in terms of crime control: if young people were in the company of known offenders, police had the right to find out who they were and what they were doing. Police said that it was their duty to be suspicious and they had the powers to stop and search when necessary. One beat officer told his side of the story with respect to a particular Asian youth:

> I'll tell you a story about one that happened to me the other day which found me in the situation where I considered the young person was acting suspiciously ... he was a school kid and I wanted to see what was in his school bag and he refused to let me search his school bag. He gave me a mouthful of cheek so I took him back to the police station and intended to have him cautioned. He gave me false addresses, blah, blah, blah, the whole kit and caboodle. I was pacified in the sense that the young person turned around and said well, 'I made a mistake. I should have done what you wanted to do in the first place and I'd have been gone.' And I said, 'Well, that's all I wanted to do.' He was eventually released and given a verbal caution by me. And in five minutes he was down at the newspaper complaining about police harassment.

This officer admitted that it was a difficult situation because it was part of the duty of beat police to know who they were dealing with: 'who the crooks are up the town and who the good guys are'. His basic argument was 'if they have nothing to hide, they have nothing to fear'.

In response to charges of police racism, police typically ignored the inherent ambiguity of most areas of policing, and swept aside instances of police brutality, concentrating instead on unambiguous situations and serious offences. One officer commented:

> Well, you couldn't possibly be accused of being a racist here because ... I mean, if he's got a balaclava and he's got a boot full of drugs, well, how can we be racist, whatever nationality he was, if our information is correct, he will be arrested, but it's just that we have such a large [ethnic] population in this area and mainly that's who we deal with.

Similarly, police dealing with major drug investigations did not see targeting particular ethnic groups as discriminatory, since 'we're not targeting the entire community, we're just targeting criminals within that community'. It was taken for granted that police were able to discern with great accuracy the guilty and the innocent among members of a community.

The cultural diversity of the New South Wales population has a significant impact on the task of policing. Police officers in the 1990s find themselves in frequent contact with members of ethnic communities, many of whom speak a foreign language and are suspicious of the police. The research evidence suggests that officers have difficulties both in overcoming language barriers and in gaining the trust of minority groups. Responses to the survey give the impression that officers were much more ready to blame community attitudes and cultural differences as the cause of the difficulties, and much less willing to acknowledge that police attitudes and ineffectiveness were at least partly responsible for the problems.

The case study of relations between police and ethnic youth is illustrative of the problems of police racism and its varying interpretations discussed in Chapters 1 and 2. Community workers complained about police harassment and mistreatment of ethnic youth. Police defended their actions as appropriate because it was their job to be suspicious and to enforce the law. Stereotyping was seen as both a result of, and justified by, 'bad experiences' that police had in dealing with certain minority groups. Harassment was not considered a problem since 'if they have nothing to hide, they have nothing to fear'. In response to charges of racism, police typically justified their actions in relation to serious offences and unambiguous situations, ignoring the fact that most policing situations are fluid, ambiguous, and concerned with relatively minor offences.

It is against this background of changing social environment and emergent 'race relations' problems that many of the police reforms in New South Wales were introduced. The next chapter will describe in some detail the recent history of administrative reform and philosophical change in the NSW police, especially the initiatives directed at improving relations between police and minorities.

Notes

1 In a similar survey carried out in 1978 (NSWEAC 1980), only 43 per cent of the respondents reported having contact with 'immigrants' (defined as 'residents of Australia who are of non-Anglo-Saxon origin') many times a week. This may be regarded as evidence that the frequency of police contact with

NESB people has increased substantially over the thirteen years. However, the 1978 survey was based on a simple random sample of about 700 NSW police officers, while the 1991 survey was stratified by rank and based on a random sample of officers who worked in areas with at least 15 per cent NESB population. The 1991 sample, therefore, may have produced a *higher* frequency of police–NESB contact because of the choice of patrol areas, but it may also have produced a *lower* frequency of such contact because of over-sampling senior officers who tend to have less direct contact with citizens. In general, the two surveys are not directly comparable.

2 One category of police contact with visible minority groups not captured by Table 5.4 is the activity of special squads on drug trafficking in certain ethnic communities. These officers work extensively with informants in the communities to investigate middle- to upper-level drug traffickers, although they occasionally also deal with vice and gambling matters. One group targeted has been the Asians. Other areas not covered include less stressful situations in which police interact with ethnic communities in crime prevention or safety education programs. The fact that these situations were not mentioned by any of the respondents even though an 'other' category was provided in the questionnaire was perhaps an indication that these were not considered 'usual circumstances'.

3 About 6 per cent of the police officers in the survey mentioned 'alcohol-related offences' among Aborigines as an 'other' category of circumstances not explicitly canvassed in the questionnaire.

4 The 1978 survey of police officers estimated that about 2.9 per cent of NSW officers were of 'non-Anglo-Saxon origin' (NSWEAC 1980: 9). This proportion has no doubt increased, but there was no reliable estimate of the figure in 1991. An analysis of the ethnic background of twenty-one classes of new recruits at the NSW Police Academy in the late 1980s and early 1990s shows that the average proportion of NESB recruits (based on parents' birthplace) in each class was 7.4 per cent, with the figure closer to 10 per cent in recent years (NSW Police Service 1994: 41). These figures suggest that the proportion of NESB officers in the NSW Police Service is probably less than 10 per cent. In 1991, about 11 per cent of the sworn officers in the NSW Police Service were female (Sutton 1992).

5 Since multiple responses were available for this question and the one on 'reasons for difficulties', the percentages do not total 100.

6 The cases and quotations used in this section were drawn from written notes kept by youth workers.

7 The existence of organised youth gangs was disputed by another police officer, although he had personally received death threats: 'I've yet to see anything that convinced me totally that we've got organised youth gangs here. They're a loose affiliation of kids whose only common link is, generally speaking, a very low education background ... They have a very low respect in regard to other people's property and life ... They're a loose, unbound affiliation of street youths.'

8 Australians still have a tendency to refer to white Anglo-Australians as 'Aussies' or 'Australians' while NESB Australians are called 'migrants' regardless of their residence or citizenship status.

9 It is ironic that such behavioural patterns have consistently been displayed by Australian politicians, business entrepreneurs, and even police officers when accused of wrongdoing.

CHAPTER 6

Under New Management

Unlike countries such as Britain and the United States, police forces in Australia are mainly organised along State or Territory boundaries. A survey by Bayley (1992) of the organisation of police forces in five English-speaking countries found that Australia has the least number of autonomous forces: seven State forces and a federal force, compared with 43 in Great Britain, 461 in Canada, and over 15,000 in the United States. Since the area covered by the seven State forces is about the size of the United States excluding Alaska and Hawaii, police forces in Australia are the largest in terms of geographical coverage (*ibid.*: 512–14). They are also among the largest with respect to the number of officers per force and population covered. According to Bayley, the average size of Australian police forces in 1988–89 was 4978 police officers and the average population covered was 2.3 million.

The New South Wales Police Service, which consisted of about 13,000 police officers and 3000 civilians in 1992 and an annual expenditure of close to a thousand million dollars (NSWPS 1992), is the largest police force in Australia. It serves the entire State population of around 6 million, covering an area three times the size of the United Kingdom. The functions of the NSW Police Service, like other Australian police forces, are primarily those of law enforcement, protection of life and property, order maintenance and crime control, although the State police also regulate traffic and work with the Australian Federal Police and other Commonwealth law-enforcement agencies to enforce federal laws.[1]

The recent history of the NSW police, as Finnane (1995) points out, has not been one characterised by the continuing of 'long-standing traditions' or 'bureaucratic inertia'. In terms of effecting organisational change, the NSW police reform efforts have been substantial and impressive, even if these efforts have not all been successful. To appreciate the nature and scope of change, as well as the organisation's reactions to change, it is important to examine the conditions under which the reform programs were introduced and the intentions behind the reforms. The purpose of this chapter is to provide an overview of the recent history and organisation of the NSW Police Service, and to describe the changes it has undergone since 1984 and the strategies adopted for implementation.[2] It will become obvious that the majority of the reforms were directed at the gamut of policing activities, including administration and management, operations, recruitment and training. Strategies for improving relations between police and minorities were not the primary focus of the reform programs, although they were a natural extension of the philosophy of community-based policing which underpinned many of the changes.

Prelude to Change

The 1980s to early 1990s was a period of rapid and constant change for the NSW police. However, change was historically not a feature of the police force. The social climate of the 1960s and 1970s, as Swanton *et al.* point out, created increased pressure on policing during the time of Police Commissioner Norman Allan (1962–72):

> Allan's ten years in office saw the emergence of the great social issues of the late sixties and seventies – the Vietnam moratorium protests, Aboriginal Rights, Women's liberation, Abortion Law Reform, relaxation of censorship which, whilst a long way off when he took office, burst on the New South Wales scene in quick succession accompanying the sudden and massive break with traditional values by young people; all of which placed great strains upon the police force in the field of order maintenance. [Swanton *et al.* 1985: 389]

For most of the period after World War II, rumours of corruption and malpractice both within the police force and among other government institutions were widespread and persistent. Commissioner Allan's term of office was plagued by public controversies and political embarrassments. At the time of his resignation, the reputation of the NSW police was 'at a low ebb' (Finnane 1995). The need for reform was pressing when the Labor Party was returned to power in 1976. By the late 1970s, with continuing allegations being made of police corruption, especially in relation to the policing of drugs, gambling and prostitution, and the lack of capacity of successive Police Commissioners to reform the force, relations between the police and the government were 'exceedingly poor' (*ibid.*).[3] Much to the resentment of the police, the government decided to extend the powers of the Ombudsman to investigate complaints against the police; as well, it repealed the 1970 *Summary Offences Act*, effectively decriminalising certain public order offences.

The new government was sensitive to the changing needs of the population, especially the rapid increase in people of non-English-speaking background (NESB) following the relaxation of immigration restrictions. In 1977 the then Premier Neville Wran established the first Ethnic Affairs Commission in Australia to conduct an inquiry into the needs of ethnic communities in New South Wales. The commission was subsequently established as a permanent government authority to encourage full participation of ethnic groups in the social, economic and political life of the community and promote the unity of all ethnic groups, while recognising their diversity (NSWEAC 1985: 2). In 1978, it conducted a survey on the work experience of police officers with immigrants and Aborigines (NSWEAC 1980). This survey 'arose out of the discussions between the Commissioner of Police, Mr Mervyn Wood, and the Chairman of the Ethnic Affairs Commission, Mr Paolo Totaro' (*ibid.*). John Avery, then a police inspector involved with training and development, 'made the project his own'. The survey drew just over 700 responses from a random sample of police officers – a response rate of 95 per cent; it provided a wealth of information about police contacts with immigrants, police perception of problems with immigrants and Aborigines, communication difficulties and suggestions for change.

Change in the police organisation, however, did not come swiftly. There was a small group of people within the organisation who were supportive of improving the accessibility of services to minority communities, but the organisation itself was able to ignore many of the social and political changes occurring at the time. The role of external agencies, according to a senior member of the force, was important for pushing the police to be more accountable as an organisation:

> You have so-called minority groups, ranging from the Women's Co-ordination Unit, the Child Protection Council, the civil libertarians' movement, you have the Ombudsman, the Privacy Committee, you obviously have the media generally pushing very strongly ... I mean, it wasn't one particular group wanting one particular thing. It was simply external pressure on the organisation to say, you must emerge from this cocoon in which you currently reside and re-enter the real world.

One powerful driving force pushing the police organisation towards change was the Lusher inquiry into the NSW police administration (Lusher Report 1981). The inquiry's terms of reference were very broad, including an examination into the 'structure, organisation and management policies' of the Police Force and the Police Department, as well as the 'structure of the relationship between the Police Force and the Executive Government'. The report made more than 200 recommendations in a wide range of areas, including management, recruitment, training, promotion, working conditions and police corruption. The most significant developments following the Lusher inquiry were the creation of the New South Wales Police Board and the appointment of John Avery as Police Commissioner in 1984. Major organisational and ideological changes in policing were pursued in subsequent years.

Changing Concept of Policing

The appointment of John Avery as the NSW Police Commissioner in 1984 by the newly formed Police Board was a turning point in the policing history of New South Wales. In the years that followed until his retirement in 1991, Avery was to be responsible for introducing some significant and fundamental changes to the concept of policing in New South Wales. Yet the task facing Avery was difficult from the very start, given his 'academic' image and the fact that he was promoted above others in more senior ranks. One of his former colleagues, now a senior member of the force, explained:

> First of all, his appointment was a surprise to many. Avery himself was seen as an 'academic', which is a term – when police officers refer to an academic ... it meant that they have never really done anything at all. They've been off wandering around universities and not doing some real police work. So in that sense it was a general feeling that this bloke wasn't really a cop. That seemed to fly in the face of the fact that he spent 35 years operating as a grassroots police officer. What it said was the fact that he managed to go off and get a BA and MA had removed those 35 years police experience ... The other aspect was that he was, in a seniority-based system, he was what we'd call then the Executive Chief Superintendent, which is about the third layer down the organisation.

Compared with his predecessors, Avery was an exceptional commissioner. Long before his appointment at the top, his thoughtful and visionary approach to policing was demonstrated in his book *Police: Force or Service?* (1981) which details his view of the role of police in society. In the book Avery recognises the 'importance of community participation in the process of social control' and argues for a 'closer relationship between the police and the citizens involving a responsibility to assist each other to maintain the peace in the community' (*ibid.*: 2, 73). Using a survey of telephone calls to four police patrols in Sydney, he demonstrated, as researchers in other countries did, that 'law-enforcement' calls constituted only about 20 to 30 per cent of the calls to the police.

However, contrary to the opinion of those who suggested that police be relieved of their 'extraneous duties' such as community service, Avery maintains that these duties 'bring police into a normal form of contact with the community and allow police to establish a relationship with them which is not affected by dramatic crisis situations' (*ibid.*: 56). Not surprisingly, Avery's vision permeated his reform agenda as Police Commissioner.

Avery's push for more accountable, community-based policing practice coincided with a similar trend to reconsider the role of the police in Western industrialised societies. In fact, the influence of overseas debates and the role of the international exchange of ideas were significant factors in pushing along police reforms in New South Wales. An officer who was involved with these early developments explained her involvement in a major seminar on the future of policing in the United States in 1984:

> It was run by Harvard [University], collecting together the top academics, police chiefs ... Together, we talked about: Where was policing going? What had been done? ... some police officers started thinking about change – what would it look like? what would the structure of the police force look like? What happened was that I got involved in it. I came back from America in '86, but had a lot of contact with them over time, as well as with Mark Moore, who was the Professor of Criminal Justice Policy and Management at Harvard ... He and Avery met and talked ... and pretty much what was developed with Sir Gordon Jackson ... and Sir Maurice Byers [of the Police Board] was a plan for change.

The visit of Professor Moore was said to have 'greatly assisted the executive in developing a strategy to achieve a more open and community-based system of policing' (NSWPD 1986: 4).

Many advocates of police reform see community-based policing as the answer to many policing problems, including those between police and visible minorities. The idea is that if the police are held accountable to the local community (which may consist of a number of ethnic groups), then it becomes their reponsibility to establish a constructive relationship with members of that community. Police cannot serve the needs of the local (ethnic or non-ethnic) community satisfactorily unless they abandon any prejudice they have, reach out to its members, establish a sense of trust among them, and involve them in the policing of their community.

Advocates of community-based policing argue that the existence of large, urban police forces is a relatively recent phenomenon. Until the passage of the *Metropolitan Police Act* in England in 1829, the tasks of surveillance and order maintenance were largely the responsibility of private citizens. The evolution of the English police model to the present-day organisation of police can be traced to the progressive movement in the late nineteenth century in the United States, where political control of the police became a major issue. As a result of a movement to rid police of corruption, police departments in the United States became committed to crime control as their primary function; they developed a paramilitary organisational structure, with central command and functional specialisation; and they gained independence from the political system. This trend accelerated in the 1940s to 1960s, when technological advances and statistical reporting pushed policing practices towards the achievement of rapid responses to alarms, the allocation of patrol resources to optimise response time, and the use of serious crime statistics as performance indicators. Doubts about the appropriateness of this style of policing were raised in the United States amidst the civil rights movement, which brought out the conflict between the crime-fighting role of the police and individual political rights and freedoms. At the same time, research on police work was raising new questions about the effectiveness of random patrol, rapid response and detectives' investigation procedures (Kelling and Moore, 1982; see also Moore 1992).

Advocates of community policing see a fundamental overhaul of the ideological and organisational basis of policing as an effective and necessary step towards greater police accountability. The gentleness of the label 'community-based policing' in fact disguises some extremely radical measures which turn traditional policing upside down. A full embrace of the community-based policing model involves several major shifts in emphasis in policing style (Sparrow et al. 1990). We will look at them in detail.

Proactive: preventive policing rather than reactive policing

Acknowledging the limited utility of motorised patrols, rapid response to calls for service and retrospective investigation of crime, those who advocate community-based policing emphasise the 'problem-solving' approach to policing. This approach releases expensive police resources traditionally consumed by reactive policing, and puts these resources into removing the conditions and opportunities which are conducive to the occurrence of offences. Instead of rushing around from call to call and never stopping long enough to get to know the victims and their communities, police are now encouraged to become familiar with neighbourhoods and people within these communities so that they are in a position to solve their problems, which may or may not be directly related to the occurrence of crime.

Reducing fear and maintaining order rather than fighting crime

Advocates of community-based policing point to the obvious disjunction between the police self-perception that they are predominantly crime-fighters and the reality that police officers spend most of their patrol time dealing with non-criminal matters involving disputes or emergencies. For many years, these 'social service' calls were considered peripheral to real police work. Consequently, police resent these tasks and receive no training in handling disputes and maintaining order. They rely, instead, on the actual use, or the threat, of law enforcement or physical force to restore order. Community policing suggests that police may serve their community better by not denying the importance of their order-maintenance role and by addressing matters such as vandalism and disorder which may help to reduce the community's fear of crime.

Accountability to the community rather than operational autonomy

The ideals of community-based policing place a great deal of emphasis on the involvement of members of the community in defining and assisting police work. Rather than asserting that police operational decisions are police matters, the new approach to policing makes clear that police must be accountable to the community they serve. Accordingly, police must listen to and give credence to the wishes of the community, for ultimately the success of their work depends on the consent and support of the community.

That these principles constitute a radical departure from traditional policing philosophy and practices cannot be over-emphasised. In fact, community-based policing raises some 'fundamental questions abut the proper limit to and scope of police activity' (Weatheritt, 1987: 19). Flowing from the principles of community-based policing are concrete initiatives which police organisations may decide to implement: the establishment of programs such as Neighbourhood Watch and Safety House, the setting up of community consultative committees, the increased use of foot patrols (beat police), and putting additional resources into community liaison. With minority ethnic communities, there may be additional initiatives such as: group-specific or language-specific community consultative committees, the recruitment of police officers from ethnic groups, the appointment of special ethnic liaison officers, the institution of cross-cultural training courses for police officers, and offering incentives for police officers to acquire ethnic language skills and understanding of multicultural issues.

In New South Wales, the changes can be discussed in three main areas: organisational restructuring; a new approach to recruitment, training and education; and the development of community-based programs.

Organisational Restructuring

The Lusher inquiry questioned the appropriateness of the organisational structure of the then NSW Police Force, which was characterised by 'a para-military rank structure, a high degree of specialisation and job definition and detailed rules, procedures and documentations of events' (Lusher Report 1981: 87). The inquiry suggested that by continuing with its rigid structure, the Police Force was holding on to 'a style of policing which is likely to alienate it from the community at large' (*ibid.*: 87). The inquiry also criticised the force's lack of explicit organisational objectives which could assist in organisational planning. However, it was the excessive concentration of authority and its attendant inefficiency and discouragement of lower-rank initiatives which received the most pointed criticism:

> The concentration of authority in the hands of executive police officers … results in a loss of initiative in the middle and lower ranks. Certain talents of younger police officers are underutilized. Examples have been brought to the attention of the Inquiry where innovation and creativity have been discouraged. A new idea has to pass through so many hierarchical levels that it is unlikely to find acceptance at all levels. Senior police have frequently adopted a defensive attitude towards suggestions for change … Disappointments and frustrations experienced at lower ranks as a result of these obstacles and discouragements often turn to acceptance and conformity which are carried through into the top ranks, thereby perpetuating negative attitudes towards change. [*ibid.*: 96–7]

The inquiry's recommendation for greater decentralisation of authority and a more flexible organisational structure was in line with the dominant thinking in the fields of organisational theory and public administration at the time. The report quoted an article by Dunphy (1976) about the need to 'build continual change into organisations so that adaptation and re-organisation is a normal part of ongoing operations'. Dunphy contrasts features of bureaucratic organisations with those of organisations capable of coping with change and discontinuity. The flexible organisation is characterised by: decentralised power, short hierarchies, radical delegation, participative decision-making, fewer classifications, multiskilling, high accountability, and so on. The need for decentralisation and flexibility was also emphasised by two powerful government inquiries in the 1970s: the Royal Commission on Australian

Government Administration (1976) and the Review of NSW Government Administration (Wilenski Report 1977).

The organisation restructuring that followed the appointment of Avery, however, went further than the recommendations of the Lusher Report. It was also more explicitly directed at the achievement of organisational objectives. During his first two years of appointment, Avery's attention was focused almost exclusively on attacking institutionalised corruption within the police force. One officer explained to me that decentralisation was designed to assist Avery's fight against police corruption: regionalisation and decentralisation were structural changes which broke up the 'Criminal Investigation Branch, the Traffic Branch, and other big headquarters branches, and really shifting and decentralising authority and power', thus preventing a resurgence of the 'corrupt inner core'.

By 1986 a set of corporate objectives was formulated in a two-day workshop involving the combined executive of the Police Force and Sir Gordon Jackson of the Police Board. These objectives, which have only been slightly modified in subsequent years, were:

- Increase feelings of safety and security in the community by giving priority to crime prevention and detection programmes.
- Provide policing services which are more responsive to the needs and feelings of the community.
- Encourage greater involvement of citizens in policing.
- Influence changes in driver behaviour, with the object of reducing road deaths and injuries.
- Improve management and organisation to optimise use of resources.
- Further extend practices aimed at minimising corruption within the Police Force. [NSWPD 1986: 16]

By the following year the government had adopted community-based policing as the principal operation strategy of the NSW Police Force and regionalisation 'as a vehicle for its implementation' (NSWPD 1987: 24–5). The main thrust of regionalisation was to replace functional division by geographical division. New South Wales was divided into four Regions, which included 24 districts, 73 divisions and 478 patrols. Each Region was under the control of an Assistant Commissioner. Region Commanders would report to the State Commander. Each patrol was to be headed by a Patrol Commander. There followed a progressive devolution of centralised areas, such as the Criminal Investigation Branch and the Traffic Branch, to regional command. The restructuring was said to have reduced the chain of command from fourteen to seven levels and brought 'senior Police decision-makers closer to citizens and their problems' (NSWPD 1986: 16).

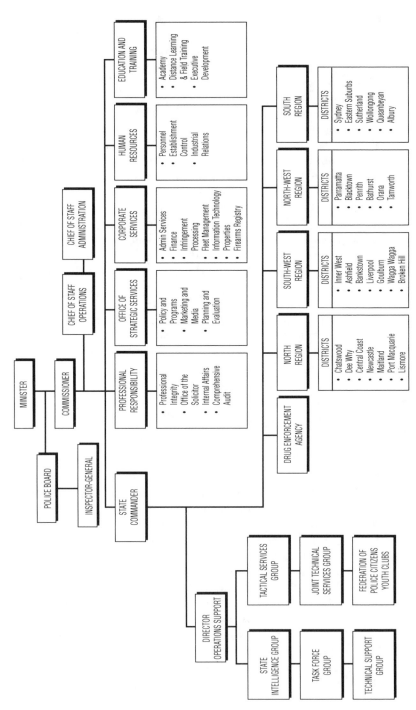

Figure 6.1 The organisation of the New South Wales Police Service, 1 July 1992.

By 1988, the Police headquarters structure consisted of five components: State Command, the central operational command; Policy, Planning and Evaluation; Professional Responsibility; Procurement, Finance and Data Transmission; and Education/Personnel. The State Executive Group, chaired by the Commissioner, consisting of the State Commander, Executive Director, Assistant Commissioners and Region Commanders, was to be responsible for 'overall policy development, planning, priority determination and performance evaluation' (NSWPS 1988: 13). The organisation has since been modified a number of times, although the command structure remains the same. The organisation structure of the NSW Police Service at the time of the research is shown in Figure 6.1.

In spite of being a dominant trend in private as well as government organisations, decentralisation was not a popular concept in the police organisation at the time of its introduction. It was opposed by many police officers and the two police unions. Many opposed because they lacked understanding of the concept, but a great deal of resistance was due to the fact that regionalisation broke up the traditional power bases of the organisation and demanded a higher level of professional accountability. A senior officer explained the chain of accountability in the decentralised system:

> One of the things which Avery used to say was that if something went right and he was looking for the person who he could give credit, he would have seven people able to claim credit. If something went wrong, there was no one available ... And so ... [with regionalisation] the Patrol Commander, District Commander, or Region Commander would be responsible for the entire range of policing services in that geographical area. And it didn't really matter whether you were a detective, or a traffic man, or general duties person, or emergency services person, or anything else. You are accountable to that one chain. There was a lot of resistance to that notion.

In the end, decentralisation was achieved using a change strategy that can be characterised as 'transformative' in a 'directive/coercive' mode, rather than incremental or consultative (see Dunphy and Stace 1990: 90). However, it was considered to be a necessary strategy at the time. A senior officer who regarded himself as a 'change agent' of the organisation agreed with the strategy:

> The decentralisation was a massive and forced change ... It wasn't a democratic change. They were forced, and I'm absolutely convinced that in an organisation like this, the only way to achieve change is – they won't adapt, they won't change, they're far too comfortable the way they are – the only real way to achieve it is with force.

Organisational restructuring was accompanied by another major change: the shift from a seniority-based to a merit-based promotion system for police officers. This was another issue examined in great detail by the Lusher inquiry. The inquiry considered the organisation's approach to promotion as of 'central importance' in terms of attracting police recruits of high potential, maintaining the quality of supervision and management, and affecting the morale of the police force (Lusher Report 1981: 468). The inquiry recommended that 'promotion should be to a position and not to a rank', and 'merit and not seniority should be the dominant criteria for selection' (*ibid.*: 554–5). This approach was again consistent with the New South Wales government's preferred direction for change (see Wilenski Report 1977). Even this initiative was very much related to Avery's campaign against police corruption, since professional integrity was considered a crucial dimension of merit. The move also facilitated younger officers who were not resistant to change to move up to positions where they could exert an influence:

> Of course, what [merit-based promotion] did was give [Avery] an opportunity to break up any old systems which may have been in place to facilitate the corrupt officers getting to positions of authority. A key component of a person's appointment was their ability to pass an integrity test in the sense of any person nominated for promotion had to get a clearance from the Internal Security Unit and the Internal Affairs Unit. That is, if there was anything in their history which suggested that ... if dishonesty plays any part in your career then you were not promoted. It also ... was the beginning of the process of allowing younger people to compete for positions, although that took quite some time to open up.

The surprising aspect of this massive transformation of the organisation is its eventual success in terms of organisational acceptance. As one officer put it, 'now four years down the track [of regionalisation], you wouldn't find an opponent in the organisation'. One patrol commander described from his personal experience how he benefited from promotion by merit and the devolution of power and budget following regionalisation:

> [Promotion by merit] changed everybody's approach to their careers, of course ... I received elevated promotion very early, and I've attained a position now which under the old system I could not have achieved even by the age of 60. I'm 49, so I've achieved something that was unattainable before. With regionalisation, of course, the major changes there are the flattening of the organisation and the rank structure, and the accountability that – at my level, where I have the freedom to act within my own area of responsibility, and some of the things we put together here, whereas years ago, policy would have been dictated from someone else.

There were also losers in this change process. Merit-based promotion and the use of the 'integrity' criterion created a great deal of discontent among those who favoured the seniority system. The NSW Police Association criticised the new system as 'legalised favouritism' and the assessment of integrity was seen as unfair. The system was subsequently fine-tuned following the recommendations of a Select Committee (Finnane 1995).

Changes to Recruitment and Training

Recruitment

The Lusher inquiry was highly critical of the approaches taken by the NSW Police Force in both recruitment and training. With respect to recruitment, the inquiry found that the procedures and criteria did not 'have any link with a clear statement of objectives as to the type of person being sought or the nature of the job or jobs to be done', and the recruiting system failed 'to recognise the need to compete actively in the market for the appropriate talent and skills needed by the Force to deal effectively with its present and future responsibilities' (Lusher Report 1981: 304). The inquiry recommended that the minimum height and weight restrictions should be reduced to remove some of the barriers against the recruitment of some ethnic minority groups, although it did not support affirmative action to increase the number of ethnic recruits. It recommended the removal of restrictions on the entry of women into the Police Force, provisions for lateral entry, and improvements in the procedures for processing applications.

Changes to recruitment criteria were introduced in 1986 as part of Avery's reforms. Height restrictions were abandoned, and educational and physical requirements were updated. Job-related agility test and aptitude tests were also introduced (NSWPD 1987: 103). By 1988 a set of recruitment objectives was developed, with a stated commitment to recruit more women and ethnic minorities:

- To provide an adequate number of suitably qualified and experienced persons for the Police Service.
- To ensure that applicants selected reflect the ethnic composition of the community.
- To ensure that an increasing proportion of recruits are women.
- To ensure that applicants with the highest possible academic achievements are attracted to the Service. [NSWPS 1988: 59]

In February 1990 the NSW Police Service introduced a new battery of job-related aptitude tests for screening applicants. These include:

observation skills, verbal comprehension, drawing conclusions, reasoning skills and decision-making (NSWPS 1990).

While the 10 per cent target for recruitment from NESB people has generally been reached or even surpassed (NSWPS 1988a: 29), efforts to attract more Asian-Australians to the Police Service have not been very successful. Members of some minority groups have found that joining the police can place them in danger of being ostracised or threatened by sections of their own communities. I was told anecdotes of recruits of Vietnamese descent facing threats from their own community. This trend is consistent with the experience of other countries. Sullivan (1989) explains that one of the main barriers to attracting minority members to join the police in the United States was related to the negative image police officers had among minorities. This image is especially pronounced among immigrants from countries in which police were corrupt or oppressive. There was a general recognition within the NSW Police Service that the organisation cannot recruit members from a certain visible minority group and expect them to work solely within their own community. The Ethnic Client Consultant cited cases where ethnic police officers resigned after being placed in their own ethnic community. She felt that these officers needed a lot of support and protection.

Racial prejudice within police ranks and among the general public can deter visible minorities from joining the police. One Aboriginal officer, who maintained that he himself had not had any problem throughout his nineteen years of service ('The odd joke or two, which happens, but it hasn't been directed at me personally'), described the negative experience of a female Aboriginal officer who was stationed at an 'elite area':

> she was having problems due to community pressure. The community where she was working, I believe she felt, discriminated against her because they didn't feel that they should have an Aboriginal person in that community. It got to the stage where she was thinking about resigning, but we were able to overcome that problem there by transferring her to another area.

There has been a great deal of effort devoted to the increased recruitment of police officers from Aboriginal communities. The number of Aboriginal applicants to the Police Service has been extremely low, from a low of two in 1990 to a high of thirty-two in 1992 (NSWPS 1994: 18–20). However, the actual number of Aboriginal recruits admitted would have been much lower. In 1992 a bridging course was developed to help Aboriginal people who wanted to join the Police Service to obtain the necessary educational qualifications. The bridging course was a one-year Tertiary Preparation Course, assessed externally and run by the NSW

Department of Technical and Further Education. However, the capacity of the course to maintain the current level of applicants has been placed in doubt following recent changes to its organisation (*ibid.:* 17). The working party which reviewed recruitment policy concluded that a significant increase in Aboriginal applicants would 'only occur with a complete turn around in the perception of policing by the Aboriginal community' (*ibid.:* 17).

Police Training

The Lusher Report's criticisms of police training in New South Wales ranged widely. Not only was the method of teaching said to be 'very traditional', but the training programs were heavily weighted towards procedural and operational techniques, with little emphasis on social and behavioural sciences or the role of police in the community. The Police Academy also made very limited use of non-police staff, while service to the academy was given little recognition within the organisation. The length of recruit training was seen as inadequate, and there was no systematic effort to evaluate the effectiveness of training programs. The academy's accommodation and facilities were also considered unsatisfactory. Lusher recommended sweeping changes to the system of police training, and many of the report's recommendations were taken up by the Police Board. The academy moved to Goulburn (a country town about 250 kilometres from Sydney) in 1984 and has since reached a residential capacity of 648 beds. Following one of the Lusher Report's recommendations, an Interim Police Education and Training Advisory Council was set up in 1985 to advise the Police Board on education policy.

The Interim Council produced four major reports between 1985 and 1987. As a result, the Police Academy adopted a totally new educational philosophy, a redesigned recruit training curriculum, and a different policy in relation to the staffing and administration. The new approach 'called for police training and education to be built upon progressive adult education principles including experiential learning, case study, educational contextual studies and the importance of practicum' (NSWPS 1991: 11). A Dean of Studies was appointed in 1987, followed by the appointment of other non-police academics. A Police Education Advisory Council was formed in 1988 to advise the Police Board, the Police Commissioner and senior officers on educational policy, course development and evaluation of the education programs (*ibid.:* 18).

The new Police Recruit Education Programme (PREP) was considered crucial for a cultural change in the police organisation, including the realisation of the community-based policing ideal. The program consists of five phases, lasting eighteen months: eight weeks of residential training in Phase I, followed by four weeks of field observation in Phase II, then fourteen weeks of residential training in Phase III, followed by forty-nine weeks of on-the-job training (Phase IV), ending with a two-week final assessment in Phase V. The PREP course broke away from the 'traditional' teaching methods criticised by the Lusher Report, as a member of the academy's staff described:

> The old training basically was drill, firearms, hands-on and law – lectures on this, lectures on that, highly didactic. Students are sitting there in ranks with their notes and a highlighter pen, teacher out front ... and every now and again they'd say that's assessable and they'd all go bzzzz and go away and learn it that night. And every now and again ... the lecturer would say, that reminds me of Mad Smith, and he'd go on about the story of Mad Smith. In other words, they got that rote learning, plus war stories and what they really learned was the war stories and that had to be policing and that was it.

The initial reaction to the employment of non-police staff was hostile and, according to this member of the academy staff, there were enormous 'start-up problems':

> We started PREP but the trouble was that you couldn't escape the cultural constraints of the past, you couldn't escape the enormous impress of history. Goulburn was a refugee camp for middle-aged police officers in the country who had arrived in that time in their police careers where they were forced to move back to Sydney and didn't want to go, so it was a refugee camp for some and really didn't attract very good people ... Anyway, because of the staff development problem I was determined that we'd have ... a Study Guide for each of the subjects and they would be well designed as self-study guides so that whatever the staff told them, at least they could read something different. So it was from the start a ... very print-oriented knowledge-manipulation and regurgitation system. And after the first year I was aware that there were enormous problems. We were getting better in the Academy, but I know the Field [training] was dreadful.

The problem with field training arose because the field trainers had come through the traditional police training that was based on a totally different model of police work:

> You see, PREP was based on a professional model of police work, in contrast to the limited expert model, the artisan model that preceded it. But the people who had to deliver it in the field were products of the old artisanal system ... so it was always going to be difficult, and was always going to take five or ten or fifteen years to really settle down.

PREP was evaluated in 1990 by a team of academics from the Centre for Applied Research in Education (CARE) at the University of East

Anglia in Britain. While the general assessment of the program was unequivocally positive (CARE 1990), the Phase IV fieldwork and aspects of the teaching style at the academy were found to be problematic. In other words, for both staff and students, there was a gap between theory and practice, between what was taught at the academy and what was seen to be 'real-life' policing:

> [The CARE Report] said that the field training was in a state of collapse, that there was accelerated de-training and cynicism, cheat-sheet mentality, culture shock, ... no support, the students were thrown into the front end of policing, the sharp end – reactive, mobile, fast pursuit – within weeks of leaving the Academy ... There still was an antagonism between theory and practice, between 'bullshit castle' and reality.

Many attempts have since been made to fine-tune the training system. To strengthen the Phase IV program, the Police Service introduced two new initiatives in 1991: the creation of a Distance Learning and Field Training Directorate with two quality control officers, and the designation of 'Demonstration Patrols'. The role of the Distance Learning and Field Training Directorate was to 'ensure the attainment and the updating of the knowledge and skills of field officers to enhance operational effectiveness ... providing links between the academy and the field to ensure that corporate goals are realised' (NSW Police Board 1991: 51). Demonstration Patrols were modelled after teaching hospitals; they were supposed to provide probationary constables with a model for 'best policing practices'. Constables were to be given more support and have more experienced training staff to assist them. The Police Academy has been negotiating with universities to integrate the recruit program into a university degree. The PREP program had already gained recognition of its academic status in 1989 by being granted advanced standing by universities and Colleges of Advanced Education.

Training in Cross-cultural Awareness

Police recruits received their first training in multicultural issues and cross-cultural awareness in the core course *Policing and Society* in the PREP program. The course gave students an introduction to the historical and contemporary social context of policing. The section on 'Multiculturalism and Policing' aims to provide students with knowledge and an appreciation of 'the variety of cultures in Australian society ... and the threat posed to good policing by stereotyping, prejudice, discrimination and racism'. Police reactions to some of these training initiatives were not always favourable, as a member of the Police Academy staff observed:

[They did not take it well] because it upset their view of the world – that Aborigines get too much, and they deserve their plight, and people of non-English-speaking background ought to come here and learn the language and all the old stereotype[s] ... Well, [the course] changed the good ones, but you see, I think it gets back to an issue of recruiting ... our recruits are simply reflecting the broader society ... I had one guy get up in class and tell me this is a load of bullshit, this is not what policing is about ... very worrying stuff. The danger ... is that we may simply be legitimating, allowing the police force to say, here, look at all this training we do in these issues, when in fact we're not making any difference at all.

Cross-cultural awareness workshops were sometimes organised at the patrol level at the initiation of the local command. Resistance was especially strong during the early years of Avery's administration. The Ethnic Client Consultant, herself from an NESB, spoke of her personal frustration in trying to deal with the resistance: 'I absolutely loathed it, because you end up defending the entire ethnic population.' She also recalled instances where people from other agencies who helped run cross-cultural training for police had 'burst into tears' and vowed never to 'have police here again'.

The *ad hoc* nature of the training and the lack of adequate time for debriefing meant that cross-cultural training, instead of 'better than nothing', could be counter-productive or simply preaching to the converted. The experience in New South Wales was that often police attitudes became more polarised once they started working in the field:

the young PREP students are OK, ... they're bright-eyed and bushy-tailed, they listen and they're enthusiastic. And then they go out and the reality somehow doesn't coincide with what they've learnt and they get disillusioned and apparently students who come back after their training in the field tend to be fairly fixed or bigoted. So racism, if you do a survey prior to them leaving, or when they first come and compare it to their attitudes when they finish, you'll find there's a difference. They've *polarised* a lot more, and tend to be a lot less tolerant, if you like.

This observation was confirmed by a recent study of ethnocentrism and conservatism among a cohort of 412 NSW police recruits. The researcher found that 'the Academy has done a good job in reducing or at least containing racist and authoritarian attitudes of recruits ... [but] once recruits hit the streets, much of this good work is swept away' (Wortley 1993: 7).

The NSW experience seems to be consistent with what Southgate (1984) found in Britain: that cross-cultural awareness training could reinforce existing prejudices if not conducted properly. Southgate has also suggested that training and education must be seen to be relevant to police operations and pitched at a practical rather than an abstract level. This was what the Ethnic Client Consultant found eventually when she started taking a different approach to training. Instead of appealing to police officers' commitment to social equity, the trainer emphasised the practical skills and professional consequences of not following guidelines:

> A lot of the bleeding-heart type training was not working ... We really should concentrate, don't tell them it's because we want social equality but say this is the way you've got to do it. If you don't do it these are the consequences, all right? Your case is going to be chucked out of court, or you're going to have the Ethnic Affairs Commission write and complain about the fact that you've discriminated. That is how I try and deal with cross-cultural stuff.

It is ironic that police training in cross-cultural issues, which has often been recommended by government inquiries (e.g., HREOC 1991) as a way to combat police racism, is often counter-productive in practice. The approach being advocated strongly by one of the Police Academy staff was that police training should be more broadly conceptualised as aiming to produce officers who 'actually see themselves as the uniformed branch of the movement for civil liberties', rather than specifically instructing them not to discriminate against visible minorities. Policing should be predicated on a fundamental respect of people, regardless of their social or ethnic status:

> It's not about policing the criminal classes or the scumbags, or the hoons or whatever ... but recognising peace keeping, ... recognising division and inequality in our society, and recognising marginalised groups and the fact that they are forced, unlike rich people, to occupy public places and not have their own privately policed pavements. My view is that's more important fundamentally than going through the cosmetic notions of teaching them about pre-1788, or some of the more arcane elements of Chinese or Welsh or Italian or Aboriginal or Lebanese culture, but to cultivate in the student police officers a love of conversation and curiosity about people generally. They've got to like people, and if they're good communicators and they like people, they'll learn about people, not these abstract strangers or stereotypes. I mean, a lot of multicultural training is 'human awareness training', as they call it. Human awareness training – my God, people of West Indian extraction really are human! I mean, look at the premise that starts from – because all I know from my own reading as a police educator is that the only certainty to 'de-racify' people who are racist is that they either stay the same or they get worse.

This view was supported by another officer, who saw the problem as a more general one of intolerance:[4]

I think ... it's a general problem of attitude and that's why I think we don't need specific cross-cultural stuff. What we need is general attitudinal stuff. So if you can get a police officer to overcome his or her prejudice to the gay community, the chances are you're going to get an officer who's not bigoted to ethnic minorities or what have you. You know, if someone is sympathetic to domestic violence issues, it's the same person that's going to be sympathetic to the problems that any disadvantage of the beleaguered group has. ... I think if you've been effective in terms of educating the person, then there's a chance they'll strike across the board.

The difficulty of conducting effective cross-cultural training, together with the resistance to such training by officers, is symptomatic of the problems of imposing cultural change from the top.

Developing Community-based Initiatives

Responsibilities for community policing initiatives originally rested with the Community Relations Bureau, which was established in 1984 and staffed by over 200 police and public service personnel. The objectives of the bureau were wide-ranging, including the development of community policing programs, community and media liaison, the formulation of relevant departmental policies, contribution to police training and assisting operational police with the establishment of community contacts. The Community Policing Section within the bureau consisted of units for administering specific community policing programs (such as Neighbourhood, Business and Rural Watch, Safety House) as well as specialised units with community liaison coordinators dealing with youth, Aborigines, ethnic groups, gay people, and elderly people. In 1987, Community Consultative Committees were introduced as one of the bureau's programs (NSWPD 1986; 1987; NSWPS 1988). Following regionalisation, the Community Relations Bureau ceased to exist. Community liaison coordinators were transferred to the Programs Branch. They were no longer responsible for coordinating activities throughout the State; rather, they took on an advisory role, leaving the implementation of programs largely to local patrols.[5] Further restructuring in 1991 was accompanied by a 'streamlining' of the management structure which reduced the number of branches from six to three and the number of staff from about 109 to about 84. Community liaison coordinators were given the new title of 'client group consultants'. During the time of the research project, the development of community-based programs was the responsibility of the Policy and Program Branch within the Office of Strategic Services.

Client Group Consultants

The renaming of community liaison coordinators to 'client group consultants' reflected the gradual shift towards a customer-oriented style of policing (see Landa 1994; Hughes 1992). It also meant that the hands-on role of the former coordinators became a more advisory and policy-oriented one. The following discussion focuses on the role of two client group consultants most relevant to visible minorities: the Ethnic Client Group Consultant and the Aboriginal Client Group Consultant.

Ethnic Client Group Consultant

The Ethnic Client Consultant's duties involved liaison, negotiation and mediation between ethnic communities and the police. The consultant also had a 'media and marketing' role in terms of issuing press releases, contacting the media, and giving advice to police on how the ethnic media could be accessed. Besides dealing with the outside community, the consultant liaised with other government departments and provided advice and expertise on ethnic issues within the police organisation. Internally, the consultant was responsible for program development; providing policy advice to the Minister, the Police Board and the State Executive Group; coordinating the development of police and public service education programs; instigating relevant research and program evaluation; and monitoring the Ethnic Affairs Policy Statement (see Chapter 7).

The consultant told the researcher that her work had been facilitated by the adoption of community-based policing as an operational strategy. It made the 'mainstreaming' of minority issues a much more natural and achievable task. Instead of someone at headquarters trying to 'market the idea' and convince operational police to meet the needs of ethnic communities, community policing encouraged Patrol Commanders to find out for themselves the ethnic composition and needs of their local communities and to design methods for meeting these needs. The client consultant was there to provide advice and support for their initiatives.

Aboriginal Client Group Consultant

Liaison with Aboriginal communities did not begin with the Avery administration. An Aboriginal Liaison Unit was established in 1980 as an operational section directly responsible to the Deputy Commissioner of Police. After its establishment, the unit expanded from one police officer to a staff of eleven, including one public servant. In 1985 the unit became a part of the Community Relations Bureau. Following regionalisation, however, the unit was devolved in 1988 and all positions were allocated to the four regions. As a result of that, two Regions (North-west and South-west) disbanded their units, and the number of officers working in these units dropped from ten to two. In 1986, three Aboriginal Community Liaison Officers (ACLOs) were appointed in Bourke and Walgett as a pilot program. The number of ACLOs by mid-1991 was thirty-two. An Aboriginal Client Group Consultant was appointed in 1990. The consultant was responsible for 'advising the police executive on Aboriginal issues and for developing policy and programs for the Police Service' (NSWPS 1990: 16).

A 1992 draft of the Statement of Duties of the Aboriginal Client Consultant listed a wide variety of responsibilities, including policy development and evaluation, identification of Aboriginal people's needs, the development of structures and strategies to enhance service delivery, and various advisory, advocacy and public-relations functions. The major projects of the consultant in 1992 included the development of an Aboriginal Policy Statement for the NSW Police Service; the establishment of Regional Aboriginal Coordinators; the training, education and industrial issues for ACLOs; assessment of the Aboriginal Community Justice Panels; action to reduce the over-representation of Aboriginal juveniles in the criminal justice system; and others.

The Role of Client Group Consultants

The effectiveness of client group consultants in a decentralised system became an issue both for the consultants themselves and for their clients (see Landa Report 1995). A senior administrator expressed concern that ethnic and Aboriginal programs have suffered owing to a lack of clarity about the role of the client consultant, who quickly became identified within the police organisation as 'the person carrying the program'. This was in fact the opposite of what was intended. With regionalisation, the implementation of programs was no longer the responsibility of the Program Branch, but operational police had tried to push this responsibility back to headquarters, so that client consultants got stuck with 'a lot of running around, doing courses and seminars and workshops' instead of looking at 'bigger issues'. The senior administrator saw a need for client consultants to work out a framework and priorities for the program area, and not be involved in the implementation of programs. The trouble, however, was getting operational police to pick up that responsibility:

> there wasn't an acceptance in the operational area that [ethnic affairs] was their issue. In other words, what had happened, I think, was John Avery and the Executive saying ethnic affairs issues are important to the Police Service because we're in a multicultural society, and there is a recognition of that. But

what has tended to happen is that unless you spend a fair bit of time gathering support in operational areas ... the normal thing you get is 'Look, I've got all this other work to do, I can't be taking on, yes, it's an important area, but da, de da, de da'. So there's [the Client Consultant] there, perfectly identified to take them. She's the coordinator, so what happens is she's trying to roll the program out, they're trying to roll it back in again.

Client consultants often found themselves sandwiched between demands from the communities and the lack of cooperation from operational police. The Ethnic Client Consultant's role, for example, became very difficult as a result of the lack of support within the police organisation on the one hand, and the pressure from central agencies such as the Ethnic Affairs Commission on the other (see Chapter 7). From the communities' point of view, the client consultant was also identified as *the person* within the Police Service to take care of their needs. The responsibility given to the Aboriginal Client Consultant was seen to be 'massive' by the officer who previously occupied the position:

When I came into this job, ... I realised I was given a massive responsibility ... which puts me in a position where I got over 60,000 Aboriginal people on one side of me and 14,000 police officers on the other side ... I said to my boss, well, you have to face it, we are dealing with a relationship that for 200 years has been based on conflict and absolutely nothing else.

One strategy to improve the effectiveness of the current system, according to the senior administrator, was to 'strong-arm' the operational areas, making it clear to them what their roles were. In his view police training should not be run by Programs people, but people in Training would need Programs people to assist with the development of curricula. Similarly, community-based policing programs should be initiated and implemented by the operational commands, with Programs people providing advice and assistance.

Inadequate funding also limited the effectiveness of the work of client consultants. The former Aboriginal Client Consultant was critical of the inadequate resources allocated to the position to carry out its State-wide function:

You are not given a car to cover the whole State – I don't have access to a vehicle other than through the car pool, and if I don't get in early, I don't get a vehicle either. Then I get in, well, I cop a lot of criticism because I spend the budget. I use funding out of our budget and I have said to my boss when I first started. I said my clients are not in Police Headquarters. My clients are scattered all over the State. I said you've got to consult with them, and they say, we don't spend as much money as [name of Aboriginal Consultant]. And I say, fair enough, you look at the Gay Consultant whose clients are concentrated in the Metropolitan area. She does not need any outside travel budget. I mean, the same with a lot of the things that the Youth [people] are doing. The biggest problem with youths is in the Metropolitan area. So that does not require a lot of travel either, but my communities are scattered from one end of the State to the other.

The lack of resources meant that the consultant had to be selective about where efforts were directed:

there are 180 odd patrols in the Police Service, and 90 of these patrols have a significant Aboriginal population. Probably about 15 or 20 of them are contentious, but 11 of them extremely contentious, which means I can concentrate my efforts on 10 towns, 10 patrols – forget about the rest of the State – and try to work with these ones, but when you are just one person, you don't have any resources.

There did not appear to be a consensus about what the position required. While conceding that the Aboriginal Client Consultant's job was 'more of a field job' than that of the Ethnic Client Consultant, the senior administrator nevertheless disagreed with an approach where the client consultant 'immediately got in a car or the plane and went to wherever the issue was' every time there was a problem.

Community Liaison Officers

Community Liaison Officers were predominantly civilian officers appointed to specific patrol areas to assist with community relations, although in some areas police officers were also designated as Ethnic Liaison Officers (see below).

Ethnic Community Liaison Officers (Civilian)

In 1987, four civilian bilingual Community Liaison Officers were appointed at Fairfield and Cabramatta as a pilot program. These officers were to play 'a major role in establishing dialogue and facilitating understanding between Police and the large multi-cultural community in that area' (NSWPD 1987). By 1992 there were six civilian Ethnic Community Liaison Officers (ECLOs), two in Cabramatta, two in Fairfield, one in Marrickville and one in Bankstown. The officers spoke a range of languages, including Vietnamese, Laotian, several dialects of Chinese, and Croatian; one officer was fluent in five languages: Vietnamese, French, Spanish, Italian, and Japanese.

The officers admitted that when the ECLO positions were first filled, no one really knew what they were supposed to do. They were given no training or direction, and had to find out for themselves what they needed to do. So they used their community network and consulted with groups and community workers to identify the community's critical concerns. They also helped with translation and interpretation at the station. ECLOs saw their main job as trying to 'improve relationship, to market the police ... to the ethnic community'. This marketing role included visiting ethnic organisations and local schools, arranging for police officers to talk to the community, getting involved in Neighbourhood Watch, organising Blue Light Discos[6] and Community Consultative Committee meetings. Often ECLOs have to provide information, give advice, refer people to appropriate agencies, and even assist clients by showing them around the court.

One officer pointed out that the role of the ECLOs was not well understood by the community or the police, especially in the beginning:

> It was very new to the community, and also to the Department. Also, at the station police officers were not sure who we were. Some thought that we would be working for the Headquarters and report back about them. And some of the community members also were thinking that we are undercover police. So we have to make it very clear to both sides that we are just public servants ... Remember at that time the [pilot] project only lasted 12 months, and half of the time of the project had gone and we were still finding out how to fit in with the community and to fit in with the police. Some of the police just don't understand our role, that we have to deal with the community. We have to go out a lot to liaise. Some of the callers ... expect us to be able to be interpreting in many languages.

A great deal of the effectiveness of the ECLOs depended on the support and interest of the patrol commander. One ECLO found that he was not getting any cooperation from his commander and no one seemed interested in any of his ideas or suggestions. However, most ECLOs found that they were eventually successful in securing cooperation and trust from the police they work with:

> When we first [came] on the job, we actually shared our office with the beat police, so had very close relationship with them. We get them out a lot ... We'll organise something and ... we'll get a police officer there to talk ... And most of the police officers are cooperative. They're good, but still, ... you have to build the trust anyway. So at first they might not understand what we're doing, whether what we're doing is worthwhile ... and after a while they see the results and they think, yeah, this is right. So we're getting more and more cooperation.

One of the tasks the ECLOs set for themselves was to encourage people to report crimes to the police, and they felt they have made progress in that regard:

I do think [that people are now more willing to report crimes] because the police has created means convenient for people to report. I would like to emphasise on firstly the Dragon Line, where people can ring police and speak their own language including Vietnamese or Chinese. And, secondly, we organise police lecture for migrants and join the radio interview at SBS [multicultural] radio station to encourage community and to inform them of the ways to report to police, either by telephone, special line, Dragon Line, or writing letter in their language. We also advertise very often on newspaper the Dragon Line and also a police station telephone number.

The achievements of these officers were said to have been impressive, in terms of both gaining community confidence and increasing the reporting of crime. The fact that these officers spoke a community language seemed to have made a great deal of difference to the community's attitudes towards approaching the police. One beat officer felt that the ECLOs were a great help in his work:

I think they save me from doing a lot of work ... which I would consider mundane with the community-based side of the work that I do ... organising meetings and sending out invitations to meetings and just doing the legwork that's sometimes required to get certain things up and running. ... Generally speaking I'm quite full of praise for the work they do. ... I'm trying to use them at the moment for things like Neighbourhood Watch meetings, especially in areas where there is a predominance of Asian-speaking people ... They may want to participate in some of these community schemes but are put off by language and the fear of being different, looking different.

Ethnic Community Liaison Officers were often seen as (and sometimes called) interpreters by the police and, depending on the patrol, quite often used as interpreters. One ECLO said she was asked to interpret 'a lot'; another said she 'helped out' whenever possible:

I'm a qualified interpreter ... if someone come to the Police Station asking for assistance and they can't get the message across and if I happen to speak that language and happen to be around, I'd help out ... [Professional interpreters are] pretty costly, and because ... this station would have so many different ethnic [people] coming up every day, ... we just don't have the resource to get the interpreter for every case. So if we can sort it out, we just sort it out. ... But if it's a crime, reporting of crime, or victim, or whatever, and [they] really need assistance, we get the interpreters.

ECLOs were, until 1991, Ministerial employees. A review had been under way to enhance their employment status. In 1991 they were appointed as temporary staff by the Police Service (NSW Police Board 1991: 48). Officers felt uncertain about their status and were not happy with the level of resources allocated to their work:

There's support but not the resources ... we never had any training or seminar or anything at all. Even when we have to go to a meeting or something we have to use public transport. There's no allowance for us to use our own car ... If we have meeting at night time we roster ourselves on the afternoon shift, starting at 2 o'clock, finishing about 10 or something like that. We are very short of resources. Like doing translation, we have to bring our own dictionary and sometimes when we have to go to some seminar, but [if] it costs [too much] we can't go.

At the time of the research, a training program for ECLOs (both civilian and police) was being developed along the lines of the ACLO training program (see later).

Ethnic Community Liaison Officers (Police)

Apart from the few civilian ECLOs, patrols with a significant percentage of ethnic populations were to designate police officers as community liaison officers. According to the Ethnic Client Consultant, it was not at all clear to what extent this had been implemented or even if the idea was a sound one to begin with:

I'm not even sure if it's a good idea because I think that's when you marginalise things, when you have *a* person looking after ethnic liaison. Same things happen to me at a station: 'Go and talk to so and so, that's the ethnic liaison officer.' ... We do have them in some places, but not in others.

The problem, according to another officer, was not simply that the appointment of a liaison officer allowed the rest of the police to abrogate their responsibility in relation to ethnic issues, but also whether such a person was actually given the resources and opportunity to perform meaningful work:

you can appoint someone a liaison officer and then keep them working on their regular shifts and never give them the opportunity to make the sort of development network that needs naturally to flow and in building relationships that take time ... my point is that depending on the Patrol Commander's view of things, you could say, yes, I've got a liaison officer, but the next question would be: How much time do you give that person? How long have they been working at it? Do you change them every three months so that the moment they get some network they've got to get going? So that you can appear to be very sensitive to the issue and actually be doing nothing at all, or you can be very sensitive and see this as a very viable way of lessening the problems that you confront.

Aboriginal Community Liaison Officers

The number of Aboriginal Community Liaison Officers grew from three in 1986 to thirty-two by mid-1991, covering all four Regions. The intention of the scheme was spelt out in an undated internal police document:

> This scheme was established for the purpose of allowing an Aboriginal person from the local community to act in the capacity of Liaison Officer at the Police Station to encourage Aboriginal people to avail themselves of service offered to the community at large, to become directly involved in assisting their own community and, hopefully, bring about improved understandings and relationships as far as Police and Aborigines are concerned.

The scheme was said to have contributed to dramatic improvement in relations between police and Aborigines. It acted 'as a solid foundation base in bridging the gap and provides the necessary support to this delicate and sensitive area of policing'. The Aboriginal Client Consultant saw it as a great success. In spite of earlier scepticism and mistrust on both sides, the scheme was said to have worked well and was accepted by both police and Aboriginal people. There was, however, an absence of female ACLOs at the time. This was a problem when Aboriginal women needed assistance, especially in relation to sexual assault or domestic violence.

It was not easy for Aboriginal officers to work in police stations. One ex-officer spoke of the feeling of intimidation any Aboriginal person working among the police would experience:

> One of the biggest problems was that no one really did any planning for Aboriginal Liaison Officers to physically appear behind a counter in a police station, which it does not seem as much of a problem, but if you are black, and you walk into a police station, you are in another side of town. I mean when I started..., one of the biggest personal problems I had, my first six months there was walking into a police station and being allowed on the other side of the counter.

Another ex-officer reported receiving racial remarks from police officers at the station (Landa Report 1991: 84).

There was also some concern that ACLOs did not appear to have well-defined statements of duties. One Statement of Duties, for example, showed that the ACLO was responsible for a host of ill-defined and all-encompassing tasks such as patrolling on foot and liaising between police and the community, fostering generally police–community relations, overseeing the welfare of prisoners, visiting social events and licensed premises to 'oversight behaviour', and 'reducing tension between police [and] Aboriginals by removing misunderstandings and generally facilitating info exchange'. In another patrol, however, the ACLO was given strict instructions on how to act:

The ACLO WILL
1. Speak with all custody prisoners of aboriginal descent upon their arrival at the station off the prison van, *after* seeking permission off the supervising sergeant.
2. Speak with all members of the aboriginal community who attend the police station seeking their assistance.
3. Liaise daily with the patrol commander or patrol tactician.
4. Be accountable for their daily activities as per attached log to be submitted daily to patrol commander.
5. Speak with all prisoners brought to the police station by [name of patrol] *only* upon request of the arresting police OR the supervising sergeant.
6. Inform the station staff of their absences from the station, indicating where they are going and when they are due back.
WILL NOT
1. Read telephone message pad or occurrence pad.
2. Enter the inquiry office *except* to walk through to the custody area upon permission being given to the supervising sergeants.
3. Contact the Aboriginal Legal Service of their own volition, *unless* the defendant specifically requests they do so.
4. Enter the Detective's office, Sgt's office, Intelligence Office *unless* their assistance is sought from that area. [Undated internal document]

The officer who provided the above document saw the situation as totally unsatisfactory:

This is just how patronising ... They say you have to talk to Aboriginal offender people of Aboriginal descent, but you will only speak to them with the approval of somebody else. You are not allowed here, you are not allowed there. ... I mean, I gave that to the Commissioner ... I said this is just totally unsatisfactory because you cannot have Patrol Commanders going around devising their own Statement of Duties to suit themselves. There's basic things that all the Liaison Officers should have in their Statement of Duties, but you can still leave it flexible enough so that you can modify it to each community.

An ex-officer felt that there was a lack of trust and confidence in the ACLOs among police officers. One example was that the ACLOs were not told about Operation Sue, where 135 police officers took part in a raid on ten properties in Redfern in February 1990. The justification given was that

[The ACLOs] stood to be double losers out of it. They would have lost credibility with their community either way had they known about it. We'd have written them off completely and I wasn't prepared to put them at that risk. [Chief Superintendent Peate, quoted in Landa Report, 1991: 84]

One of the ACLOs involved disagreed:

> Well, I questioned Supt. Alf Peate about that whole situation. I said, look, it doesn't matter, I'm employed here as Aboriginal Community Liaison Officer, we should be informed of everything that has to do with Aboriginals, regardless, regardless if we're in trouble we, we still cop it anyway from the blacks and the whites, so it doesn't matter and also from the coppers, but because of our low status as ACLOs I suppose they felt, why should we tell them anyway, they would only go back and tell the blacks ... What I picked up ... was that we're not going to tell you because we don't trust you. You know, that's saying to me that they have got no confidence in me.

Like the ECLOs, the ACLOs' working conditions were part of the 'low status' these officers were given:

> There's no career structure in it, I mean, they work, they work overtime, they work outside normal hours. They are not entitled to penalty rates, they are not entitled to overtime, they are not entitled to shift allowance, they are not entitled to climatic allowance. Yet you send a cop out in the bush and they get every one of them. Yet these guys are working on call 24 hours a day which police are not.

One ex-officer told of a meeting of ACLOs with Commissioner Avery in 1989 where they set out their grievances:

> I think [the police] are only using the Aboriginal Community Liaison Officers as token blacks to do their dirty work. No, I've argued with Commissioner Avery ... we brought all the Liaison Officers together and met in Redfern or in the inner city for a meeting. We invited the Commissioner along, the Koori Network Committee which is made up of all public servants in the Police Department ... We raised a lot of issues with him. One was, we appreciate whoever set up the Community Liaison Officer Scheme, that's fine, but if he is going to set up these liaison officers around the State to solve most of the problems, or Koori problems ... he's got to provide the resources to go with it, and we have got no resources, or we didn't have any resources.

One example of not being given resources was once again related to travel:

> we needed some funds at least with a taxi or bus or whatever. We didn't have money ourselves, we walked everywhere. In the Metropolitan area we covered most of the area ... but we couldn't get reimbursed or anything at all. So [name of ACLO] and I ... worked out a budget and submitted it to [name of superior officer] and saying, OK, this is what we need ... and this is our budget ... came to about $7000. He came back to me and he said ... I can't do that, we've just got no money.

The work of the ACLO can be very stressful, especially in some areas where police–community relations are tense, but it was believed that these officers were making a difference:

> In some areas where I've spoken to community members, they rail on the ACLOs but they're very quick to call on them when they need their help. And in some cases, that's what adds to some of the stress in the job. It's very stressful, but on the whole most of them are active members of their own communities, that's my observation. I can think of one or two cases where that isn't the case ... It's hard, but in terms of the success in bridging that gap between police and Aborigines, it's making the difference.

Like the ECLOs, the employment conditions of the ACLOs were under review and they were 'temporary employees' in the Police Service at the time of the research.

Training for ACLOs was *ad hoc* or non-existent prior to 1991. Since then, a program has been developed in the Police Academy which involves an intensive 'train the trainer' methodology. Phase I of the training was run in August 1991 and was seen to be a great success. A substantial proportion of the teaching was eventually to be carried out by Aboriginal people themselves. The subjects covered in the training include: dealing with domestic violence; dealing with Aboriginal young people; conflict resolution; basic skills in stress management, counselling and networking; and some simple knowledge about bail procedures and criminal offences.

Community Consultative Committees

The Concept

The establishment of Community Consultative Committees (CCCs) was formally adopted as a community-based policing strategy in New South Wales in 1987, although CCCs had existed among Aboriginal communities in Taree, Forster and Walgett before then (NSWPD 1986). These committees were designed 'to bring Police closer to the community they serve and to deal with the issues which are of most concern to the community' (NSWPD 1987: 78). Patrol commanders were told that CCCs provide an 'invaluable' resource for the commander 'when allocating resources and evaluating operational strategies in the patrol' (NSWPS *Community Based Policing Paper No. 6*: 1).

Patrol Commanders were also given suggestions about the process of establishing a CCC:

- Research the composition of the community.
- Call a Public Meeting.
- Invite selected community representatives.
- Publicise the Meeting via the media, posters, letters, telephone, word of mouth.
- Organise nominations in advance.
- Choose a venue which won't be intimidating or difficult to get to (this may exclude the Police Station).
- Contact local community representatives by letter inviting them to a meeting to discuss policing issues in the area. Follow up the letter with a telephone call. [*ibid.*: 5–6]

The composition of CCCs was to reflect the demographic profile of the patrol area. For example, they might include representatives of minority ethnic groups, Aborigines, young people, and so on, if some of these groups were disproportionately represented among offenders in the area. Committee members should ideally consist of:

- local residents (representative of the community in terms of age, sex, ethnicity, aboriginality and sexuality),
- people who work in the area,
- people who have an interest or contribution considered worthwhile, and
- representatives of Government and non-Government agencie ... and community organisations such as Neighbourhood Centres, minority group organisation and so on. (*ibid.*: 10).

With the appointment of Aboriginal and Ethnic Liaison Officers, language-specific CCCs were also established in some areas.

A Case Study

One patrol commander found the task of establishing a Community Consultative Committee with NESB representatives a particularly trying one. He went through all the steps recommended: research into the demographics of the area, identification of the problems and needs of the community, appointment of a coordinator and liaison officer, visits to ethnic newspapers, publicity via the ethnic media about the proposed CCC, invitations to ethnic organisations to join the committee. However, only ten people turned up at the first meeting, six of whom were from one particular ethnic group (out of approximately 120 different groups in the area). The next meeting, held a month later, attracted only three members. The patrol commander concluded that there was 'either a disinterest or ignorance shown towards the implementation of a Consultative Committee for the benefit of those persons' (Patrol Commander Course Project Contract 1989: 14).

Undeterred, the patrol commander developed and implemented a set of strategies. He obtained staff input through a short questionnaire survey, conducted a survey through five major ethnic newspapers to establish whether group members were interested in becoming a member of the CCC, obtained input from coordinators of Neighbourhood Watch committees, consulted with council representatives, and held a dinner-meeting with representatives of ethnic groups and a cultural awareness workshop for police officers, as well as conducting various surveys of ethnic group members.

Responses to the staff survey and to the invitation to a staff development seminar on ethnic affairs were both 'disappointing'. This was put down as an attitude based on 'lack of knowledge and understanding of ethnic cultures, background and their needs' (*ibid.*: 19). The patrol commander resolved to provide further training and lectures on the aims and objectives of the Ethnic Affairs Policy Statement for the police officers. However, responses from the ethnic press were even more disappointing. Only one communication was received following the newspaper stories. The commander decided then to concentrate on communicating with group leaders rather than individuals. No useful suggestions came out of the Neighbourhood Watch meeting, the members were 'more interested in *their own watch area* rather than this project concerning Non-English Speaking persons' (*ibid.*: 24). The dinner-meeting, however, turned out to be an 'outstanding success', with all the group leaders expressing interest in becoming members of the committee. The cultural awareness workshop was attended by forty police officers. All 'genuinely showed a keen and enthusiastic approach towards this workshop and all actively participated in all exercises conducted by the lecturers' (*ibid.*: 30). Most officers were said to have found the workshop valuable in understanding other cultures and interview techniques using interpreters.

A CCC meeting was then arranged and the response to this meeting was considered 'satisfactory': about a dozen community group leaders were present and all 'participated enthusiastically and expressed their desire to attend all forthcoming meetings' (*ibid.*: 40a).

Other Experiences

Holding the interest of the members of a committee was an ongoing problem, as one officer pointed out in relation to a faltering CCC:

> So we'd sit there and spend *hours* talking about trivia and people who participated in these groups are people who do it in their own time. A lot of them are professional people who are not being paid to attend these meetings: ... they can't, this is a waste of time, what the hell are you doing? And then you complain about the fact they're not attending ... I finally said to [the Patrol Commander], drop it, there are other things you can do which are more effective, forget about it if it's not working. Try something else ...

Sometimes, though, it was a loss of interest on the part of the police that contributed to the demise of CCCs. One senior officer noted that police officers responsible for organising CCCs failed to understand the principle on which they were based:

> One of the more interesting comments I heard was in [name of District] where one of the officers ... concluded that [CCCs] are a waste of time, because all that people did was bring along their problems, and that they were ... piddling, little problems that really had nothing to do with police. I said that I was struck by his analysis, but I felt if John Avery had been doing the analysis he would have thought that in fact they were serving a very useful purpose. Because what might be piddling to a senior police officer, to a citizen or groups of citizens, it could probably be a major issue. And in bringing it to police, they have probably tried every other avenue available to them and we're in a certain amount of desperation. So, rather than being, in his view, a failure because they haven't gone into big things, I think the view might well be that they had been, if nothing else, had been a forum for expression of those thoughts or concerns, and provided an opportunity for them to be addressed.

Although by 1990 almost every patrol had established Community Consultative Committees, there had not been any monitoring of their composition or effectiveness. The 1987–88 *Annual Report* mentioned 'teething problems' in relation to this initiative. Police were given feedback from existing CCC organisers as to how to make their CCCs more effective. Organisers were advised to 'set achievable goals', to be conscious of not letting committee meetings 'become a forum for personal complaints' or 'degenerate into a social event', to ensure that committee members were representative of the community, to hold meetings after office hours, not to 'stack the meeting with Police', and to consider the involvement of appropriate non-police resources in resolving issues (NSWPS *Community-Based Policing Paper* No. 6: 8–9). The composition of the CCC was often a bone of contention. Critics of the police felt that members were not truly representative of the interests of the community; they mainly represented business interests, or interests of conservative, middle-class sections of the community. Others saw the whole activity as a mere public-relations exercise which was not meant to do anything.

Beat Policing

The Concept

Beat Policing is perhaps the most symbolic aspect of community-based policing – the fact that uniformed police officers, instead of driving around in fast cars and doing random patrols, actually spend some time getting to know the local community, listening to their problems and finding ways of dealing with them. In New South Wales the term 'beat policing' did not appear in the *Annual Report* until 1988. In 1986, fifteen Foot Patrol Squads were established:

Each Foot Patrol consists of 10 uniformed Police, under the control of a Sergeant. Members carry portable radios, make patrols on foot and also utilise public transport. They concentrate on trouble-prone areas where crime, vandalism and hooliganism are likely to occur. [NSWPD 1986: 46]

By 1988 'sector and beat policing' was introduced, with the beat officer being responsible for providing service to a small geographical area. The concept was seen to be crucial for the implementation of community-based policing:

The fundamental priority for the future will be built around the professional community-based police officer working with the particular community of his/her beat to solve (or contribute to the solution of) local problems, supported by a responsive command structure and the assistance of specialists. The introduction of sector and beat policing is in line with this concept. A sector will consist of a number of beats. The Constable delegated a 'beat' will be responsible for providing service to that area in the broadest possible sense. For example, assisting persons in difficulties, conciliating in disputes between neighbours and working with the community to solve local problems. [NSWPS 1988: 10, original emphasis]

It was not until years later, however, that the beat policing concept became more developed. An operational statement drafted in 1991 described in more detail the aims and objectives of the Beat Policing Program. The overall aim was to 'provide a beat policing service capable of efficiently and effectively meeting the community's needs and wants by achieving a safer environment'. Five broad objectives were identified:

- **Planning**: Identify principal crime areas and problems relating to maintenance of law and order.
- **Problem Solving**: Mobilise all available appropriate resources and policing methods to contribute to the solutions of problems identified.
- **Community Organising**: Motivate and mobilise members of the community to address crime and social issues.
- **Information Sharing**: Gather and share appropriate intelligence with other patrol members and the Patrol Intelligence Office, and with the community.
- **Jobs**: Ensure that urgent matters are given highest priority and that routine matters are followed-up when time permits. [NSWPS, Beat Policing Program 1991, Operational Statement]

Acccording to this statement, Beat Policing was not equivalent to foot patrolling. The goal of Beat Policing was not simply to provide a highly visible police presence: it aimed both to reduce fear and to actually prevent crime. Partnership with the community and public accountability were also important elements of Beat Policing that were not traditionally part of foot patrolling. Unlike officers on foot patrol, beat police worked as a team, made flexible use of transport options, and combined law-enforcement activities with community relations and problem analysis.

Implementation

With the State government's 1991 decision to allocate an additional 1000 police officers to Beat Policing in patrols with a high workload, beat police constituted almost 10 per cent of the total police strength. There were indications that Beat Policing, besides being popular with the public, was gaining acceptance within the police organisation. One officer explained that an overwhelming majority of respondents in community surveys wanted foot patrols. Beat officers were seen as 'more approachable' and 'more available'. However, within the police force there were initially mixed reactions to the introduction of Beat Policing, and a certain amount of resentment because of the high profile enjoyed by the beat officers. One officer claimed that beat officers were gradually gaining internal acceptance because they were making 'as many, if not more, arrests than other police', they were 'getting more intelligence information' and were 'doing real police work'. When questioned about his use of traditional policing measures of success, this officer admitted that the performance of beat officers was still predominantly measured in terms of the amount of charges and arrests, the number of intelligence forms submitted, and so on. This was partly because 'Beat Policing had to be. ... recognised by the policing culture as a worthwhile exercise.' A senior officer even quoted some preliminary statistical analysis and made the remarkable claim that 'for every beat police officer who is put into a patrol, car theft goes down by half a car a month'.

Like the overall strategy of community-based policing, Beat Policing was directed at all communities. It was not designed to service any particular minority group. Yet the concept of local accountability meant that beat officers could not ignore the fact, for example, that there were large numbers of people in their beat who were Aboriginal or from minority ethnic groups, and that it was their responsibility to provide equal and appropriate service to these members.

As part of their community organising function, beat officers met regularly with residents and business people in their area. Beat officers were encouraged to help organise and motivate the community to develop strategies for solving problems within the community. They were usually involved with programs such as Neighbourhood Watch, Business Watch, Community Consultative Committees, Safety House, and so on. These were in fact what most people conceived of as community policing:

> My concern is that when you talk to police officers about community-based policing, they talk about Neighbourhood Watch, Community Consultation, Safety Houses as though they were what community-based policing is all about. I think the Avery notion was a much more pervasive notion than simply a few public strategies but nonetheless those elements are very important elements, but what it has allowed police officers to do is pay lip service to those strategies in many respects and just continue unabated in the old form.

The concept of Neighbourhood Watch, for example, was not always appropriate for organising ethnic communities, as one officer explained. Much depended on the pattern of home ownership and homogeneity of the community:

> It's very difficult with Neighbourhood Watch ... because Neighbourhood Watch is geared to those people who are sort of middle-class, upper middle society ... And of course then we have the language stuff ... If you've got 100 languages just in Fairfield, how do you do it? ... You know, unless you want to set up Neighbourhood Watch or Safety House just for the Vietnamese or just for Chinese, it's not going to work. And I think we should stop trying to push it – it's inappropriate.

The claim that Neighbourhood Watch was essentially a middle-class, suburban phenomenon, however, was challenged by a senior officer, who saw it as a 'very useful forum for people to make contact with police in non-traumatic circumstances', even though he acknowledged that some committees were better run than others.

This chapter has provided an overview of the major changes and programs developed by the NSW police since the appointment of John Avery in 1984. The organisation was decentralised and its rank structure simplified. Recruitment criteria were modified to attract more women and members of visible minority groups. Police training, especially PREP, was totally restructured and reconceptualised. Having adopted community-based policing as its main operational strategy, the organisation introduced a wide range of community-based initiatives. The appointment of community client consultants and liaison officers reflected a new willingness to reach out to the needs of the minority communities. Similarly, the establishment of Community Consultative Committees and the expansion of Beat Policing were designed to set up processes of consultation and 'partnership' with the community.

It is clear that the majority of reforms were directed at overhauling the tattered image of the NSW police in the early 1980s following persistent rumours of corruption and malpractice. The social climate and political conditions were favourable for the wide-ranging and fairly radical changes which followed. The influence of management theory was also substantial throughout the reform process. The Lusher inquiry, for example, drew on the work of Australian management professor Dexter Dunphy to argue for greater decentralisation of authority and a more flexible organisational structure. Avery's search for appropriate reform models also received direct input from American management professor Mark Moore. The managerialist approach was also in line with the major reorientation of the Australian public sector in the 1980s towards effiency and productivity (Yeatman 1987). The push for decentralisation and merit-based promotion, for example, had been endorsed by the NSW government following the Wilenski Report (1977). With his initial attention focused on the fight against police corruption, Avery achieved 'transformative' change in the police organisation using a 'directive/coercive' method (Dunphy and Stace 1990). There was little doubt that, in spite of the depth of Avery's vision of community-based policing, he did not have a great deal of support within the organisation. He was considered an 'academic' and his swift and decisive assault on traditional policing values and institutionalised corruption created a great deal of discontent.

The essentially top-down method of implementing reforms was, of course, inherently problematic. The rules were suddenly changed before the majority of the members caught on to what was happening, let alone understood the deeper philosophical justifications. Officers interviewed readily acknowledged that there were weaknesses in the implementation of some of these initiatives, especially during the early stages. Even though many were optimistic about the prospects of success, the cracks were already beginning to show: some programs were poorly defined or inadequately resourced, others were tokenistic or difficult to sustain. I will provide a fuller assessment of the overall achievement of the reform program in Chapter 9. Before this final assessment is made, however, it is informative to examine more closely the organisational responses to change and the processes of resistance, reaction and repair which were set off as a result of change. Two such case studies will be presented in the next two chapters. Chapter 7 traces the development of the Police Service's Ethnic Affairs Policy Statement; it is a study of how the police organisation resisted change imposed by an external agency. Chapter 8 recounts the events leading to the development of the Police Aboriginal Policy Statement; it is a study of how the police organisation tried to control and repair the damage caused by adverse media publicity. Both provide valuable data for understanding the processes of change in the NSW Police Service.

Notes

1 Apart from drug offences, organised crime and fraud against the Commonwealth, the bulk of criminal offences are governed by State or Territory laws.
2 The main sources of information used in this chapter are official documents and interviews with key police personnel involved in the design of the changes.
3 A reform-minded Attorney-General of the newly elected Labor government was reported (by one of the police sources interviewed for this study) to have made the remark 'We'll get the cops!' upon taking office.
4 This officer conceded, however, that police attitudes were much more negative towards Aborigines than towards other ethnic groups: 'I find that some of the prejudice against Aborigines is a unique prejudice. It's of a different scale. It's not intolerance, it's prejudice. It's, you know, I hate Aborigines. With ethnics, it's more of an irritation. I mean, it's just, why can't the buggers learn English? It's an irritation; it's not a deep-seated prejudice.'
5 Moves to integrate the NSW Police Department and the Police Force were under way in 1987, with the Commissioner of Police appointed as the departmental head. In 1988 the integrated organisation formally adopted the name 'New South Wales Police Service'. The integration was formalised by the *Police Services Act* 1990.
6 Alcohol- and drug-free discos organised and supervised by police and volunteers for young people.

CHAPTER 7

Ethnic Affairs Policy Statement:
The Paper Chase

In response to rapid demographic changes in the population brought about by immigration, Australian governments at both federal and State levels have introduced mechanisms to ensure that government services are accessible and non-discriminatory. At the federal level, the principle of access and equity was translated into a strategy in 1985. The strategy aims to overcome 'barriers of language, culture, race and religion which impede the delivery of government services to all residents' (Office of Multicultural Affairs 1992: 1). In New South Wales, a similar program had already been introduced in 1983. The Ethnic Affairs Policy Statement (EAPS) required public sector service agencies to 'develop structured plans for reform, with the aim of making their operations more responsive to the needs of a culturally diverse society' (NSWEAC 1990: 6). The way the NSW Police Service responded to the EAPS requirement is the subject of this chapter. It is a case study that shows not only why policy fails, but also how the police organisation resists change imposed from outside.

Formulation

Requirement

In 1977 the New South Wales government established the first Ethnic Affairs Commission in Australia. The commission was initially formed to conduct an inquiry into the needs of the ethnic communities in New South Wales. It was established as a permanent government authority in 1979. Its objectives are:

- to encourage full participation of persons comprising ethnic groups in the community in the social, economic and cultural life of the community;
- to promote the unity of all ethnic groups in the community as a single society consistently with the recognition of their different cultural identities; and
- to promote liaison and co-operation between bodies concerned in ethnic affairs [NSWEAC 1985: 2]

Pressure to formulate ethnic affairs policies came in 1983 in the form of a memorandum from the then Premier, Neville Wran, to all Ministers. Every government department and statutory authority was to prepare, by December 1984, an Ethnic Affairs Policy Statement setting out 'how ethnic affairs policies are to be incorporated in the delivery of mainstream services' (NSWPS 1988a: 4). According to documents obtained by the NSW Ombudsman, the then Minister for Police and Emergency Services and Minister for Corrective Services, Peter Anderson, wrote to Commissioner of Police Abbott on 19 January 1984, explaining the intentions of the EAPS. The Statement was to be prepared with the objectives of:

(i) eliminating and ensuring the absence of discrimination in access to services on the grounds of race, or ethnicity;
(ii) promoting equal access to services for members of racial or ethnic minorities; and
(iii) promoting services which are culturally sensitive and appropriate to potential clientele. [Quoted in NSW Ombudsman 1994: 15]

The Commissioner was asked to consult with the Ethnic Affairs Commission to ensure that the statement met the requirements.

The policy statement was supposed to cover not only service delivery, but also other functions which might affect the delivery of service, such as planning, policy, research and training of staff. The requirements of EAPS included a review process, and a detailed strategy, as well as annual reporting of progress:

Each departmental E.A.P.S. addresses those issues, firstly by conducting a thorough review of current operations, in order to identify barriers to equal access to people of non-English-speaking background. The Statements incorporate goals which specifically identify the steps needed to ensure equality of access. They also outline detailed strategies for Departments/Authorities to follow. Each Department/Authority will be required to report annually to the Ethnic Affairs Commission so that the implementation of strategies can be monitored and the achievement of goals assessed. [NSWEAC 1985: 7]

EAPS documents were to be submitted to the Ethnic Affairs Commission for assessment. The commission had 'delegated authority to approve them or call for revision' (NSWEAC 1990: 6).

Process

The NSW Police Service did not publish its EAPS until 1988. I was not able to find out the reason for this delay. However, there was evidence that on 23 March 1987, the then Chairman of the EAC, Mr Totaro, wrote to the Commissioner of Police, advising him that the Police Service EAPS 'requires substantial reworking to bring it up to an acceptable standard ... the document requires restructuring and considerable clarification' (quoted in NSW Ombudsman 1994: 15).

Another document obtained by the Ombudsman provides some insight into the problems that the task of formulating the EAPS had created for the police force. A Special Project Officer in the Police Policy Unit wrote a submission to the Senior Assistant Secretary of the Police Department on 17 August 1987, referring to the lack of 'EAPS structure, function and co-ordination outside the Community Relations Bureau'. The officer suggested that for the EAPS program to be viable, there needed to be a commitment by senior management. The officer also recommended that the appointment of the EAPS coordinator be at 'executive management level', and that an EAPS structure be developed within the organisation. The submission emphasised the importance of developing 'timely, accurate and EAPS relevant data bases' and incorporating EAPS 'as an integral part of the corporate objectives and strategies'. Senior executives were asked 'as a matter of urgency' to approve and provide the necessary resources to develop appropriate mechanisms for the implementation of EAPS (quoted in NSW Ombudsman 1994: 16).

Far from appointing an EAPS coordinator at executive management level as recommended by the submission, the Police Service made the Client Consultant for Ethnic Minorities, a relatively junior officer, 'largely responsible for the carriage of the Police Service's EAPS commitment' (NSW Ombudsman 1994: 17). When it was finally released in 1988, the EAPS document explained the delay in the following way: 'Completion of this policy document has occupied a protracted period of time owing to significant changes within the Police Service and rejection of previous plans by the Ethnic Affairs Commission' (NSWPS 1988a: 5).

Content

The policy statement was said to have been developed 'in consultation with the relevant Headquarters and Region commands' (NSWPS 1988a: 18). The statement 'commits all portions of the Police Service to provision of services that are both accessible, ethical and appropriate to all members of ethnic minority groups, in accordance with the statement of values' (*ibid.*: 18). Community-based policing was to provide 'the framework to facilitate the more equitable, efficient and effective delivery of policing services to ethnic minority groups within this State' (*ibid*.: 5). In fact, community-based policing was seen as 'precisely the key for all administrative policies and practices to be aligned to "Mainstreaming Ethnic Affairs Policies"' (*ibid*.: 27). The program objectives for 1988–89 were listed under nine headings relating to providing acessible and non-discriminatory service to NESB people: administrative policy, recruitment, information services, staff development and education, interpreter service, research, community participation, EAPS awareness, and EAPS implementation. Each area encompassed a range of strategies, designations of responsibilities and target dates. In addition, 'development to date' and 'service deficiencies' were also outlined for each area.

Implementation

The 1988 Ethnic Affairs Policy Statement called for a 'sound EAPS co-ordination mechanism and an effective way of monitoring and evaluating implementation progress'. The proposal was to have Regional Commanders nominate a senior officer in each Region to be an EAPS coordinator. These coordinators were 'to act as resource persons, to monitor the extent to which the Department's multicultural policies are uniformly adhered to by the respective Region, District and Patrol Commander, and to ensure that reports submitted by these officers are compiled into one report which will then be forwarded to the Commissioner'. District Commanders would nominate an EAPS officer to 'assume local responsibility for EAPS strategies' and report to the Regional Commander. Likewise, branch and unit directors would nominate a branch or unit EAPS coordinator (NSWPS 1988a: 24). The document explicitly designated the Ethnic Client Consultant as the Police Department's EAPS coordinator. This officer was to be responsible for 'reviewing and coordinating the Department's multicultural policies and recommending amendments to them; monitoring and reporting on the extent to which they have been implemented across the Department and the preparation of an Annual Report on progress and forward plans to the Minister of Ethnic Affairs' (*ibid*.: 24).

The document stressed that the role of the various coordinators must not be regarded as an additional function, but as a part of the normal responsibility of the office-holders, since 'multicultural policy does not represent a new initiative'. An EAPS Implementation Committee was to be established to 'monitor implementation target dates and identify areas of responsibility'. The committee was to meet twice yearly and a representative of the Ethnic Affairs Commission would be invited to attend (*ibid*.: 24–5).

The period following the release of the 1988 EAPS document was one during which the police organisation was undergoing massive reorganisation and changes. There was very little documentation of what actually happened in relation to the implementation of EAPS. According to documents obtained by the Ombudsman, a large committee was formed in 1988 to oversee the implementation of EAPS, although 'the records provided were not minutes and did little more than list the people who participated in various meetings' (NSW Ombudsman 1994: 19). After that, however, nothing much seemed to have happened:

> The reality seems to be that in 1988 the Police Service issued a comprehensive EAPS but that, apparently, was the end of that. No EAPS Annual Reports (or draft reports) were produced to the Ombudsman until the 1994 Status Report, which was submitted to the EAC on 28 April 1994, pursuant to the much later 1992–95 Police EAPS Strategic Plan. [*ibid.*: 20]

I was able to obtain some additional information regarding the implementation of the 1988 EAPS by interviewing key informants. The Ethnic Client Consultant did not think that the concept of EAPS coordinators had been effectively implemented:

> We've had four EAPS coordinators for four Regions, who are the Staff Officers, Operations. I found that it really wasn't working well because the four Superintendents really didn't understand EAPS at all … They still exist. I mean, because I haven't had a meeting of the EAPS coordinators for a long time, but they know that they are responsible for EAPS … in implementation. But they didn't understand it, so what's the point? They didn't understand it themselves … They didn't understand the sort of overall philosophy of what it was meant to do.

The client consultant considered the task of being the Police Department's EAPS coordinator an additional burden which was not part of her job as client consultant. She also found the annual reporting responsibilities extremely onerous because it was not just a matter of collating standard information from the various Regions; she had to sift through a great deal of 'management garbage':

> I … find the EAPS job cumbersome because we had to have an annual reporting, and all the various Regions were sending stuff that was just dreadful garbage. They were not doing any of the things we suggested they do … They were sending me piles of, you know, six-inch high, which I had to sift through and most of it was just management garbage. Nothing was being done or … in many areas, nothing has been done. They get a little note, saying 'What have you done for ethnic minorities?' So they quickly think of something they've done for ethnic minorities or make it up. So I thought it was a dreadful

waste of my time. It took me months to get that sort of thing organised and the chasing up, you know, ringing them up, oh, where is it, where is it, it was just dreadful.

An Assessment

Awareness of Policy

The EAPS targeted for special attention sixty-two patrols in New South Wales which, according to the 1986 Census, had more than 15 per cent NESB population. Patrol Commanders in these patrols were to 'develop objectives, strategies and evaluation mechanisms to improve access and services provided for the ethnic groups within their communities' (NSWPS 1988a: 20). I was able to obtain some useful information about the level of awareness of EAPS from my survey of police officers who worked in these patrols. The results indicate that the EAPS was not widely known or understood throughout the organisation, even among officers working in patrols with sizeable proportions of NESB people.

Officers were asked in the survey to respond to the question, 'What do you understand to be the NSW Police Service's policy in relation to providing police services to minority ethnic communities?' Just less than half (45 per cent) of the respondents were able to mention the *general idea* of making police services available and accessible to all, regardless of people's cultural, linguistic, or religious background. A small minority (12 per cent) mentioned one or two practical initiatives which were consistent with the policy, without being able to articulate the policy itself. Some examples of these responses were: recruitment of ethnic officers; to liaise with minority groups and gain their trust; to recognise the variety of cultures in Australian society and understand the threat posed to good policing. Finally, about 43 per cent of the respondents either did not provide an answer or did not mention any relevant aspect of EAPS. In fact, 23 per cent of the respondents did not write anything down, indicating either a lack of knowledge or a reluctance to provide the answer. About 8 per cent of the respondents said they did not know of any such policy, 5 per cent provided some comments which were largely negative or cynical about any such policy, while 7 per cent provided irrelevant answers. The cynical or negative responses, though representing only a small minority of the responses, revealed a deep level of hostility towards any policy of access and equity towards minority groups. A sampling of these responses is illustrative:

- We go overboard, too much focus in this area!! [*A sergeant*]
- It appears that if you are from a minority race, then donate to police projects, and you will get preferential treatment! [*A senior constable*]

- Everyone to bend and bow apart from minority. [*A sergeant*]
- Ignore them until they go away (i.e. become assimilated). Meanwhile use large amounts of whitewash and don't lose votes. [*A senior sergeant*]
- EEO [Equal Employment Opportunity policy] is prejudicial against healthy males of Anglo-European background. Preference given to minority groups at expense of general community. [*A constable*]

Table 7.1   Knowledge of NSW Police Service ethnic affairs policy

Q: What do you understand to be the New South Wales Police Service's policy in relation to providing police services to minority ethnic communities?

Response		Percentage of respondents
No response or did not mention any relevant aspect of EAPS		43
Blank (no response)	23	
Don't know	8	
A cynical or negative comment	5	
A positive but irrelevant comment	7	
Mentioned one element of EAPS only, not the policy itself		12
Mentioned making police service available/accessible to ethnic and non-ethnic communities alike		45

Note: Total number of respondents = 332.

Table 7.2   Acceptance of policy, by rank

Q: How much do you agree or disagree with the following statement? 'People from different cultural groups should have equal access to police services.'

	Percentage of respondents who:						
Rank	Strongly agree 1	Agree 2	Slightly agree 3	Slightly disagree 4	Disagree 5	Strongly disagree 6	Average score
All ranks	62	31	4	1	2	1	1.566
Probationary constable	54	44	2	0	0	0	1.488
Constable	61	31	6	1	2	0	1.512
Constable first class	68	29	0	0	0	3	1.452
Senior constable	45	39	3	0	7	7	2.032
Sergeant	62	27	3	3	3	3	1.649
Senior sergeant	69	25	6	0	0	0	1.361
Inspector and above	94	6	0	0	0	0	1.059

Note: Total number of respondents = 332.

These results (see Table 7.1) suggest that the police EAPS has certainly not filtered through to rank-and-file officers, and even at the level of paying lip-service to the policy, officers in the survey showed a remarkable lack of concern regarding ethnic affairs. It was a well-known joke in the organisation that many officers were only concerned about the details of EAPS and EEO policies when applying for a new job or a promotion.

Acceptance of Policy

Even though many respondents were not aware of the official policy towards ethnic minorities, an overwhelming majority (97 per cent) agreed with the principle that people from different cultural groups should have equal access to police services. This opinion did not vary very much by rank, except that respondents at the rank of senior constables did not agree with the principle as strongly as the rest, and those at the most senior rank (inspector and above) were 100 per cent in favour of it (Table 7.2). There was little variation by the respondent's duty. Thus, there appears to be wide support and acceptance of the spirit of the EAPS throughout the ranks of the Police Service.

Outcomes

After regionalisation, the responsibility for implementing programs in the police force no longer rested with any central body, but with individual patrols. Apart from Beat Policing, there appeared to be no centralised system for collecting data or monitoring to determine the extent of implementation and the degree of success. A recent report noted 'severe gaps in the collection of data for planning and evaluation purposes' in the area of ethnic affairs:

> there appears very limited information at headquarters level of what the component parts of the Ethnic Client Group Program do, aim to achieve, actually achieved, etc. For example, there is no data currently on the work of Ethnic Liaison Officers, which have been attached to most patrols, nor any indication whether the employment of such officers has improved the equality of access to police services for ethnic groups. There is also no data concerning what specialist ethnic programs exist and little indication that the special needs of ethnic groups are met in the mainstream programs. ... With the limited data currently available, there is no way of evaluating the progress on ethnic issues raised in the Ethnic Affairs Policy Statement (EAPS). For example, EAPS identifies 62 patrols with ethnic populations greater than 15%. Patrol Commanders were asked to develop objectives, strategies and evaluation mechanisms to improve access to existing services by ethnic groups, however, no data exists to determine whether this has occurred nor whether increased access has been achieved. [Ingram 1991: 28]

The 1988 EAPS laid out strategies and target dates for various strategies to be implemented, but it did not specify any concrete outcomes or indicators of performance against which results could be measured. In fact, the development of suitable indicators of performance for the Police Service as a whole was the preoccupation of the Office of Strategic Services during the period of my research. The quantitative indicators being used generally to measure police performance in the NSW Police Service have been: crime statistics; road safety statistics; personnel statistics such as attrition, sick leave and overtime; and complaints statistics. None of these statistics can be disaggregated for analysis of performance in relation to ethnic or Aboriginal communities. Since 1988, community surveys have been conducted at six-monthly intervals. These surveys canvass specific aspects of people's opinions of the NSW Police Service, their support for community policing programs, and their fears and concerns about crime. Some of the results pertain to 'ethnic groups', based on whether the respondent speaks a language other than English at home. The 'ethnic' sample is usually quite small (183 out of 1300 in the sample for October 1991 to March 1992) and although some interesting trends are found, it is impossible to link these results with any specific programs undertaken.

In the absence of systematic data, assessments of the performance of the NSW Police Service in the areas of ethnic and Aboriginal affairs policy tended to take the form of complaints and criticisms raised by external bodies or individuals (e.g. NSWEAC 1992; HREOC 1991), or high-profile cases of police 'failure' (e.g. *Cop It Sweet*; Operation Sue), followed by desperate attempts by the Police Service to control the damage brought on by negative publicity (see Chapter 8). Although high-profile reports and negative feedback from sections of the community do signal some instances of failure in performance, they often provide little or no indication of the extent of failure, the reason for failure, or whether there has been a deterioration or an improvement in the rate of failure. Neither do these cases show which police initiatives have succeeded and which have failed. While they have to be taken seriously by the police organisation, these cases have to be analysed in context and with the aid of better-quality information before useful remedial actions or programs can be taken.

What Went Wrong?

Social science researchers have offered various explanations for the failure of policy. For example, the models proposed by Elmore (1993) of social program implementation provide a useful catalogue of ways of understanding policy failures.[1] The first model represents a popular view of organisations as machines. When organisations are conceived of as hierarchical, rational, and goal-oriented, policy failures are explained as the result of 'bad management': 'lapses of planning, specification and control' (Elmore 1993: 319–20).

The second model recognises that organisations are not at all like machines, but organisational behaviours are dominated by *discretion* exercised by individual members and *routines* developed to manage assigned tasks. Implementation failures result from individuals or sub-units resisting change by continuing to do what they have always done. Of particular interest in this model are the actions of the 'street-level bureaucrats' (Lipsky 1980) who are relatively autonomous from supervisors and immune to changes in policy: 'Bureaucratic routines operate against the grain of many policy changes because they are contrived as buffers against change and uncertainty; they continue to exist precisely because they have an immediate utility to the people who use them in reducing the stress and complexity of work' (Elmore 1993: 328). Within this model, there is very little scope for change or control imposed from the top. It is also impossible to predict with any accuracy the impact of change.

The third model focuses on the social and psychological needs of individual members of the organisation. Implementation is seen as a process of mutual adaptation, accommodation and consensus-building between those who make policy and those who implement it. Far from being something that can be controlled from the top, implementation relies on individual commitment and cooperation. Thus, implementation failures are not the results of bad management or bureaucratic resistance, but a lack of commitment among those responsible for implementing the policy. Techniques for enhancing implementation include involving implementors in decision-making, giving people a sense of ownership in the new policy, and encouraging mutual support and innovation in work groups.

The final model conceives of organisations as fields of conflict and bargaining where many sources of power exist. For example, 'mastery of specialized knowledge, discretionary control over resources, a strong external constituency' can be used to 'enhance the bargaining position' of people within an organisation (Elmore 1993: 340). From this view of organisation, the success or failure of implementation is never absolute, nor is it permanent.

While it is true that none of these models captures completely the workings of organisations, each highlights an important dimension of the policy process and, for the purpose of this book, a way of explaining policy failure. It is obvious that all four models could have explained why the NSW Police Service's EAPS would not make a great deal of difference to police practice. There is some truth in the criticism that the failure of EAPS was due to poor management. Although the 1988 EAPS document did provide 'clearly specified tasks and objectives that accurately reflect the intent of policy' and a 'management plan that allocates task' to sub-units, it was short on details about performance standards and objective measures of performance. Certainly there was not in place a 'system of management controls and social sanctions sufficient to hold subordinates accountable for their performance' (Elmore 1993: 319–20).

A more important explanation, however, is found in a combination of bureaucratic resistance, lack of organisational commitment, and inter-agency politics. Police research has long documented the wide discretion exercised by street-level police officers and their general indifference to policy changes initiated by headquarters. It was therefore not surprising that EAPS did not make any difference to actual police practice. In addition to this, however, there was another layer of resistance flowing from inter-agency conflict. The EAPS was, above all, seen as a bureaucratic document, as one senior officer in the Police Service pointed out:

> I knew this game pretty well because I'd been working in central agencies which is about central agencies bashing up functional departments to do things and provide huge reports, whether it's on management plans for EEO [Equal Employment Opportunity], or whatever, which sit on the shelf over there, and no-one ever implements. They're done and you've fulfilled your requirement, signed it off, and it's completely useless to the organisation. As the Ethnic Affairs Policy Statement was. Great document to read; totally meaningless. Absolutely useless. But we fulfilled our requirement to Ethnic Affairs and then everyone forgot about it.

The EAPS was seen to be forced upon the police organisation, which found the exercise time-consuming and irrelevant, given that the organisation itself was undergoing radical changes precisely to achieve the same goals:

> The fact is ... we *were* addressing ethnic minority issues for a long time ... The EAPS stuff is bureaucratic. All right, I mean, I can understand the rationale for that, but nevertheless it's a bureaucratic exercise. And there was a lot of resistance to it. You know, a lot of people here feel that this is a waste of time ... I think what I'm saying is that community-based policing is far more effective than EAPS, yes. Because through community-based policing a lot of the needs of the communities are identified, whereas EAPS is coming from a central level down. This is coming from the grass-roots level and I think *far* more effective.

People in the organisation admitted that trying to implement policies and programs from headquarters was generally an extremely difficult task. The client consultant's role became very difficult as a result of lack of support within the organisation on the one hand, and lack of understanding from the Ethnic Affairs Commission on the other:

I found ... the pressure from the Ethnic Affairs Commission a bit hard to take as well ... Some of them are very pleasant, but some I found very arrogant and pushy and I was having to bear it all because I was just *the only person* who dealt with ethnic minorities. So they've got a problem, I'm the one who's going to cop it. Somebody doesn't do something somewhere, doesn't provide an interpreter, I get abused.

Yet it was precisely the *marginal* status given to ethnic affairs by the police organisation that the Ethnic Affairs Commission was trying to change. One officer from the commission explained:

The Police Service were not providing us with [an annual report on the implementation of EAPS], and that happened the first year after 1988, and the second year after 1988. All endeavours we had to actually get the Police Service to provide the report were stonewalled at a whole range of levels. We were always told there's going to be a report on women and minorities, or there's no infrastructure. One of the structural reasons for that was that the Police have an ethnic affairs officer – an officer for client liaison with ethnic communities ... but because of that client liaison role, she had immediately assumed Ethnic Affairs Policy responsibility, which is not the way the program is meant to be implemented. The program is meant to be implemented right through an organisation. There can certainly be a role for an Ethnic Affairs Policy person or an ethnic advisor, but that person shouldn't be a superhuman person who can make the whole organisation change. Especially one like the police.

This officer thought that there was a 'clear lack of understanding' in the Police Service about EAPS and what it was intended to do. It took the Ethnic Client Consultant a long time to 'realise that rather than being a sponge of ethnic affairs issues, what she needed to be for [the EAC] was the key to the organisation'.

More recently, the Ethnic Affairs Commission has adopted a 'strategic plan' approach to the development of EAPS (see NSWEAC 1991). Seen as being more 'flexible', this approach was welcomed by the police organisation. In 1991 the responsibility for the formulation and implementation of EAPS shifted to the Office of Strategic Services. Where the 1988 EAPS was the product of one police officer sitting in a room and writing, the new EAPS aimed to be more of a 'living, breathing document', with inputs from operational police. The exercise was quite different to the first, according to a senior officer in the police administration:

the critical thing is, if you're going to develop a strategic plan in operational area, the first step is to get operational input into the development of what you're doing. ... So this time we've said that the process is more important than the document. It sounds a bit glib. But in fact unless you've got some operational standing out there, that people in the field have had an input into that – and you're not going to agree with everything they say, you can thrash those things out – but it's got to have credibility in the field. Cops have got to believe that what comes out has some relevance to them and that it's achievable and that it has a fair degree of commonsense. A lot of the stuff in the past hasn't had those three elements.

The new EAPS Strategic Plan (NSWPS 1992) was acknowledged by the Ethnic Affairs Commission 'in glowing terms': 'The EAPS Strategic Plan is not only comprehensive in its coverage, but also noteworthy in that it is clearly linked to the overall Corporate Plan of the Police Service' (quoted in NSW Ombudsman 1994: 23). Ironically, the EAPS concept has since been replaced by the 'New South Wales Charter of Principles for a Culturally Diverse Society'. Public authorities are now required to submit a 'Statement of Intent' in response to the Charter. The difference between the EAPS and the charter approach, as far as I can gather, is that public authorities will now have to table their reports in Parliament, rather than to the Ethnic Affairs Commission. The effectiveness of the charter in changing police practice remains to be seen.

The EAPS case study is a powerful reminder that a statement of policy is no more than that – a paper exercise. The police organisation is notoriously difficult to control, both from outside and from inside. However, the EAPS program was based on nothing more than a memorandum from the Premier to Ministers. As such it had very little 'muscle' in securing compliance from agencies. As one of the interviewees said, 'A lot of it has been bluff, but quite an effective bluff.' It is also instructive that a major argument put forward by the Police Service for the delay in formulating an EAPS as well as its lack of commitment to monitoring and annual reporting was that the organisation was undergoing major changes and was already pursuing similar goals through its community-based policing strategy. The argument appears reasonable, except that community-based policing ran into exactly the same problems as EAPS: there was not a great deal of understanding of the concept; there was little monitoring or evaluation; resistance was evident in some pockets of the organisation; and there was limited involvement of the community in decision-making (see Chapter 9).

Notes

1 The models are an adaptation of the framework developed by Allison (1971).

CHAPTER 8

Cop It Sweet: *Reform by Media*

Even though the NSW Police Service had formulated an Ethnic Affairs Policy Statement by 1988, no similar policy statement in relation to Aboriginal affairs existed during the period of my fieldwork. The television documentary *Cop It Sweet*, described briefly in the introduction of the book, was instrumental for the development of an Aboriginal Affairs Policy Statement in 1992. This chapter examines the processes and events which led to this development. It describes the reaction to the film within the police hierarchy, the attempt at damage control, and the subsequent repair work carried out in improving relations between police and Aborigines. The *Cop It Sweet* scandal provides a rare glimpse into how a police organisation, one that was in the middle of a great wave of change, reacted to external pressure to reform.

Cop It Sweet

The controversial television documentary *Cop It Sweet* was filmed over a six-week period in Redfern by freelance journalist Jenny Brockie, with police permission at a 'senior command level' (NSW Police Board 1992: 17). The content of the documentary was based on a collage of police work in this inner-city area, which has been well known in recent years as a site of tension between the police and the Aboriginal community. One account of the documentary neatly summarises the images presented:

> *Cop It Sweet* ... was a shocking account of six weeks in the life of the Redfern police ... [T]hese real-life coppers artlessly revealed the bovine obstinacy and banal prejudice that sustains hostilities with the Aboriginal community ... They spoke automatically of 'coons' and 'gooks' and pubs 'full of lesbians'. Asked to explain what he meant by a 'suss' car, one policeman suggested a red

Laser with an Aborigine driving it ... These ludicrously young officers, who were sharp enough to sense that what they learned at the police academy was 'bull——', knew nothing about the people they were policing and were unable or unwilling to find out. As one officer remarked: 'I really don't stop and talk to them that much, to tell you the truth.' ... Towards the end of the program the police found a young Aboriginal man swearing on a street corner. [The man was subsequently arrested.] ... Back at the station, the man demanded to know what he had done. 'You swore,' said the policeman. 'You're kidding,' said the man incredulously. In the preceding hour, most of the obscene language had come from the police. In other circumstances it might have been comic. Here, it was almost harrowing. [*Sydney Morning Herald*, 7 March 1992].

The broadcasting of *Cop It Sweet* sent shock waves through the NSW police bureaucracy and the Australian community. Even though it was clear that some of those depicted were inexperienced officers working under extremely difficult conditions, the film raised disturbing questions about the style of policing, the quality of police training and supervision, the justice of the criminal law, and the culture of racism in Australian society. Most significant of all, the film revealed some of the more offensive aspects of the police occupational culture. Police culture is situated in the 'back region' of police organisation, rarely disclosed to the outside world (Ericson *et al.* 1989). Most of the academic accounts of police culture were based on observational studies of street-level police work. What the producers of *Cop It Sweet* managed to do was to make aspects of this culture visible to the public in a way that called police executives to account. The film-maker's own description of what she discovered echoed many of the research findings:

My experience of general duties police is that they feel misunderstood, undervalued and constantly under siege from politicians, the media, welfare groups and their own bureaucracy. All this as they daily ricochet from the boring to the volatile, the trivial to the life-threatening. ... The police I met did feel separate from, rather than part of, the broader community. It had driven many of them to a siege mentality – the 'us and them' syndrome. ... Racist language, was, at the very least, tolerated among police, though there was an awareness there'd be trouble if it was revealed to the world outside. But that was a question of tactics. Keeping it in house was what mattered. Keeping the lid on things. Always keeping the lid on things. [Brockie 1994: 177–8]

Instead of worrying about the racist language they used, police officers were more concerned about whether or not they were wearing their hats when the cameras were rolling. This was because 'they knew what was important to their bosses' – a knowledge subsequently validated by a senior police official's remark that disciplinary action was in order because of the 'standard of the officers' dress' shown in the documentary (*ibid.*: 178; cf. Van Maanen 1983).

As mentioned before, the documentary offered nothing particularly new or shocking about police–Aboriginal relations in Australia (see Chapter 1). What it uncovered, therefore, could not have been all that surprising to members of the police force. Yet it was a picture of police work at great variance with the organisation's rhetoric of community policing, non-discriminatory practices, and professionalism. It was this gap that required explanation. It was the damage done to the credibility of the organisation that required control. Even though none of the activities portrayed in the documentary would be considered illegal, the need for damage control was no less urgent. In this way, the media was more effective than the law in demanding accountability from the police.

Negotiating the Public Discourse

In spite of the predictability of its content, when the highest-ranking executives of the Police Service viewed *Cop It Sweet* for the first time, it was reported that they 'nearly fell off their chairs' in amazement. Media and public reaction to the documentary were also unusually strong. Part of the explanation for this reaction may be that television images are powerful and convincing:

> The visual capacity of television allows it to bind its messages to the context in which they were produced ... Television appears most valid because statements made by its sources can be contextualized in the real places in which they were made ... Television's capacity to bind messages to context and thereby validate its messages accounts for the fact that survey research in Canada, Britain and the United States consistently shows that readers find television news more believable, fair, and influential than radio or newspapers ... [Ericson *et al.* 1991: 23–4]

Viewers may have read or heard about the problems of police–Aboriginal relations in Redfern, but television allows them to see the problems as if they were there. Police managers do not directly supervise or control the work of line officers; they rely on written and verbal accounts provided by these officers to inform them of what goes on in the streets. The television images are thus particularly revealing and, where there are clear breaches of rules or regulations, extremely embarrassing for the organisation. Another reason for the public outrage has to do with what is not shown. As one analyst of the film medium points out,

'Cinema is an art and a medium of extensions and indexes. Much of its meaning comes not from what we see (or hear) but from what we don't see or, more accurately, from an ongoing process of comparison of what we see with what we don't see' (Monaco 1981: 136–7). Viewers of *Cop It Sweet* could well imagine the likely behaviour of these police officers if the television camera had not been present. As a letter writer to the *Sydney Morning Herald (SMH)* states, 'What is most frightening about the actions of the officers shown in the program is that they are those of the police on their best behaviour for the cameras' (*SMH*, Letters, 7 March 1992).

Of course, not all reactions to the documentary were hostile to the police. One letter writer complained of 'journalistic manipulation of the issues' and 'public blind spot to Aboriginal lawlessness' (*SMH*, Letters, 7 March 1992). Another supported the police who 'work day to day with racial tension, drunkenness and violence' and defended the officers' swearing and racist comments as 'ways of coping' with their work (*ibid.*).

As Ericson *et al.* (1989) point out, police organisations have in recent years recognised the importance of cooperating with the media as a way of sustaining the organisation's image of being open and accountable. They often employ full-time public-relations officers who disseminate information and stage 'media events'. Proactive media strategies can, in the long term, protect the organisation from its environment and enhance the organisation's legitimacy. When the organisation is under attack, as in this case, a proactive approach is important for containing the damage done to its image. According to senior police officers, the State Executive Group had an opportunity to watch *Cop It Sweet* one week before it was broadcast. A meeting was called and senior representatives of operational, policy, and disciplinary branches got together to discuss ways of responding. The damage-control operation was well orchestrated and professionally executed:

> I think firstly that there was genuine concern of what had happened ... The issue was ... you need to do something and you need to be seen to be doing something ... I think another standard approach in damage control is to stress the positive ... The critical part of the strategy was in fact to get on the front foot. So by the time the program went to air we'd already had the written stuff prepared. Tony [Lauer, the Police Commissioner] knew what he was going to say. We had approached the media channels before the program even went to air, so that at 7 a.m. the next morning he's on [various radio talk shows]. In other words, get out there first, don't sit back and wait for the questions. And then he did [television interviews]. You don't take them all on, you pick the ones that you think will have the maximum exposure. You make sure you're well briefed about the issues and generally you're open about it. In other words, if there's criticism there, you accept it if it's right – not everything ... So part of that is about stressing the positive but

accepting that there are things to do and trying to identify what those issues are. [*A senior administrator*]

A proactive approach meant that instead of being on the defensive, the police organisation was seen to be already doing something about the problem. The front-page headline of the *Sydney Morning Herald* read, for example, 'Police shake-up over TV racism' (6 March 1992). The message was unequivocal that the racist behaviour was unacceptable, and something was being done. Deviance was portrayed as 'individual and incidental' and located at the lower ranks of the organisation (*cf.* Punch 1985: 152), while senior management was presented as being clearly in control: an internal investigation had been ordered by the Police Commissioner into the conduct of 140 officers stationed at Redfern; the Commissioner was 'dismayed' by the behaviour of some of the officers, but was 'confident their attitudes did not reflect those of the overwhelming majority in the force'; and the transfer or dismissal of some officers was one of the options being considered. The Assistant Commissioner in charge of Training and Recruitment supplied the positive news of the Police Service's achievements in recent years in terms of improved training and standards (*ibid.*). There was, of course, still a lot of bad news on the same pages. Police–Aboriginal relations were still tense, with a spokesman for the Aboriginal Legal Service and a local activist both claiming that 'nothing had changed' because 'police still regarded Aborigines as the enemy' (*ibid.*).

Critics of the police were not impressed by the slickness of the media campaign, although the thoughtful ones did appreciate the enormity of the problem and the fact that the organisation was genuinely trying. The then NSW Ombudsman commented:

[Police Commissioner] Tony Lauer talks about how we've made great strides in this and great strides in that ... he articulates very well, but it's all fairy tale. I mean, he believes what he's saying and he's got procedures in place but it takes a long time and, you know, you go forward two steps and something happens and they go back five sometimes. And I mean his responses to *Cop It Sweet* were very clear and not bad press but I don't think it convinced anybody ... I watched *Cop It Sweet* for instance ... I mean, it was exactly what I expected, you know, what's new? It was only revealing to people that don't know the area. And so to say it's isolated – he's just fooling himself and he believes it. And, you know, the changes just aren't any great leaps in these things ... But in fairness there are some areas where [community liaison] is working very well ... I think they really are sincerely trying to do it.

The media coverage which followed in the next few days focused on various issues, such as the injustices of the offensive language provisions of the *Summary Offences Act* (NSW)[1] which 'gave police an open ticket to arrest Aboriginal people' (*SMH*, 7 March 1992); the futility of scapegoating the inexperienced police officers portrayed in the film (*SMH*, Letters, 10 March 1992); the increased rate of detention of Aborigines in prisons and the lack of progress in implementing the recommendations of the Royal Commission into Aboriginal Deaths in Custody (*Sun-Herald*, 8 March 1992).

What the NSW Police was not prepared for, however, was a second bombshell in a week: the screening on ABC television news of clips from an amateur video, showing two NSW police officers with their skin painted black and nooses around their necks, mocking two Aborigines whose deaths had been the subject of investigation by the Royal Commission into Aboriginal Deaths in Custody. The tape was made in 1989 at a police fund-raising party in Eromanga, a town in Queensland. This time the outcry was led by the Prime Minister, Paul Keating, who called the video 'sickening' and said that the officers' behaviour 'brings disgrace on themselves, on their police force and on Australia' (*SMH*, 13 March 1992). Again the Police Commissioner ordered an inquiry. The two officers were placed on restricted duties and the Commissioner offered an 'unreserved apology' to the family and friends of the dead Aborigines, Lloyd Boney and David Gundy. The Commissioner's office issued a statement to the media which, apart from offering apologies and expressing disappointment, attempted to broaden the debate to the historical role of police in enforcing 'protection' of Aborigines and racism in the wider Australian society:

> We readily acknowledge there are problems between the police and the Koori community.
> But when one considers that the NSW Police, in line with Government policies of the day, were forcibly removing Koori children from their mothers as late as the 1960s, one can start to fathom the extent of the historical friction between both camps. ...
> I remain firm in my belief that the problems confronting the Koori people go well past the police and into areas of health, unemployment, alcohol abuse, housing and education. ...
> Of course, the ABC footage reflects badly on police, but it also shows up the depth of a wider community malaise.
> The actions of these few officers mirror a broader social problem and this episode is a shocking and stark indictment on the attitudinal ambivalence many of us feel. [*Police Service Weekly*, 23 March 1992: 3]

This broader view was also taken by the Prime Minister, who put the onus on white Australians to change their attitudes towards Aborigines. Royal Commissioner Hal Wootten saw it as a reflection of the deep-seated racism in Australian society (*SMH*, 13 March 1992).

Organisational Reaction and Repair

Reaction

Within the police organisation, there were mixed reactions to the events and varied opinions as to where the blame should be laid. After the initial shock and disbelief, members of the organisation began to distance themselves from the negative picture that was painted. Distancing consisted of condemnation, denial, and criticising the messenger. Many rank-and-file police officers openly condemned the racist language and unprofessional practices of those portrayed in the documentary. An executive of the Police Association explained:

> The interesting statewide response was that the police at Redfern were subjected to a level of abuse and, I guess, rejection that I have never experienced in my twenty-odd years of policing. And that the general view was that the behaviour of the Redfern police was not only seen as being unacceptable but it caused great discomfort to police generally throughout New South Wales ... It was interesting in talking with some 80 police at Redfern that the thing that they objected to most of all was the fact that they had been rejected by their own peers. Some would suggest that that was significant in terms of the police culture – that is that for the first time we've seen what I call the great body of police publicly rejecting the behaviour of a group at Redfern.

The culture of secrecy and solidarity among police officers might have been partly broken at a time of crisis, but several letters to the Police Association's official journal regarding *Cop It Sweet* presented some dissenting views. One letter condemned those who criticised the Redfern police as acting out of 'mindless self-interest' which threatened to destroy camaraderie among police officers:

> This letter is ... about and directed to all those persons, police or otherwise who have had the gall to ring Redfern Station to register their self-righteous indignation about the police and their behaviour on that programme. Who the hell do they think they are? I've even seen letters to the editor in a Sydney newspaper from police officers in which their holier-than-thou drivel is espoused. Stand and be counted – how many of you have submitted your green form to relocate to Redfern and to volunteer to work a night shift on Redfern One ... let's think twice before jumping on a band-wagon; camaraderie amongst police does not mean conspiracy – it means comradeship and good fellowship; qualities, I fear we are in danger of losing to that of mindless self-interest ... [A police sergeant, *NSW Police News*, April 1992: 35]

Another letter reinforced stereotypes of Aborigines and attempted to justify police practices by laying the blame on Aborigines themselves:

To our branch this show depicted that it is the Aborigines who are racist when it comes to police. The Aborigine arrested for indecent language showed this openly when he swore at the sergeant declaring by what right he had to dare to enter an Aborigine area and to get out immediately – hence the language ... If police are inclined to be racist, and I am not suggesting that they are, then the Aborigines have given them plenty of cause to take this view. As well as committing plenty of offences against the law, they often show open animosity against police especially when drinking – which is often. In my own experience, for many years I had a lot to do with Aborigines. In those days the Aborigine Protection Act was in force, which in part prohibited them from drinking intoxicating liquor. I can assure you that the Aborigine of the 50's was a much happier and peaceful person than he is today – there being a few exceptions of course. The day the Government accepts the fact that intoxicating liquor is one of the main problems of Aborigines the sooner relations between Aborigines and whites, especially Police, will improve ... [Secretary of an organisation of retired police officers, *NSW Police News*, June 1992: 45–6]

Many within the police organisation saw *Cop It Sweet* as unbalanced and unrepresentative, thus denying that there was a systemic problem. Some of the comments from senior police were concerned with the lack of balance, and questioned the professional judgment of the documentary producer:

I don't believe that it was a balanced presentation. For example, I had two of the Aboriginal Liaison Officers from Redfern here yesterday and I asked them were they interviewed by the ABC journalists and ... they nodded and I said I didn't see you in the program and they said, well, they didn't like what we said ... I really think they went in there with a preconceived idea of what police and Aboriginal relations was all about and that's how they presented eventually. It doesn't justify what I saw recorded, I'm not seeking to do that. [*A senior police executive*]

The program *Cop It Sweet* ... was I think far from a balanced program. It was in my view quite boring television, an attempt to copy the American *Cops* type program, but we don't have the same kind of activity here that keeps it interesting ... My own suspicion is that they got a bit desperate – there wasn't much dramatic happening and they put together what they could. That doesn't detract from the fact that some of our young officers were behaving in a manner that ... we disapprove [of] as an organisation, but I think it is a reflection of community attitudes rather than specifically police attitudes. [*A senior civilian officer*]

There are some police that I suppose are cowboys ... I know some police that are down there [in Redfern] that have done a lot of good work with Aboriginal youth which wasn't portrayed ... It portrayed a lot of the negativity. I don't think it was reflective of the whole Patrol. [*A senior police officer*]

In fact, the organisation was in the middle of another 'repair' job when *Cop It Sweet* went to air. During the previous year, the National

Inquiry into Racist Violence by the Human Rights and Equal Opportunity Commission (HREOC) had come out in strong condemnation of Australian police forces as the main perpetrators of racist violence against Aborigines (HREOC 1991; see Chapter 1). One consistent reaction to the commission's report, *Racist Violence*, within the NSW Police Service was that the research was methodologically flawed. One officer remarked about the inquiry's study of police treatment of Aboriginal juveniles:

> you realise that all the people they interviewed were offenders, don't you? I'm not saying it's not possible; it could have happened, but bear in mind that they're allegations. Bear in mind they are the criminals. They've all got an axe to grind if you like ... I think the general consensus is that the report is exaggerated and not a true picture. Because I think police are extremely careful about what they do with Aborigines because of all the flak they've received. There's also a high degree of provocation that goes on ... We have young police who ... go to Walgett wanting to do the right thing. They've been educated and taught to be sensitive and they go there and they confront 50 per cent of the population that is abusive and violent and aggressive. I mean, what is that going to do to anybody? [*A civilian officer*]

This also echoed the general criticism by the police of an earlier Human Rights and Equal Opportunity Commission report on the Redfern raid in 1990 (Cunneen 1990b). As a newspaper editorial pointed out in that case:

> Instead of answering the most telling of the specific criticisms of the raid, [Police Commissioner] Mr Avery has attacked the report for its lack of balance. In particular, he says, it failed to take proper account of 'the operational constraints and responsibilities placed on police in the [Redfern] area' and 'the positive initiatives undertaken by police to seek to improve the quality of life in Redfern.' ... Mr Avery's response will not do. A strong criticism emerging from the Human Rights Commission report is that positive policies, however imaginative and sincerely applied, can be thoroughly undermined by one single misguided policy such as the resort to the heavy-handed methods characteristic of the Tactical Response Group. [*SMH*, 24 May 1991]

The *Racist Violence* report took the police organisation by surprise. They did not think that they would be singled out in the report as the prime perpetrators of racist violence. One member objected to the scapegoating of the police by the inquiry:

> by having what was seen as a heavy police focus ... the report did a disservice in failing to recognise that many other government agencies had failed to accept their responsibility and that ultimately the problems, which should have been shared not only within the agencies and bureaucracies but within communities, were in fact being sheeted home to police. [*A police officer*]

The frustration felt by those who have been the 'reformers' within the police force was evident in the account by a member of the police organisation who attempted to establish a dialogue with the critics regarding the issue of over-policing (see Chapters 1 and 2). This officer tried to put forward a dissenting view at a public seminar on Aboriginal people and the criminal justice system that over-policing was a more complex issue than looking at 'a simple system of ratio of police to population' in a particular area:

> if that was the only criteria they were going to use to judge whether they're overpoliced or not, they missed the point, because the way the government responds ... is to depend upon the police agency to keep the lid on these communities ... and the way we staff towns like that is on a workload basis. So that the more reports of crimes you get, the more police you get. It's a sort of vicious cycle and in lieu of any other agency doing anything constructive, what you do is you find you get more and more police because the communities – the downward spiral of disintegration that takes place in these communities because of poverty, unemployment, alcoholism, and consequentially, domestic violence, child abuse, bad health and hygiene, all those issues manifest themselves in crime and none of the other agencies pick the tab up. And what the government does is ask the coppers to pick the tab up. That issue of over-policing, I was trying to say to this conference, is a very complex issue ... and the response I got from the audience was one of derision.

The organisational response to *Racist Violence* was, according to one officer, to 'not take it seriously'. The official response was that 'Staffing levels will be increased in patrols with high Aboriginal and non-English-speaking populations and police officers will be warned that racist violence will not be tolerated'(*SMH*, 27 May 1991). It took the commitment of a few members to make sure that the organisation did not simply sweep everything under the carpet:

> I suppose at the end of the day there are some individuals in here who are serious about improving the quality of service to minority communities, but the organisation as a whole doesn't give a shit about it ... We didn't take it seriously when it was happening, then there was the media circus with the likes of [name of journalist] talking about individual allegations of racist behaviours and that, we then thought we'd better do something so we responded again with some releases ... then it stopped there – stopped dead. And that's where the whole show would have stopped, right ... What happened here was a few people ... decided that we needed to pick up the ball and run with it. So, in any organisation you're dependent on some ratbags doing something about it, so we picked it up and said, well, we need to set up a mechanism internally that's going to take it seriously, and is going to respond to it and that's where we set up our Working Party on the report. ... What we tried to do was to involve operational police ... in working up our response to the recommendations.

The working party met over twelve months and came up with additional recommendations to deal with structural obstacles to combating racism. A status report was made to the Police Commissioner and an implementation schedule was developed. The final recommendations went to the different commands for comments. Meanwhile, *Cop It Sweet* came along and the Commissioner established another working group to advise him on what action might be taken by the organisation in response.

Repair

Opinions varied within the police organisation regarding what went wrong with Redfern. One of the most frequently raised criticisms was the quality of supervision:

> the reality is that – notwithstanding the Redfern film was a one-hour clip of six or eight weeks – the behavioural characteristics must have been known ... to the patrol command. I can't see how that could have been avoided ... At the same time, bearing in mind the experience of Operation Sue nine or twelve months earlier, you must query the role of the District Commander I would have thought ... The reality is that the behaviour was so open that it's very hard to say that people didn't know it was going on ... Whilst you may not have fully agreed with it, there was obviously no one totally opposed to it.

Another diagnosis was the gap between training and practice – Redfern was a difficult patrol to work in and police training did not adequately prepare officers for the type of work they had to engage in. One constable explained:

> I found that Redfern is a place that's extremely difficult to police. It's extremely hard. The incidence of crime is not petty ... The huge housing commission complexes and the high density of population in a small area creates a lot of difficulty. Alcohol's a really visible problem in the area, maybe more so with Aboriginal people than white people ... Why it's difficult to police is because you're making important decisions quickly and often Redfern police have a high workload so they're constantly going from one job to another – at whatever age level they are or whatever amount of experience of policing that they have – flying by the seat of their pants ... Redfern police are dealing with difficult situations maybe three or four or five times a day ... What that woman says on the film when she says the [Police] Academy is 'bullshit' ... she's saying that we have to make split decisions, we had to make them quickly and the Academy doesn't teach us this.

As a result of the scandal, a review of the quality and effectiveness of cross-cultural training was undertaken. *Cop It Sweet* was to be incorporated into a video for police training, and a senior lecturer in multicultural studies was appointed to the Police Academy.

Some officers attempted to broaden the organisational response to the documentary beyond simply improving supervisory practices and police training, towards assisting local police to develop meaningful strategies and consultation with the Aboriginal communities. One officer proposed that a proper debriefing session should be conducted with all the police officers working at Redfern to allow officers to reflect on the problems and collectively come up with some plan of action to improve the situation. Another proposed a comprehensive program of consultation with the Aboriginal community in Redfern. These ideas were not immediately adopted by the police executives. One officer tried to establish a consultation mechanism through the Police Association (the police trade union) (*SMH*, 17 March 1992), but his effort was met with scepticism from the community and obstruction from the association. A frustrated officer thought that once again the police organisation gave up an opportunity to do something substantial about the problem:

> We've had the window open up before, you know, Operation Sue gave us an opportunity to do something. The National Inquiry report gave us an opportunity to do something. There've been lots of individual instances where we could have taken opportunities to improve our game. This one absolutely shattered the window and we've got this huge opportunity to do something. What do we do? Bring in the repair people and whack up a bit of four-by-two so no one can get in. Basically that's where we are; we're hoping it will go away ... Nothing's changed, absolutely nothing has changed. We'll wait for the next disaster in Redfern and we'll go into this cycle again ... I'm not even sure if it's we're not taking it seriously, or we don't understand the issues.

One example of senior police not understanding the underlying issue was given in relation to what was said at a meeting:

> One guy said to me ... he said there's so many recommendations going, you don't change these people (talking about the Aboriginal people) 200 years they've been like this, you're not going to change them, and I said to him, we're not trying to change them, it's *us* we're trying to change – he sort of missed the point.

The organisation's public show of openness and emphasis on the positive did not prevent an internal witch hunt. Questions were asked about who had allowed the filming to take place, what procedures had or had not been followed, and how the organisation could ensure that it never happened again (Brockie 1994: 179). An officer who took an active part in pushing for change had mixed feelings about the initial outcomes:

> What *Cop It Sweet* did do, it raised the level of debate within communities within this nation to the point where ... for the first time the issue in debate

didn't centre exclusively on policing. I also believe *Cop It Sweet* has been instrumental in forcing a government response to the [Royal] Commission on Black
Deaths in Custody. Unfortunately, it appears that from a Police Service view-
point, their only understanding of *Cop It Sweet* was to see it strictly in terms of
unacceptable behaviour of a few ... In fact what I saw from the Police Service
response was to justify police education and training, was to reject the behaviour and basically to call on our Internal Affairs people to conduct a fairly
close investigation to identify those constables and sergeants who were either
directly seen in the film as behaving unacceptably or were ultimately found to
have some level of responsibility in terms of supervision.

It was not until a year later that the full consequences of the organisational responses to *Cop It Sweet* and the 'bad taste' video became apparent. Initially, disciplinary actions were taken against thirteen of the
officers whose behaviours were broadcast in *Cop It Sweet* and the amateur
video. The two former Bourke police officers featured in the amateur
video were transferred and closely supervised for two years. They were
also paraded and counselled by the State Commander and required to
attend 'an educational course designed to encourage empathy and
understanding with ethnic and minority groups'. One constable at Redfern received a disciplinary transfer and was to be directly supervised.
Other police ranging from probationary constables to an inspector were
paraded or counselled. The Commissioner justified the disciplinary
action as reflecting a 'problem-solving' approach meant to 'impact positively on long-term attitudinal and cultural change', since little benefit
could be gained by 'banishing' these officers, who 'have already been
widely criticised and ridiculed in the public arena and within the ranks
of their own profession' (*Police Service Weekly*, 11 May 1992: 13). The NSW
Aboriginal Legal Service and the widow of David Gundy were reported
to be outraged at the lenience of the punishment (*SMH*, 25 April 1992).

Subsequent developments prompted a previously sceptical member of
the organisation to comment on the positive effect of the documentary,
'We need a *Cop It Sweet* every week.' One of the positive developments
involved a 'historic' meeting between a group of Aboriginal elders and
senior police, including the Commissioner, in May 1992. The meeting
was 'part of a consultation process the Commissioner is undertaking to
improve the relationship between Police and the Aborigines' (*Police
Service Weekly*, 15 June 1992: 31). The State Commander also visited
various centres in the North-west area and met with both the police and
the local Aboriginal communities. In October 1992 a two-day forum
attended by senior police and Aboriginal leaders from around the State
considered a draft Police Aboriginal Policy Statement and the formation
of a Police Aboriginal Council. The policy statement was subsequently
launched in December – this was a significant event in the history of

police–Aboriginal relations in New South Wales, since such a policy statement had not existed until then. What was more significant, however, was the fact that the statement was developed through extensive consultation with the Aboriginal community. In this statement, the NSW Police Service 'is committed to providing a service to Aboriginal and Torres Strait Islander people, which is appropriate to their needs and free from racism and other forms of discrimination'. Furthermore, 'Appropriateness will be determined through a comprehensive and ongoing process of consultation. This consultation will involve the general Aboriginal community, including Aboriginal people who have come under police notice.' A strategic plan was to be developed and monitored by the Police Aboriginal Council; the policy statement was to be evaluated every twelve months by the council, and 'changes considered necessary by Aboriginal people will be considered by the Council'.

In a 1993 speech on police accountability, the Commissioner expressed his belief that police organisations should not give in to the 'natural desire to retreat when under attack or scrutiny':

> Some have made the analogy of a police organisation being much like a turtle. If it is bashed about, the turtle simply sucks its head, arms and legs into its shell ... It does not matter how hard or ferociously you bang on top, it remains tucked away from public glare. The temptation to behave like a turtle must be resisted. [Lauer 1994: 65]

Ironically, being more accountable meant being more open and accessible to outside scrutiny. This in turn could lead to more damage to the organisation. Some senior officers within the police organisation thought that the succession of adverse media coverage in recent years was not the result of any deterioration of the quality of police work; rather, it reflected a more mature, more open and a more accountable police organisation:

> The impression often held by politicians and the community is the police stuff up more now than they used to. My view is completely the opposite. I think that in the old days we covered them up ... And I think that, if you like, the price of being a more accountable organisation is more visibility and I think that it's desirable ... I think we stuff up less but we hear a lot more about it. ... In the old days we basically said nothing, said 'no comment' and did no preparation, put our heads down and copped it. Now ... it's certainly more sophisticated in terms of being more open-minded for a start, recognising we make mistakes or continue to make mistakes, and that's particularly more so now when you're trying to change things. You always make more mistakes when you introduce some of these substantial changes as we have in the past five or six years. [A senior administrator]

The lesson of *Cop It Sweet* appeared to be that openness was to be a virtue of the higher rather than the lower levels of the organisation. While the Commissioner allowed the ABC program *The 7.30 Report* to follow him around from morning till night for a week, Jenny Brockie was allowed only limited filming of the police 'under the tightest supervision' for her subsequent documentary on the Campbelltown Local Court (Brockie 1994: 179).

Media, Scandal and Reform

The accountability of police has been much debated by both practitioners and academics in recent years. In general, accountability refers to the 'institutional arrangements made to ensure that police do the job required of them', but there is considerable disagreement regarding which should be regarded as the appropriate institutions to which police are accountable (Brogden *et al.* 1988: 151). Certainly, police are supposed to be accountable to the law: illegal activities are punishable by criminal law, while other failures to perform their duties properly may be dealt with by civil remedies or disciplinary procedures. Police regulations or codes of practice, criminal and civil courts, administrative review tribunals and citizen complaints procedures are instruments of accountability available to the general public. More recently, however, there is increasing recognition that police should also be subject to democratic political control, since law-enforcement policy is not so much a neutral legal decision as a political choice (*ibid.*: 161; Lustgarten 1986). Goldring and Blazey have argued that police in Australia should be subject to the same mechanisms of accountability as other public sector employees:

> They are accountable to their departmental superiors, in hierarchical systems. They are accountable financially, through the audit systems. They are accountable to the ombudsman and to the courts for their administration. They are accountable in many ways under the managerial techniques which have now become part of public sector administration. [Goldring and Blazey 1994: 153]

The role of the media as one of the mechanisms of accountability is seldom discussed in the literature (Skolnick 1994), although the participation of the news media in exposing police corruption is well known (Sherman 1978). It may be argued that in the case of *Cop It Sweet*, the media had succeeded in securing accountability where the hierarchical structure, the audit systems, the Ombudsman, the courts, the managerial techniques, and the democratic process had failed. The documentary and subsequent media coverage had revealed, publicised and helped dramatise the problem of police–minorities relations, so that police executives were forced to defend the organisation (*cf.* Sherman 1978). Just as police bureaucracies demand routine giving and taking of accounts between subordinates and supervisors, media scandals require police executives to provide credible accounts to demonstrate that they are in control of their organisation and that appropriate actions are being taken to rectify the problems.

Criminological literature has long documented the role of the media as a generator or amplifier of 'moral panics' regarding crime and deviance (e.g. Cohen 1972; Hall *et al.* 1978). This literature highlights the processes engaged in by the media in the social construction of deviance. In general, research in this tradition has focused on what are conventionally known as 'street crimes' or violent crimes (see, for example, Fishman 1978; Voumvakis and Ericson 1984). More recently, researchers have argued that, in fact, 'deviance is *the* defining character-istic of what journalists regard as newsworthy and, as such, becomes inex-tricably linked with journalists' method' (Ericson *et al.* 1987: 4; original emphasis). Media workers do not simply concentrate on street crimes and violence: they are engaged in the policing of all forms of organisa-tional life (Reiss 1983), especially that of public institutions. Organisa-tional deviance in the form of corruption, procedural irregularities, or unfair practices is as much a preoccupation of the media as individual deviance, especially among the 'quality' media outlets which take seriously their 'fourth estate' function (see Ericson *et al.* 1989). The important role of the media as an active agent of criminal justice reform is an area that deserves more extensive exploration and analysis in criminological research (see also Fisse and Braithwaite 1983).

The significance of the media's role as an agent of reform lies in the power of the public discourse of deviance and control that they help to generate. By painting a picture of deviance, corruption or injustice, media stories contribute to the sense of urgency regarding the need for action to combat such corrupt or unjust practices. But the media are not alone in this enterprise of moral crusading – the public discourse is a product of negotiation between media workers and information sources (Ericson *et al.* 1989). Organisations whose deviance is being exposed are capable of, and are routinely engaged in, shaping and developing this public discourse to minimise damage to their organisational image, as well as to project a sense of order and control by reporting on remedial actions being undertaken to rectify the problem.

As already mentioned in previous chapters, police researchers found a fundamental difference between the 'street cop culture' and the 'man-agement cop culture' (Reuss-Ianni and Ianni 1983). Ericson *et al.* (1989) find that a similar split between the two cultures of police reporters: the 'inner circle' reporters who typically work for popular media outlets and who are trusted by the police to carry stories which enhance the popular image of the police, and the 'outer circle' reporters who typically work for quality media outlets and who are prepared to engage in 'investigative reporting' and to present stories which expose deviant police practices. The authors argue that while inner-circle reporters orient their work to both the street cop and the management cop culture, outer-circle reporters are primarily oriented to the management cop culture:

> It is arguable that emphasis [by outer-circle reporters] on police propriety and efficiency through the portrayal of deviance served in the long run to enhance police management. The typical response to police malfeasance is to demand more resources in the form of more laws or rules, more equipment, and more personnel ... In the long run and in the aggregate, outer-circle reporters contribute to this reform politics on behalf of police management. They actually join with the police management culture in the policing of efficiency and propriety ... [*ibid.*: 113–14]

Typically, police forces seek to enhance their organisational image by having specialised media units in charge of providing information to the media. In large police forces, however, there is a recognition that authorised police officers in other units should be able to give factual information to the media in matters of public interest. The areas of 'enclosure' and 'disclosure' are carefully guarded, so that 'confidence', 'secrecy', 'publicity' and 'censorship' are judiciously employed (Ericson *et al.* 1989: 9). Nevertheless, large police organisations are porous, with numerous sources of information available to journalists, so that it is not always possible to 'patrol the facts' nor to avoid negative publicity. Ironically, when police deviance becomes a major public issue through media coverage, police organisations must seek access to the media to control the damage.

Public scandals also require substantial repair work within police organisations. Since scandals threaten to expose organisational weaknesses and reveal systemic abuses, organisational representatives must 'energetically seek to restore and bolster up the myth system' (Punch 1985: 7). They do so by 'attempting to minimize the issue, by claiming that it is an aberration caused by a few individuals, and [by seeking] scapegoats', while critics may insist that it was not a matter of a few 'rotten apples', but a 'rotten basket' (*ibid.*: 15; Sherman 1978). Police organisations are more likely to be successful in this negotiation of public image if they can demonstrate their ability to control themselves. The adoption of immediate and visible reforms is essential:

To be successful reform may require that heads will roll, that chiefs and
senior personnel be removed and replaced, that a new style of control be
implemented, that opportunity structures and enforcement patterns be
altered, and that new norms and values be broadcast internally and externally
as a reassurance that police behaviour will be changed. [Punch 1985: 16]

Scandals can also precipitate further factions and divisions within the
organisation. Management may attempt to locate the problems at a
lower level, while rank-and-file officers may resist this scapegoating by
pushing the blame upwards (*ibid.*: 7). The traditional solidarity and
secrecy of the 'street cop' culture at times break down under the strain
of external scrutiny and official investigations (*ibid.*: 121–2).

The power of the media should not, however, be overstated. Police
organisations have two choices when confronted with adverse publicity.
They could retreat into their shell as Tony Lauer mentioned, or they
could try to control the damage by proactively engaging in the negotiation of the public discourse. Increasingly the latter strategy is found to
be more effective in protecting organisations from further adverse publicity and allowing organisations to steer public debates in a less damaging direction. The ultimate success of a scandal in effecting change
depends critically on the extent to which the organisation is willing and
able to take seriously its responsibility to be publicly accountable. As
Braithwaite and Fisse found in their research on the control of corporate
crime: 'companies with little will to comply sometimes draw lines of
accountability with a view to creating a picture of diffused responsibility
so that no one can be called to account should a court look into the
affairs of the company. Everyone is given a credible alibi for blaming
someone else' (Braithwaite and Fisse 1987: 227).

The willingness of the NSW Police Service to take accountability seriously was demonstrated by some of the actions and policies which
emerged from the aftermath of *Cop It Sweet*. Its ability to take accountability seriously was the result of years of reform which have begun to
change the police culture at least at the upper management level.
Although senior management did try to portray the problems as individual and incidental, as well as being located at the lower levels, and
there was a tendency for scapegoating and conducting witch hunts, these
were accompanied by serious attempts to consult with Aboriginal communities and to improve police training. In fact, many of the initiatives
announced as corrective measures had been planned and developed
before the scandal. *Cop It Sweet* provided reformers within the organisation with powerful ammunition to push for further changes – it was a cat-
alyst for implementing the necessary reforms. Instead of activating
inter-rank hostilities and unleashing a war of resistance by the lower

ranks against managerial control (see Punch 1985: Chapter 6), the scandal led to a fairly widespread condemnation of racism among police officers, a recognition of the deficiencies in training and supervision, and a renewed commitment by the police organisation to further reforms. There was also increasing awareness in the community that police racism could not be successfully dealt with until racism in the wider society had been confronted.

The positive outcomes of the *Cop It Sweet* scandal, however, should not obscure the possibility that racist or deviant police practices may well persist in spite of the reforms. Sherman (1978: 263) has suggested that scandal is not sufficient for reforming a deviant police organisation; ultimately police organisations must be able to control themselves. Given that some senior officers still resorted to witch hunts and scapegoating. as methods of exerting control, and that media access to the police organisation had since been curtailed in spite of the Commissioner's pledge for the organisation to be more open and accountable, the temptation to carry out piecemeal and cosmetic repair work rather than meaningful change remains strong. In spite of years of apparently radical reforms, the public image of the NSW Police Service has been marred by some high-profile cases of blundering, incompetence and unprofessional activities (Wootten Report 1991; Lee Report 1990; Landa Report 1991; Staunton Report 1991). Opponents of reform saw these as evidence that many of the initiatives were ill conceived and that the pace of change was too rapid. Police executives, however, explained the negative public image as a direct result of a new openness in the organisation. The irony of police reform is that a commitment to openness and accountability does not necessarily lead to a positive police image, but continual damage-control work by upper management in relation to scandals may lead to further cynicism and a hardening of the 'street cop' culture.

Notes

This chapter is a revised version of Chan (1995).
1 The *Summary Offences Act* was reintroduced by the State Liberal government in 1988.

CHAPTER 9

Processes and Outcomes of Change

By the early 1990s, the New South Wales Police Service had undergone almost a decade of change. The question I will turn to in this chapter is: what has all this activity actually achieved? It is easy to be dazzled by the proliferation of symbolic enterprises – the glossy corporate mission and strategic plans, the streamlining and restructuring, the surveys and the statistics, as well as the 'newspeak' among management consultants and senior officers. With so much 'happening' within the organisation, there is a temptation to assume that 'it's all happening'. On the other hand, it would be equally easy to point to *Cop It Sweet* or the report on *Racist Violence* and pass the verdict that 'nothing has changed' in spite of all these activities.[1]

The purpose of this chapter is to assess what has been achieved in the relations between police and minorities following almost a decade of organisational change. It must be recognised that what is presented is by no means a comprehensive picture; it is merely the best picture that can be put together with the available evidence. The focus of the assessment is also fairly restrictive in that there is no attempt to describe the full impact of organisational change on all aspects of policing in New South Wales. Even with a narrow focus, the assessment task was not easy, given the absence of ongoing, systematic monitoring of policy outcomes in this area either by the Police Service or by some external body. This difficulty illustrates the way change has been implemented: the lack of monitoring, feedback, and organisational learning is patently one of the weaknesses of the reform program. The impact of the reforms will be examined along four dimensions: the formulation and implementation of strategies; the activation of organisational processes; police acceptance of reforms; and the production of outcomes.

Formulation and Implementation of Strategies

As described in Chapter 6, the Avery administration had formulated and implemented major changes to the organisation within the first few years of taking office. The most important change was the adoption of community-based policing as the preferred model of operation. Thus, the Mission Statement of the service emphasised a partnership with the community: 'Police and community working together to establish a safer environment by reducing violence, crime and fear' (NSWPS 1990: 10). The 'corporate objectives' of the organisation were similarly concerned with being 'more responsive to the needs and feelings of the community', encouraging a 'problem-solving partnership' with citizens, giving priority to preventing crime and maintaining order, as well as optimising productivity, minimising corruption and strengthening accountability (*ibid.*). The community-based policing strategy made it possible 'for Police services to be tailored to the specific needs of a particular community' (NSWPD 1987: 25).

The adoption of such a strategy, of course, did not automatically give it any meaning, especially for rank-and-file officers, but it was an important first step. The strategy was given structure through regionalisation, which was accompanied by a redistribution of power, a flattening of the rank structure, and the introduction of merit-based promotion. Similarly, the strategy was given direction when community-based programs no longer resided in a marginal Community Relations Bureau but were pushed to the mainstream as each patrol became a multi-functional operational unit, with its own intelligence, investigation and community liaison activities. Finally, the strategy was given content in an educational model which emphasised professionalism and experiential learning.

In terms of improving police–minorities relations, the adoption of community-based policing brought ethnic and Aboriginal issues into the mainstream, with the role of the community client consultants moving towards policy and program development and away from direct community liaison work. The appointment of community liaison officers, the establishment of community consultative committees, the deployment of beat officers, the organisation of community crime-prevention initiatives and the provision of cross-cultural awareness training became patrol-based rather than centrally determined initiatives. Multicultural and linguistic skills received recognition in the system of appointment and promotion. An integral part of initial police training was the fostering of an awareness of the historical and social context of policing and the cultural diversity of Australian society. In other words, the NSW Police Service had managed to put in place a number of administrative, operational and educational strategies towards the realisation of the community-based policing model. This is not to imply that the strategies had all been successfully translated into meaningful activities and successful outcomes, but simply that planning had taken place and strategic directions had been determined.

Activation of Organisational Processes

Strategic Planning

The growing importance of management and planning activities in an organisation previously dominated by operational concerns was evident in the presentation of the NSW Police Service annual reports. For example, 'Operational Policing' still featured prominently in the 1985–86 *Annual Report*, both in terms of the number of pages and detailed information. By 1990, the emphasis had shifted to the organisation's achievements in relation to each of its corporate objectives. The 1991–92 *Annual Report* was structured totally in terms of five 'Key Performance Areas'; they encompassed a range of strategies, including a focus on crime prevention and problem-solving, the development and implementation of a 'Human Resources Plan', improvement of management and professional practices, increased responsiveness to 'stakeholders', and improvement of the strategic planning process.

It is obvious that a great deal of planning activity took place at the top management level. Corporate directions were said to be reviewed annually; they were developed by the Police Commissioner in consultation with the State Executive Group, the Police Board and the Police Minister. The process was 'facilitated through a series of Ministerial and Executive planning workshops' (NSWPS 1992: 21). What is not clear, however, is the extent to which these planning processes took place in other parts of the organisation. The 1987–88 *Annual Report* admitted that planning activities were not uniformly effective: 'One of the real challenges for the Police Service is to make planning part of the everyday life of line commanders, functional managers, supervisors and field operatives. Whilst *Strategic Planning* is operating effectively in some areas, it is less advanced in others' (NSWPS 1988: 13).

In the 1989–90 *Annual Report*, a bottom-up planning framework was said to have been adopted. The framework 'allows for input from the community through patrols, districts, regions and headquarters, with strategic direction from the Commissioner, the Police Board and the Minister' (NSWPS 1990: 17). It also recognised that 'Priorities will differ in accordance with identified local needs.'

One important indication that planning processes were not effective throughout the organisation even in 1992 was found in the report of the Inspector-General[2] to the Police Board:

> Planning is a concept which is reasonably well developed at the level of the Commissioner and his senior staff. Aside from some excellent examples of local, short-term planning to meet immediate short- or medium-term crime problems, there is little evidence that the total concept is either understood or practiced at the local level. [NSW Police Board 1992: 94]

In interview, the Inspector-General elaborated on his finding in relation to the Corporate Plan:

> [The Plan] sets, from the Minister's and the Commissioner's perspective, the direction for the organisation. Now subordinate levels of command are supposed to slot into this within the context of their own geographic area and prepare their supporting plans. This document is seen as largely irrelevant to the local scene. Difficult to read and to comprehend. And, to the extent that planning is undertaken at subordinate level, it is largely a paper exercise …

This finding is consistent with the results of a 'cultural' survey of police officers conducted in 1993 (Aptech 1993).[3] The survey found that members did not 'feel that they understand or share in the "direction" of the organisation'; they felt that 'decisions are not made which support the organisation's goals and that they have little ownership of the decisions which affect them' (*ibid.*: iii). Another survey commissioned by the police found that more than one-third of the respondents (members of the Police Service's Senior Executive Service) disagreed with the statement that 'most people in my command have a good understanding of what the corporate plan means' (IPC Worldwide 1994: 3).[4] The 1988 Ethnic Affairs Policy Statement (EAPS) was a good example of strategic planning which was top-down and which remained a 'paper exercise' (see Chapter 7).

Quality Control

The strategic planning process was intended to be integrated with annual performance appraisals of managers and supervisors within the organisation (NSWPS 1988: 13). As mentioned in the last section, part of the Inspector-General's mandate was to evaluate the performance of members of the Senior Executive Service in relation to their contractual obligations. Although the Inspector-General's review focused on the District Command level, his inspection also involved reviewing the operation of patrols within each District. Thus, by July 1992, fourteen of the twenty-six Districts, which included 102 of the 170 patrols, had been reviewed by the Inspector-General. One of the 'anomalies' identified in his report to the Police Board touched on accountability within the police force: 'Accountability, its meaning, significance and practice requires definition and implementation in a meaningful, objective manner. At the present time it is exacted largely through self-inspection or analysis and lacks the credibility which is vital to the integrity of the management of any police service' (NSW Police Board 1992: 94). Even among senior executives with performance contracts, there was no independent assessment of performance. The·Inspector-General explained:

> the assessment process then becomes one of an Assistant Commissioner saying, 'It's assessment time, tell me how good you are. Tell me what you've done. Tell me how you've met the obligations of your statement of duties.' So you're my boss and I write to you and say, 'I'm a genius and I've accomplished all this' kind of stuff. And that becomes the assessment ... and this has been largely the practice – you read what I have written on my own accomplishments, and you say, 'Yes, he has accomplished that much.'

A more objective system of 'service delivery assessment' was supposed to be operating within the service. In this process a team of police officers assessed whether a patrol was meeting the needs of the community:

> if necessary we do some sampling to see how the service is being delivered. The other major role is to get around and talk to ... as many members of the community as we can: on-the-spot survey, and formal interviews with the Mayor, and the leaders of the Chambers of Commerce, and other such, ethnic groups, community consultative committees, women's refuges, and talk to all those people to find out ... if their requirements are being met by the Patrol.

The problem of this exercise was, according to a senior manager, 'they only gave us six people, so they weren't serious about it'. Only a handful of Districts had been assessed in over two years. The plan was to transfer this responsibility to the District Commanders as part of decentralisation. However, the danger of relying on decentralised commands to carry out organisational policy is well illustrated by another 'anomaly' discovered by the Inspector-General:

> A greater degree of organisational discipline is required to ensure that government priorities, Police Board decisions and directives of the Commissioner find expression at the service delivery end of the Police Service ... Once the policy issues are identified, research and discussion has occurred and decisions are made, the Commissioner must have confidence that those decisions will be implemented. [NSW Police Board 1992: 94]

Two examples of areas where 'members pick and choose which organisational directives or which policies they will follow or ignore' were mentioned by the Inspector-General. The first was the Commissioner's decision that the specialty of the Licensing Police was to be disbanded and the responsibility picked up by general-duty police. This directive was largely ignored in the patrols. Another example was in the use of the new drug exhibit lockers, which required three separate keys to ensure security. Some Patrol Commanders left two or three keys together so that any one person could have access to any part of the locker, thus ignoring the policy.

In ethnic affairs, decentralisation had meant that there was a great deal of unevenness in the development and implementation of various programs. The success of these programs also depended on the commitment, interests and priorities of particular patrol commanders. The Ethnic Client Consultant was powerless to improve the quality of police services to ethnic minorities:

> Some of the patrol commanders are extremely enlightened, and they do make an effort to select the right people, but others are not and when that happens, people here in the central level really can't do very much about it ... I can ... let management know about it, but here it stops ... there is nothing I can do about it any longer. And that has happened in a few places where ... there's *obviously* a breakdown in police–migrant relations and I have no impact on it any longer.

The Ombudsman's review was very critical of the lack of coordination, monitoring and support for the implementation of community-based programs for minority groups:

> The slow change and the poor performance reported by members of community groups are the consequences of inadequate performance indicators, a lack of commitment, and the well-meaning, but unco-ordinated efforts by ill-prepared under-resourced patrol commanders. Inadequate management of Aboriginal and ethnic community issues throughout the Police Service has not helped ... there were no obvious mechanisms for monitoring the Police Service's performance in relation to the extensive range of socially related community problems ... Patrol commanders tended to assess their performance by reference to indicators like crime statistics, clear-up rates and sometimes the number of formal complaints made about police in their patrol. Patrols remained largely task-oriented and were often uncomfortable with social programs and initiatives ... In the minds of some officers, these tasks were in any event, 'nothing to do with real police business'. [Landa Report 1995: iii, 38–9]

The lack of management skills among supervisory police officers was a factor which was frequently cited as the reason organisational changes were not producing outcomes: 'It's not happening because you've got police who are being very good police throughout their career … but they have had limited exposure or no exposure to management, or how to deal with people, human relations, interpersonal skills, communication skills, grievance counselling, intervention.'

The research literature has, however, found that supervision of police work is rarely based on rational management techniques. The study by Van Maanen (1983) of an American police force, as mentioned in Chapter 4, suggests that sergeants tend to have a close and symbiotic relationship with their subordinates; officers who do not have a good relationship with their sergeants 'pay a price'. In the absence of other means of supervision, sergeants tend to 'emphasise results over means': as long as officers bring in the 'bodies' or 'numbers', they are left alone (*ibid.*: 279–80). In New South Wales the same style of supervision was seen to be prevalent, as one officer pointed out in interview:

> Well, … sergeants tended to see themselves as being at one with the constables and it was them against patrol command, and what needed to be done I suppose was to show the sergeants and the constables that it's all very well to be good mates but … you're doing a different job to the constables; you've got different responsibilities, and you're not actually at one with them, that you have to make decisions that the constables aren't going to like.

As another officer observed, constructive criticism by supervisors was never part of the organisational culture of the NSW Police Service. Not only was supervision typically superficial, there was no mechanism for identifying weaknesses or improving quality of work:

> There is no criticism within this organisation. One of the things you hear as you wander around is 'That person over there – he's bloody hopeless the way he did that, but, gee, he's a nice fellow.' It's just an amazing way of dealing with things … we don't have any checking up of anybody in this organisation. We sort of pretend to with rules and regulations and occurrence pads and telephone messages and diaries and note books, even job sheets … Now if, for instance, [as a detective] I take a case and lose it at court, then no one ever says to me, so how come you lost it? Unless the lawyer in the case gets damages, or money or something like that … there's nobody who goes back and says, gee, you know, you really should have interviewed four other witnesses and I guess Blackburn[5] is a classic example of that … where there's no checking up on people's work. There's checking up on whether they turn up, whether they wear a uniform, or if they don't, whether they've got shiny shoes, too many sick days, but there isn't checking up on 'I don't like the quality of your work.'

Results of the 'cultural' survey also found a general feeling among respondents that 'feedback on performance is not freely given, positive or negative' (Aptech 1993: i). Another criticism of the system was that even if someone's quality of work was not satisfactory, there was no way of reducing their rank in the organisation. One officer felt that many police got promoted 'overnight, from a very narrow job' and that had caused a great deal of resentment 'out in the patrols'.

The organisation's inability to define and demand quality meant that it was not possible to perform proper quality control function, as one senior police officer pointed out:

> The organisation ... has lost the ability to require performance ... You see, if a sergeant out at [name of place] isn't performing, what does one do? Because he won that position and he owns that position, and in the absence of gross misconduct or criminal conduct, it's not possible to do anything with him. You can counsel him. You can stick him on permanent night shift – but you may not get away with that either! You can deal with him in a local context but you can't say, 'You're not performing, you're out!' or 'You're not performing, you're being transferred.'... So if you can't motivate them positively and if you can't get your pound of flesh, on the punitive side, your hands are tied. You're stuck with this piece of dead wood who's too stubborn to change and too entrenched to have his behaviour modified.

One officer felt, however, that all this talk about the lack of supervision and control was detracting from the fact that police officers were already under a great deal of stress from all the changes that have occurred, including the 'growth in regulatory and watchdog groups' and the 'politicisation of administration'. Police felt that these groups were 'simply out to get them at every turn'. Even the movement towards developing best practice among supervisors was seen as a 'classic example of an organisation trying to come to grips with what are clearly complex problems but failing to understand them', so that supervisors and sergeants were being made scapegoats of the organisation.

Managing Change

Part of the problem in New South Wales was that changes to the police organisation occurred rapidly and radically soon after the appointment of John Avery as Commissioner. Both the speed and the zeal with which these changes were introduced had left a great number of people feeling dislocated and sometimes resentful. Avery's anti-corruption campaign, for example, was considered both successful and uncompromising:

> From '86 to '89, '90 ... it was their main priority ... making sure that the top hundred positions in the police force were honest ... They redefined competence with a view to promotion by merit instead of seniority and they defined

merit to include everything. So you might have someone very, very competent, but who had a shadow of sin on him or her and they weren't promoted, but you might be not the brightest person in the world but solid and honest and clean and you would be promoted and that was enormously important. And it did clean up the internal ... it did work, it got rid of systematic corruption, I'm convinced of that.

Some officers thought that the campaign got out of hand and created an atmosphere of paranoia and distrust within the organisation, so that inexperienced or incompetent people got placed in jobs because they 'keep telling them what they want to hear'. One officer described the way things turned out:

The environment that was created was that if someone said that if a policeman was crook, he was crook and if you argued against it, you were branded as being – oh yes, you're the old CIB of course you'd say that to protect a mate ... I think that the Headquarters had developed such a state of paranoia about everyone that they took in people who were totally inexperienced (I shouldn't use the word 'inexperienced', people lacking in competence ...). Because they'd never heard of them before, and we hadn't heard of them, there can't be anything wrong with them type of thing.

The so-called rivalry between 'White Knights' and 'Black Knights'[6] had resulted in the victimisation of some innocent officers, but senior police were single-minded and merciless in their efforts to eradicate corruption:

The [Police] Board tackled systematic corruption ... Avery was incredible – he insisted on suspension from your duties without pay and you weren't even found guilty, just that somebody had made an allegation anonymously and that's it, no pay. I came across one guy, a prosecutor, suspected of not report-ing of people found guilty all of their criminal record when they got a life sentence. He suspended that man for three years, not allowed to do any other work. Things got that bad he lost his house and three weeks later he was found not guilty. Imagine how he feels.

Some officers felt that Avery's anti-corruption campaign was neces-sary; they were not really concerned with the casualties which might have occurred along the way:

There had to be war declared on institutionalised corruption ... Every conflict will have its innocent victims; every conflict will have its victims who are not so innocent ... but the flushing out had to be done ... to indicate to those remaining that it would not be tolerated, indicate that it wasn't going to be worth the effort to fight and lose a war. And there had to be a clear indication that you were either on the right side or the wrong side of the fence.

Others felt that things had simply gone too far:

> overall, I think that I certainly wouldn't suggest that the changes that have occurred have been anything other than for the better, but we've made some horrible stuffups on the way and maybe that's the way change has got to be, I don't know. We still have a long way to go, I think. I mean, the principles of the change were absolutely right, but ... the problem was that we didn't know the time to put the brakes on or take the brakes off. I think we went over the critical section.

Top management was satisfied that the outcomes were worth the pain and hardship, since it would be impossible to change a large, complex organisation without pain:

> if you bring about those significant organisational changes – that always creates some havoc in the process and it has in our case and there's quite obviously a long way to go to reform the organisation ... There's no question in my mind that we've improved the organisation at the top ... through merit selection and greater emphasis on ethics. And we've certainly improved the bottom end by better recruit training programs. It's now the middle of the organisation that we need to address.

Survey results show that there was definitely a difference in attitudes between the middle-rank officers and those at the top or at the bottom (see later). Several senior officers explained this phenomenon as an inevitable consequence of the process of change:

> There was a lot of dissatisfied people throughout the organisation, particularly the supervisors, the first-line supervisors who are really dissatisfied – senior sergeants. All the surveys we do would indicate that sergeants and senior sergeants really don't ... know what their job is any more ... there used to be a clear path for them in promotion, it's not there any more.

> It's true, actually [that people at the top are very optimistic], and then it fades as you go down, and it gets worse in the middle ... Part of the reason is we actually spend a lot of time with senior people, many of them, and working with them on understanding the reason for change ... if you are trying to change an organisation and the way it behaves, at least they had to know what you were on about, and why, and then once the next phase really started then they can be both part of the change as well as allowing their people to change too, and that, I think, is why the ones at the top are much more comfortable with the language, much more comfortable with where it's going. They don't all agree, but at least they know the words and they can articulate them and it sounds like if it all works out it will be OK.

What happened was we concentrated on the top, we concentrated on the bottom and forgot those very important people in the middle – the ones that were actually keeping the ship afloat.

There is a line of resistance to change that is generally referred to as the dead wood area, consisting of sergeants and senior sergeants who have been around forever and will not be shaken out of their comfortable environment. And they represent a two-way gate. They pervert the training ... and they prevent the corporate or the more senior command message from getting down to the people who are the future of the organisation.

Community Consultation

It is obvious from the discussion in Chapter 6 that a fair amount of community consultation and liaison took place as a result of the appointment of the Ethnic and Aboriginal Client Group Consultants, as well as Ethnic and Aboriginal Community Liaison Officers. In fact, more formal structures such as group-specific Community Consultative Committees were set up for a limited number of ethnic and Aboriginal communities. The quality of this consultation is, however, difficult to determine, given that there was no systematic monitoring or evaluation of the processes.

Anecdotal evidence suggests that consultations tended to be ritualistic and that the membership of these committees was not representative of the community. For example, young people were unlikely to be represented:

> The case of consultative committees is illustrative: their membership is largely representative of other bodies, Neighbourhood Watch committees, local business interests, adult community groups, and the churches. Young people are more likely to be seen as the problem or the subject of the committee's attention, rather than as an appropriate constituent of it ... As an effective exercise of consultation with the community, it seems that there is distinct room for improvement. There needs to be a broader representation of the local population to ensure that those groups who are marginalised from decision-making procedures (such as young people and people from non-Anglo backgrounds) are included. In addition, procedures need to be established so that representatives have more influence in the determination and review of operational policy to ensure that it suits local needs and the needs of different groups within the locality. [Youth Justice Coalition, 1990: 220, 223]

The coalition reports that where youth workers are represented on the committees, 'issues which are raised in the spirit of "cracking down on delinquents" can be diverted into more constructive approaches' (*ibid.*: 221).

Officers who took part in the interviews agreed that there was a lot of misunderstanding about the meaning of community-based policing throughout the police organisation. For example, in selecting representatives of ethnic groups to become members of Community Consultative Committees, police were not particularly sensitive about who these people represent. One officer explained:

> It's ... people having the right motives, but doing the wrong thing. So it's what I describe sometimes as 'patronising'. It irritates me. It's, you know, these poor little dears from Southeast Asia who really must bring a member of their community. *Who* is their community? *Who* is this particular person representative of? I mean, ... they assume that as long as you look similar ... you're then a community leader or community representative and it's nonsense. It's so, it's so insulting, I think, and they don't realise that it is ... But that's all got a lot to do with the lack of understanding with what we are on about in terms of providing equal services.

The Ombudsman also reported dissatisfaction among Aboriginal, ethnic and other minority groups regarding the make-up of the consultative committees as well as the way they were run. Some groups were not represented and others felt that the committees were manipulated and committee members were chosen for their 'compliance':

> In some places there are potentially dangerous and divisive practices like multiple consultative committees ... Some patrol commanders are said to be incapable of handling dissent. Others are said to be doctrinaire. Others refuse to become involved or even take an interest in 'old' conflicts. [Landa Report 1995: 44]

The Ombudsman urged that the operations of CCCs be monitored 'from time to time to ensure that they are an effective means of two-way communication' (*ibid.*: 45).

Many CCCs were predominantly vehicles for police to disseminate information to communities and few saw operational issues as relevant topics for discussion. One officer explained:

> Most of the towns ... do in fact have consultative committees, [but] whether they are truly representative of the community I really don't know. They tend very often to be police-dominated information giving ... and I'm not sure that police view them as anything other than a token exercise to keep community informed. The actual decision making in terms of police resources in particular patrols or locations, I think, police have not quite made the step where they're prepared to involve community in a decision-making sense. Now I'm differentiating between decision-making and operational policing, but I guess over time police are making more and more use of them, but we've got a long way to go as to how effectively we use them.

There was also a feeling that some patrols went through the motions in terms of consulting the community, without examining what they were actually achieving. One senior officer was critical of the lack of imagination and flexibility in many community policing initiatives:

> you don't create a committee of all these earnest middle-class bored people and then look around for some problem for them to solve. You find out what the bloody problems are in the patrol and then you say which group of people are affected by that problem and which range of resources and agencies, government public/private, can you get together to help solve it. Once they've solved it if they can be off, finished, not get bored – what can we do next? The problem with Neighbourhood Watch is keeping people interested – interested in what? What kind of political empowerment do they have? ... You've got to say, well, what are the problems and they might be different constituencies, different kinds of problems, different kinds of groups – why only one group?

The danger of relying too much on consultative committees was that, instead of reaching out to the community, police became even more removed from people who should have been consulted. One Patrol Commander expressed this view:

> If you say as a measure if you've got [a CCC] you get a tick, then I say, well, what does it mean? ... I'm always very concerned about appropriate accountability and reporting back and taking into account the wants and needs of community mechanisms, but I don't think necessarily that the original Neighbourhood Watch and Consultative Committees were the appropriate ways to do that. I mean, it's a bit like preaching to those who've converted but you're not getting to those who are outside ... where does it take you?

There was also concern that police mistook the establishment of so-called community-based policing programs as indicators of achieving community-based policing:

> One of the difficulties is that we traditionally ... equate success with implementation. By that I mean that you may have 15 programs running, we're talking about community-based programs, now how to measure those – most of which exist in name only. ... The question you ask is a very basic question: what do you hope to achieve in your community as police officers? That's the bottom line ... Now if we don't consider them, then who does? So what I'm saying is let's look at outcomes. Let's be outcome driven.

The concept of community-based policing has also been unnecessarily limited by traditional mechanisms such as Neighbourhood Watch; police often forgot the wider purpose of the concept:

> It's a pretty pathetic thing where the police manager says ... community polic-
> ing is working in my patrol because my officers have attended 120 Neigh-
> bourhood Watch meetings ... so the rhetoric of community-based policing is
> weak because we haven't explored enough options, institutional options.
> Community-based policing is a broad concept that – if it has any general ele-
> mental truth, it's about building bridges, usually non-confrontational bridges
> between different groups in society and perhaps even better ones to the most
> marginalised and deprived groups and empowering them to live more safe,
> tranquil, and secure lives because they lack the resources to buy it, to purchase
> it privately.

This lack of innovation and creativity was seen to be a legacy of old-
style policing. Police officers have not yet made the philosophical switch
from traditional policing to community-based policing:

> I'm learning and discovering what particular communities want from their
> police ... My concern is that police don't quite know how to go about
> that because they haven't made the transition from thinking they know
> all about policing based on our traditional way of operating. The realities
> are that unless police begin to understand this process called community and
> what community wants it's very difficult to police appropriately and that
> community involvement should go well and truly beyond this idea of using
> Neighbourhood Watch and Safety Houses purely as a means of intelligence
> from the community ... I guess what I'm talking about is in many respects a
> philosophical change in how we police.

On the other hand, there was some concern that police were getting
too carried away by new ideas and had deserted their traditional functions. One patrol commander felt that it was inappropriate to move
policing emphasis away from crime, because 'in the end that's what the
community really expects you to focus on':

> No one that I know of would seriously dispute that we have to establish better
> relationships with the community ... that we had to become a lot more open
> in many of the things that we did and ... there was good justification for
> becoming increasingly accountable both at a local and State level, but ... I
> think there are a lot of people who thought, right, having agreed to that, what
> we have to do now is come up with a whole lot of 'you beaut' ideas. We're
> going to get a pat on the back for every idea we come up with and we went out
> like a shotgun – bang – with an idea a minute and maybe there were just too
> many pellets fired ...

One patrol commander decided that he was going to achieve practical
outcomes in solving the community's problems rather than spend
endless hours in meetings which never achieved anything:

When I came here I was told yes there is a regular consultative committee. The fact is it was regular, did absolutely nothing. It was the same people and all they wanted to do was come in and talk about the same things time after time after time ... In reality it did nothing ... What we are looking at doing is putting in place a trimmed-down system which will embrace Neighbourhood Watch and those things but will actually give a committee that's got some teeth in it ... I do think, however, that there is an awful lot of time wasted by people who simply conduct meetings so they can tell their District Commanders, oh we've had a meeting.

Some officers felt that community consultations which achieved nothing were not only a waste of time, they created unrealistic expectations in the community, who then became disillusioned and disaffected:

What we have done is probably created a lot of expectations that could never be met and it's a bit like saying I've got a 'you beaut' Mickey Mouse intelligence system and everyone says, oh, that'll be the answer to everything. No, no matter how good that system is, it's not going to eliminate crime and it's not going to mean anything unless you actually can apply the data that's come out of it. And I think it's the same with these meetings, and all these community relations things, unless there can be some level of achievement what you can end up doing is having at the end of the road a community that's very cheesed off, to say the least, because they feel that they've put a lot of time and effort into doing all these things you've wanted them to do and they can't see a return for it.

Even though the concept of community-based policing might not have been well understood or properly implemented, the above comments indicate that some members of the Police Service were at least being reflective about these issues. Tokenistic attempts to implement community-based policing were recognised and not given a great deal of weight. There was also evidence that in some patrols, community con-‛ sultations did result in some form of meaningful partnership between the police and the community. An example was cited regarding the experience in Wagga Wagga, where the police held a meeting with about forty representatives of Koori (Aboriginal) people on Koori territory to discuss policing issues. A number of positive outcomes were cited by a police officer:

[We agreed] that we would meet more regularly on a monthly basis in a very informal way to allow any sorts of issues to be belted about. There was also an agreement to provide a support group – by that I mean a group of Kooris would be on a roster system. Were a Koori offender taken into custody, the police would automatically ring them, they would attend and assist. There was an agreement that ... the Koori community would send representatives to talk to police in our training days and likewise we would do that for their particular groups on a needs basis, and [police] be involved with their young people on a whatever role they wanted us to be involved in.

Another relatively successful Community Consultative Committee in New South Wales was reported in Bull and Stratta (1994). The researchers compared two local police consultative committees in England with one CCC in a provincial city in New South Wales through a two-year period of observation. They found that the New South Wales police were more 'positive and flexible' on the issue of agenda setting: there was a 'preparedness to discuss operational matters raised by lay members, such as the way in which police questioned suspects, and a willingness to admit that the methods used by some police were unsatisfactory' (*ibid.*: 241). Police in the NSW committee, unlike those in the two English committees, 'did not feel the need always to attend in uniform, nor to underline their common identity by sitting as a group' (*ibid.*: 244). The NSW committee was also established in a more open and democratic manner, drawn from a variety of local organisations. In contrast, the English committees were self-selecting, and members were selected on the basis of being supportive of the police.

Senior police saw the road to community-based policing as a very long one and the organisation had only just begun this difficult journey:

> People are out to tell you that [community-based policing has] failed. I'm out to believe that it's yet to begin. We certainly mouthed the words. We have certainly talked about community involvement, and we have established community consultative committees, and we have got Neighbourhood Watch, we have these banners we wave around, but the core notion of policing with the community, solving problems with the community, having the community involved in solving its own problems with police assistance – is almost as far away as it ever was. What Avery has done is provide the initial means of beginning that process and I have to say there are in some places some outstanding examples of that progress towards that end, but they are simply anecdotal examples.

Police Acceptance of Reforms

How do members of the Police Service feel about the reforms which have been introduced over the years? The success of change must surely depend upon members' acceptance and support of the new policies and programs. The 1991 questionnaire survey of police officers provides an overview of members' perceptions of a range of reforms related to the policing of visible minority communities. These results are discussed in terms of officers' acceptance of policy, their participation in programs, their ratings of the effectiveness of the policy initiatives, and their ratings of the success of their patrol areas in achieving policing objectives.

Acceptance of Policy

A staff survey conducted in 1990 examined police attitudes towards various aspects of community-based policing (Performance Diagnostics Services 1990).[7] The results showed that community-based policing was more enthusiastically supported by the higher ranks and beat police. On a scale from one (strongly agree) to six (strongly disagree), respondents were asked to rate a series of statements regarding community-based policing. The average rating for the statement 'I support the concept of community-based policing' was 2.8, with higher-ranking officers showing stronger support than lower-ranking ones, and beat police showing stronger support than general-duty officers or detectives. Similar trends were found in responses to statements such as 'community-based policing is worth continuing with' and 'community-based policing will make the police service more effective'.

Respondents to my 1991 survey were also asked to give their opinion on several statements regarding the nature of police work. The sample split almost equally between those who agreed with and those who disagreed with the statement 'Real police work is about arresting criminals.' The statement was meant to assess how much officers' perceptions of 'real police work' were still governed by the traditional emphasis on law-enforcement arrests. The results show a great deal of variation, depending on the respondent's rank in the police organisation. Probationary constables and senior officers (inspector and above) were more likely to

Table 9.1 Perception of 'real police work', by rank

Q: How much do you agree or disagree with the following statement? 'Real police work is about arresting criminals.'

	Percentage of respondents who:						
Rank	Strongly agree 1	Agree 2	Slightly agree 3	Slightly disagree 4	Disagree 5	Strongly disagree 6	Average score
All ranks	13	16	21	9	25	15	3.563
Probationary constable	0	9	25	14	27	25	4.341
Constable	7	22	26	8	24	13	3.603
Constable first class	42	19	16	10	10	3	2.355
Senior constable	29	10	29	10	10	13	3.000
Sergeant	11	19	14	11	25	19	3.778
Senior sergeant	14	9	11	6	40	20	4.086
Inspector and above	6	12	6	6	59	12	4.353

Note: Total number of respondents = 332.

disagree with the statement, whereas first-class constables were the least likely to disagree. The median and mean responses form a V-shaped pattern with the lowest and highest ranks showing similar opinions (Table 9.1). These results indicate that the organisation is very divided over what is regarded as 'real police work'. The newcomers and the senior officers were less likely to consider real police work as essentially arresting criminals. When analysed by duty, detectives were the most likely to agree with the statement, compared with general-duty officers, beat police and others. Figure 9.1 compares the responses to the community-based policing question in the 1990 survey with the question about real police work in the 1991 survey. The patterns of responses show almost identical trends by rank, with junior and senior ranks more similar than the middle ranks. These results are consistent with earlier observations that middle-ranking officers had a greater tendency to resist change. However, contrary to views expressed by some of the interviewees, the groups least supportive of community policing ideas were not the sergeants or senior sergeants, but the first-class constables and senior constables.

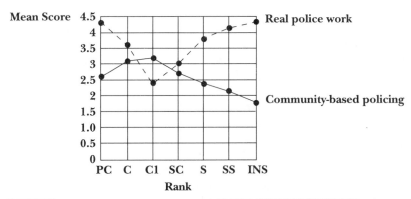

RATING	RANK OF RESPONDENT
1. Strongly agree	PC – Probationary Constable
2. Agree	C – Constable
3. Slightly agree	C1 – Constable first class
4. Slightly disagree	SC – Senior Constable
5. Disagree	S – Sergeant
6. Strongly disagree	SS – Senior Sergeant
	INS – Inspector and above

Figure 9.1 Perception of 'real police work' and attitudes to community-based policing, by rank. The graph shows the mean score of the ratings given to the following statements: 'Real police work is about arresting criminals' (1991 survey); and 'I support the concept of community-based policing' (1990 survey). The total number of respondents was 332.

Participation in Programs

Officers in the 1991 survey were also asked to indicate the extent to which they had participated in various community-based activities directed at ethnic or Aboriginal communities in their patrol areas.[8] The most frequently mentioned activities were the use of the card showing different languages (mentioned by 47 per cent of respondents), the establishment of Neighbourhood Watch (45 per cent), giving talks to community groups (45 per cent), introduction of Beat Policing (42 per cent) and liaison with community organisations (41 per cent). Other activities mentioned by more than 20 per cent of the respondents include: printing of booklets in different languages, establishment of community consultative committees, establishment of Safety House program, and research into community needs and opinions. These results indicate that officers did not report a high level of participation in community policing programs directed at visible minorities.

Ratings of Programs

The 1991 survey provides some indication of police officers' assessment of the effectiveness of the various policy initiatives. Officers were asked, in relation to a given list, whether any of the initiatives had helped them in 'providing more effective service' to NESB or Aboriginal people. Decentralisation and the appointment of Ethnic or Aboriginal Client Consultants were least frequently cited as helpful. In terms of providing services to people of NESB, the introduction of Beat Policing was most frequently cited as helpful (66 per cent), followed by provision of the card showing different languages (64 per cent), printing of booklets in different languages (59 per cent), on-the-job training (57 per cent), recruitment of officers from ethnic groups (57 per cent), establishment of Neighbourhood Watch with ethnic groups (54 per cent), and training at the Police Academy (50 per cent). With reference to providing services to the Aboriginal communities, training at the academy was nominated most frequently as being helpful (53 per cent), followed by the introduction of Beat Policing (52 per cent), on-the-job training (50 per cent), appointment of Aboriginal Liaison Officers (45 per cent). There was a great deal of variation by rank and some variation by duty. Figure 9.2 shows some of these variations by rank for selected programs and initiatives.

Training

With respect to the servicing of people from NESB, training at the Police Academy was most frequently found to be helpful by probationary constables (76 per cent) and constables (64 per cent). The percentages dropped off and then rose again with senior sergeants (45 per cent) and inspectors and above (50 per cent). On-the-job training followed a similar pattern, except that constables (71 per cent) more frequently found it helpful than probationary constables (64 per cent) did. With respect to cross-cultural awareness training, lower-ranking officers did not find it as helpful as the higher-ranking officers did. In fact, 77 per cent of the officers at the rank of inspector or above found that type of training helpful. Results concerning the servicing of Aboriginal people show a similar pattern. However, probationary constables were generally more positive about all three areas of training (Figure 9.2A).

Two other questions in the survey provided a similar assessment of the training in the Police Academy. Table 9.2 shows that when asked whether they agreed with the statement 'Academy training does not provide sufficient skills for police work with people from non-English-speaking background', the majority (65 per cent) agreed, but 51 per cent of probationary constables disagreed, as did 43 per cent of constables. In relation to the same question dealing with Aborigines, the overall results were similar (66 per cent agreed), but here 60 per cent of the probationary constables and 56 per cent of constables disagreed. These results indicate that the more recent students or graduates of the Police Academy's PREP appeared to find the training on the policing of minority groups more satisfactory.

Decentralisation, Recruitment and Appointment of Client Consultants

In response to the question regarding NESB, decentralisation of command structure was rarely found to be helpful by the respondents in the lower ranks, but 31 per cent of senior sergeants and 46 per cent of inspectors and above thought it had helped them in providing more effective service to NESB people. The recruitment of the Ethnic Client Consultant was also not considered to be helpful. However, the recruitment of police from ethnic groups was generally found to be helpful, especially by higher-ranking officers. Results regarding the servicing of Aborigines are similar, except that there was less enthusiasm about the recruitment of police officers from Aboriginal communities than from ethnic communities (Figure 9.2B).

Liaison Officers, Community Consultative Committees

The appointment of Ethnic Liaison Officers (civilian or police) was found to be helpful more frequently by the higher-ranking officers. Regarding the establishment of community consultative committees among ethnic communities, the variation showed a similar pattern with more extreme

A: TRAINING

‑ ‑ ‑ ‑ ‑   Academy training
‑ ‑ ‑   On‑the‑job training
——   Cross‑cultural training

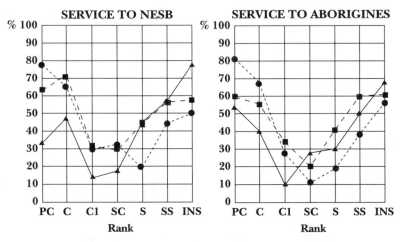

B: DECENTRALISATION, RECRUITMENT, CLIENT CONSULTANT

‑ ‑ ‑ ‑ ‑   Decentralisation
‑ ‑ ‑   Recruitment of police from ethnic/Aboriginal communities
——   Appointment of Ethnic Client Consultant
——   Appointment of Aboriginal Client Consultant

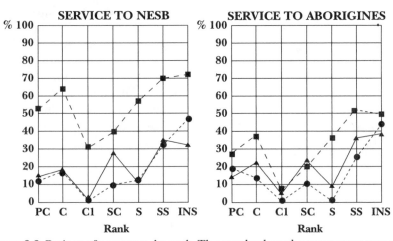

Figure 9.2 Ratings of programs, by rank. The graphs show the percentage answering 'Yes' to the question: 'Has any of the following helped you in providing more effective service to people from non-English-speaking background or Aborigines?' The ranks of respondents are abbreviated as in Figure 9.1, page 205. The total number of respondents was 332.

C: LIAISON OFFICERS, COMMUNITY CONSULTATIVE COMMITTEES

‑‑‑‑‑   Civilian Ethnic Community Liaison Officers
‑ ‑ ‑   Police Ethnic Community Liaison Officers
‑‑‑‑‑   Civilian Aboriginal Community Liaison Officers
‑ ‑ ‑   Police Aboriginal Community Liaison Officers
‑‑‑‑‑   Community Consultative Committees

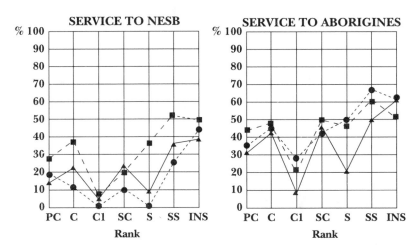

D: NEIGHBOURHOOD WATCH, SAFETY HOUSE, BEAT POLICING

‑‑‑‑‑   Neighbourhood Watch
‑ ‑ ‑   Safety House
‑‑‑‑‑   Beat Policing

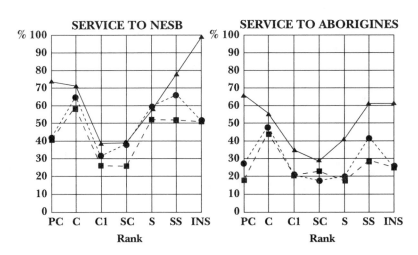

Figure 9.2 continued.

Table 9.2   Perception of Police Academy training, by rank

Q: How much do you agree or disagree with the following statement? 'Academy training does not provide sufficient skills for police work with people from non-English-speaking background.

	Percentage of respondents who:						
Rank	Strongly agree 1	Agree 2	Slightly agree 3	Slightly disagree 4	Disagree 5	Strongly disagree 6	Average score
All ranks	18	30	17	14	16	5	3.025
Probationary constable	5	26	19	16	26	9	3.605
Constable	15	27	15	20	17	6	3.155
Constable first class	22	28	22	13	16	0	2.719
Senior constable	25	32	18	4	11	11	2.750
Sergeant	20	40	17	9	11	3	2.600
Senior sergeant	35	35	9	6	12	3	2.324
Inspector and above	18	41	29	6	6	0	2.412

Q: How much do you agree or disagree with the following statement? 'Academy training does not provide sufficient skills for police work with Aboriginal people.'

	Percentage of respondents who:						
Rank	Strongly agree 1	Agree 2	Slightly agree 3	Slightly disagree 4	Disagree 5	Strongly disagree 6	Average score
All ranks	16	25	15	19	17	8	3.321
Probationary constable	2	14	24	24	10	26	4.024
Constable	11	21	12	29	22	5	3.463
Constable first class	22	19	22	16	19	3	3.000
Senior constable	21	36	7	7	14	14	3.000
Sergeant	19	33	14	11	19	3	2.861
Senior sergeant	31	37	9	9	9	6	2.429
Inspector and above	17	39	28	6	6	6	2.611

Note: Total number of respondents = 332.

oscillations. Results regarding Aborigines were similar except for CCCs; sergeants and senior sergeants did not rate them as highly for Aborigines as they did for NESB people (Figure 9.2C).

Neighbourhood Watch, Safety House and Beat Policing

In relation to ethnic communities, Neighbourhood Watch, Safety House and Beat Policing were frequently found to be helpful, especially by constables and officers at the rank of sergeant and above. Beat Policing was rated very highly by the senior sergeants (78 per cent) and inspectors and above (100 per cent). Similar patterns were found in relation to Aboriginal communities, but senior officers were less enthusiastic about Beat Policing than in relation to NESB communities (Figure 9.2D). Not surprisingly, respondents who were beat officers were consistently more likely to rate most of these programs as helpful. The only exceptions were with the recruitment of officers from ethnic groups, the appointment of Ethnic Client Consultant, and the registration of bilingual officers, where respondents on detective duty were more likely to rate the initiatives as helpful.

Achievement of Policing Objectives

Officers who took part in the 1991 survey were also asked more general questions about how successful they thought their patrols had been in achieving some of the major objectives of policing. Respondents showed a highly positive assessment of their patrol's achievements in all the objectives canvassed (Table 9.3). Very few officers (2 or 3 per cent in most cases and 7 per cent in 'reducing the fear of crime') indicated 'no success' in any of the areas. The objective 'maintaining law and order in community' was rated the highest in terms of success, while 'reducing the fear of crime' was rated the least successful. There was also much more consensus between the ranks here than in responses to earlier questions. Beat officers were most likely to rate more positively in all dimensions. One small exception was that general-duty officers were marginally more likely to rate 'securing community support of police' as a success. These results indicate a high degree of confidence among officers that their patrols were achieving many of the objectives of policing with at least moderate success.

The results in this section can be interpreted as suggesting that members of the Police Service were evenly split in terms of its acceptance of community-based policing as a concept; they were equally divided in their conception of what 'real police work' was about. Probationary officers and senior officers were much more in tune with the community policing approach, while support for this approach decreased towards the middle of the rank structure. In general, detectives were more supportive of the traditional approach, while beat officers were more supportive of the new approach. Not many officers participated in community policing activities, with typically less than half of the respondents reporting involvement in each of the listed activities. Officers' ratings of the reform initiatives varied considerably according to rank: from a low of less than 10 per cent among first-class constables to a high of 100 per

Table 9.3 Perception of success in policing

Q: In your opinion, how successful has your patrol area been in terms of the following strategies?

	Percentage of respondents who saw:			
	No success	Minor success	Moderate success	Major success	Average score
	0	1	2	3	
Securing community support of police	2	22	59	17	1.872
Prevention of crime	3	25	60	13	1.804
Increased reporting of crime	2	26	57	15	1.828
Reducing the fear of crime	7	36	50	8	1.536
Maintaining law and order in community	3	19	61	17	1.913
Involving community in crime prevention	2	33	48	17	1.770
Solving crimes	3	25	61	12	1.798

Note: Total number of respondents = 332.

cent among senior officers, depending on the item, rating the initiatives as 'helpful' to them in providing more effective service to visible minorities. Even with Beat Policing, by far the most popular initiative, the difference in proportions of favourable ratings between the senior officers and the first-class and senior constables was close to 60 per cent. In general, the same V-shaped trend emerged, with probationary officers and senior officers much more in favour than officers in the middle ranks. There was, however, a great deal of consensus between the ranks regarding the overall success of individual patrol areas in meeting the general objectives of policing. Officers were overwhelmingly positive about their patrols' achievements in crime control, order maintenance, and community service.

Production of Outcomes

As mentioned in Chapter 7, there has been little systematic monitoring or evaluation of the performance of the NSW Police Service in relation to ethnic or Aboriginal communities. The 1988 Ethnic Affairs Policy Statement did not specify any performance indicators or concrete outcomes which could be used to evaluate the effectiveness of the policy. Ironically, the 1992–1995 Ethnic Affairs Policy Statement Strategic Plan, which became obsolete following the introduction of the 'New South

Wales Charter of Principles for a Culturally Diverse Society' by the State government, contained a comprehensive 'hierarchy of outcomes', complete with strategies and performance indicators specified for each stage of development.[9] Given the absence of systematic data measuring the outcomes of reforms, the following discussion is based on rather limited, and at times only impressionistic, information obtained through interviews,[10] the 1991 questionnaire survey, and the NSW Ombudsman's report *Race Relations and Our Police* (Landa Report 1995).

Internal Reflection: Cultural Change?

A number of officers were convinced that a cultural change had taken place within the Police Service. Even though they were vague about the meaning of cultural change and were unable to offer any more than anecdotal evidence for it, the comments suggested that new police attitudes, values and methods were beginning to emerge within the organisation. For example, one senior officer felt that the old culture of secrecy and solidarity among police officers was beginning to change, with police more willing to complain about other officers' conduct:

> It's absolutely cultural change. ... The organisation of complaints within the organisation, with the people dobbing each other in [informing on each other] these days. Something like ... 40 per cent[11] of ... complaints are originated by police ... where in the past ... I understand that you didn't dob in your mate, you stuck by him [*sic*], but now, because of various court decisions that have been taken, that if you know that something is happening, and you don't dob the person in who's participating, then you're liable as well. For that reason, they're all informing on each other.

This optimism was, however, somewhat premature. The cultural change he mentioned was not happening to a significant extent. Another senior officer cited an instance of a probationary constable complaining against a sergeant for brutality; however, the probationer had to pay a heavy price for standing up:

> [It] was 2 o'clock in the morning ... [the probationer] was told by the night sergeant to come down to the cells to check on an Aboriginal youth who was arrested as an intoxicated person and was asleep in the cell, to check if he was all right. This probationary constable went down with the sergeant and the prisoner didn't wake up quickly enough so he was kicked around by the sergeant. The probationer went to the patrol commander and the sergeant was charged, criminally charged. Now the probationer went through hell, the sergeant was found not guilty, and by that time the probationer had resigned ... [but] the man has been dismissed on a lower level of proof. So it's happening, people are getting dobbed in. It's still difficult, still very difficult ...

Some officers saw change in the way police went about doing their work. Instead of taking short cuts, covering mistakes and taking little notice of the communities they serve, there were indications that officers were taking their jobs more seriously. One patrol commander felt that he no longer had to bow to a corrupt police culture as he did before:

> We've got changes, organisational changes. As far as institutionalised corruption is concerned, there were times in the police force when I even as a patrol commander wouldn't have been game to raid gambling clubs and brothels, for fear of punishment in some convoluted and sinister way. But I know, I know that [now] as a patrol commander, I will be unchallenged – if I am acting lawfully and in accordance with policy and in accordance with the law – ... not just by the police hierarchy, but by government. That's the best thing that ever happened to the Police Service.

The way patrol commanders were starting to take more seriously the idea of community consultation and needs analysis was cited as another example where police were gradually replacing traditional strategies with community-based ones:

> I see differences. I see patrol commanders that actually take things seriously, who actually worry about what people think ... what their needs are, actually engaging in sustained needs analysis, actually prioritise. There is a transformation extraordinaire, some patrols you wouldn't believe it. Go to [name of patrol] ... I've never come across policing of that sort before ... Look at our [Police Academy] Library, look at the reports ... 180 patrol commanders signed learning contracts with the Academy to go out over a six-month period, to go out and implement an applied research project that met the priorities of that patrol and they came back and produced these reports, things that they really did. Some of it is not very good and some is brilliant, but they have done it. That's fundamental, real difference.

It is safe to assume that a certain degree of cultural change did occur among relatively senior officers, but was there any evidence that officers on the streets were working differently? Certainly the images conveyed by *Cop It Sweet* did not provide any cause for optimism on the streets of Redfern. However, a police constable who worked at Redfern observed a changed style of policing from the 'old days', a new openness and accountability:

> I can remember when I first had contact with Redfern police ... and I noticed that [the person] who answered the phone identified themselves and actually said, you know, 'Redfern Police, Constable so-and-so speaking', and when I joined the Police Service there's no way that we would have identified ourselves by name to a member of the public that we didn't know, or at least had some reasonable trust in. So times have changed. People are a lot more open about who they were and were quite willing to identify themselves to people

over the phone. So therefore they are accountable for their actions ... Their attitude ... in terms of taking time with people and talking to them, in being quite prepared to assist them in lots of different areas other than just arresting them, ... quite prepared to enter into conversations about things that in the old days I don't think you would have taken the time to. I think that's important. It's breaking down the barriers ... They work hard, too, they're not shonky, they work hard.

Obviously it is often a matter of seeing the glass as half-empty or half-full, when judging whether the organisation is changing or not. An example of contradictory trends can be found in the extent to which police stereotyping of minorities had been replaced by more open and tolerant attitudes. On the one hand, the police organisation had openly and strongly supported non-discriminatory policies, not only in relation to visible minorities, but also in relation to gay and lesbian officers. As Commissioner Lauer admitted, the support of gay and lesbian police would have been unheard of in the traditional police culture:

I had occasion to go public ... about a threat to 'out' ... homosexual police. I responded on behalf of homosexual police saying they would be judged on performance and on performance alone. Again I was supported by members of Police Service and community. A few years ago that would not have been the case. For a Commissioner to stand up and say, yes, there are homosexual police amongst us, they will be judged on performance and not on any other criteria, would have seen the Commissioner pilloried. All of those are indications that the change is accepted, but [also] of the strength of the success of the change.

On the other hand, it is not difficult to find plenty of evidence that the attitudes of many officers towards minorities were still extremely racist. In the 1991 officers' survey, about two-thirds of the respondents agreed with the statement that police officers are generally not prejudiced against Aborigines or ethnic minorities. That implied that about one-third of the respondents thought that police officers were prejudiced against minorities. Voluntary comments offered by about 10 per cent of the respondents provided some colourful examples of racial stereotyping, intolerance, and hostility towards anti-racist policies.[12] For example, quite a few respondents concurred with the stereotype that Aboriginal people were lawless and were alcoholics:

The resident Aboriginals of the Redfern Patrol have *no* respect for the police, law, courts or the community. [*A sergeant*]

It is all well and fine to know characteristics of Aboriginals, their [psychological] ways of thinking etc. *But* the problem arises when they are intoxicated and stoned and have to be put into the rear of a wagon. [*A constable*]

In regards to Aborigines, they are not part of the community as such, they tend to have a lifestyle which revolves around alcohol and antisocial behaviour. Some just don't want to integrate. [*A constable*]

It is my unbiased opinion that Aboriginals generally dislike police – they have a serious problem with alcohol abuse – they are prone to committing suicide in police cells – the Royal Commission into Black Deaths in Custody have exonerated police of any blame. [*A sergeant*]

Some officers saw ethnic minorities as ignorant and dishonest. They had no sympathy with their problems with the English language; instead they felt that immigrants without English facility should never have been allowed into Australia. They were opposed to multiculturalism and other government policies to redress inequities:

I believe that the so-called *ethnic* problems in many cases are wholly the responsibility of the ethnic minority ... The majority of immigrants today are from war-torn or repressed countries and are used to living on his wits and continues on his arrival here and so cause us additional work. [*An inspector*]

[Asian] people definitely (mostly) have a language barrier when police speak to them. If they commit an offence they use a barrier where they use their original language and act like they don't understand what is going on, when in real fact they know exactly what they have done. Most Asians do not know the road rules and commit many offences and face fines. A language barrier has been erected. [*A constable*]

The police are trained in law procedures and about the protection of life and property. Aboriginal people have no respect for property or the law, and migrant people are too lazy or ignorant to learn English. Perhaps teach the migrants to speak and the policing problems will rectify themselves in relation to this area. [*A senior constable*]

Perhaps if these uneducated, unwilling, ignorant migrants were not allowed in the country, the policing factor would not be as it is today. These backward Third World countries drag down the community. [*A senior constable*]

If the Commonwealth Government was honest, it would *realise* and acknowledge that multiculturalism is wrong ... You may think I am racially biased. However, I think I can see our country turning into another Lebanon if we continue down this path much longer and I am only expressing my fears. This is supposed to be a democratic society but no one asked my opinion about multiculturalism ... If you want to live in my country you assimilate with me. If I want to live in your country then I must assimilate with your culture – they are the rules!!! that people should live by. [*A senior sergeant*]

Police should get on with policing and ethnic groups should have to learn and speak English before coming to Australia and get off the welfare lists. [*A sergeant*]

It is difficult to determine how prevalent these views are within the police force, since the silent majority may or may not share these views. It is also unrealistic to expect police reforms to effect a complete change in attitudes, given that these attitudes are fairly common among the general Australian population.

That there is evidence of cultural change within the NSW Police Service cannot be denied, although the indications are that the organisation was a long way from being transformed. The Inspector-General told the researcher that cultural change could be achieved, 'but not easily and not quickly':

> John Avery made that his mission in life and I think some people are still wondering whether he effected a culture change or simply fragmented what had been a centralised culture. I think it's fair to say ... that he broke the culture of corruption. But ... some negative aspects of culture continue to be evidenced, and they have to do with Aboriginal issues, multicultural issues, relationship of police to community.

Revelations of the Wood Royal Commission into police corruption suggest that even the culture of corruption had not yet been broken.

External Review: Service Delivery

While senior police and the majority of rank-and-file officers seemed fairly positive about the performance of the NSW Police Service and community surveys appeared to indicate a high degree of general satisfaction with police service, there have been, in recent years, some high-profile cases of blundering, incompetence or unprofessional practice. Notable cases which were the subject of major inquiries include the killing of David Gundy in 1989 during a raid by the Special Weapons and Operations Squad (Wootten Report 1991); the arrest, charging and subsequent withdrawal of charges against a retired policeman Harold Blackburn in 1989 (Lee Report 1990); Operation Sue, the raid of Redfern by the Tactical Response Group in February 1990 (Landa Report 1991) and the shooting of Darren Brennan in June 1990 during a search by the police and the Tactical Response Group (Staunton Report 1991). Other damaging publicity includes the report of the National Inquiry into Racist Violence (HREOC 1991), the findings of which have already been highlighted; the television documentary *Cop It Sweet*; and the 'bad taste' home video. In addition, a number of complaints have been raised in relation to the treatment of Indo-Chinese youths in Cabramatta (*SMH*, 20 April 1992) and the charging and subsequent cautioning of a number of Asian youths in the North Shore (*SMH*, 10 February 1992; Landa Report 1993). Even if one were to ignore the avalanche of dramatic evidence coming out of the Wood Royal Commission into police corruption, it would be difficult to reconcile the optimism of the police organisation with this long list of public embarrassments and scandals. Nevertheless, the Police Service came out of an external review of its 'race relations' programs relatively unscathed.

The Ombudsman's report (Landa Report 1995) contained both positive and negative findings. Some of the processual and management problems identified in the report have already been discussed in earlier chapters. The progress of reform, according to the Ombudsman, was 'too slow' and extremely uneven:

> Many senior officers are supportive of change to improve the policing of Aboriginal communities. Still, progress is too slow ... Absent is the visible, consistent and persistent commitment of regional, district and patrol commanders needed to bring about change. Absent too is the visible, consistent and persistent communication of those commitments to all police officers. Some patrol commanders are highly committed, but that is not universal. Without these ingredients the effectiveness of the initiatives cited by both the NSW Police Service and the NPEAB [National Police Ethnic Advisory Bureau] are diminished, if they do not fail altogether. [Landa Report 1995: ii]

The report also criticised the Police Service for not giving sufficient priority to Aboriginal and ethnic community issues such as the recruitment of officers from diverse backgrounds and the training of officers to work with minority groups (*ibid.*: v). In particular, the recruitment strategy, though it had achieved its stated target, was still a long way from reflecting the ethnic composition of the general population:

> The number of NESB recruited has been in the vicinity of the presently stated target of 10%. The 1994 EAPS Status Report showed that during the last EEO reporting period 8.65% of police recruits identified as from a NESB, while 23.08% of new administrative staff identified as from a NESB. While it was clear that a significant effort was made to achieve police recruitment targets, even if they have been met, they were insufficient to change the character of the Police Service so that its membership would ultimately reflect the make-up of the general community [more than 25% NESB]. (*ibid.*: 20)

There were some positive assessments in the Ombudsman's report. The recruit training program, PREP, was said to be 'impressive' and 'first rate' compared with international practice. The PREP materials were found to be 'highly professional, well organised and provide an integrated approach to recruit training', and race relations training was integrated into operational training instead of being compartmentalised (*ibid.*: 21, 34).

Among the community policing strategies, the Aboriginal Community Liaison Officer program was found to be the most successful and highly valued:

> Without doubt the ACLO program has been the NSW Police Service's most successful minority policing initiative. The number of ACLOs is now approaching 40 to serve a community which makes up one or two percent of the NSW population (and there are now around 150 Aboriginal police officers, approaching one percent of the Police Service) ... ACLOs have proved themselves to be a valuable resource. [*ibid*.: 49–50]

The Ethnic Community Liaison Officers were similarly 'seen as a valuable resource by those patrol commanders who can access them and by the communities with whom they help the Police Service to communicate' (*ibid*.: 50). However, the number of ECLOs was found to be inadequate: there were only ten officers for an estimated NESB population of 1.25 million.

In terms of the standard of service delivery, the Ombudsman found there was 'room for significant improvement'. The report noted that there were hardly any performance indicators for patrol commanders to measure the quality of service the patrol provides (*ibid*.: 41). Community-based policing, as currently implemented, was 'not adequately addressing minority concerns or providing a vehicle through which partnerships with Aboriginal, ethnic and other minority groups could be formed'. The report noted that there were significant gaps between 'the policing practices, procedures and programs for Aboriginal and ethnic communities as described and as implemented in the field'. Client consultants were largely 'not fully aware of operational practice'. The use of interpreters was said to be 'inadequate', as was the communication between some police officers and their non-English-speaking clients. Finally, the Ombudsman's report was critical of the lack of coordination and evaluation of local initiatives: 'Many local initiatives were piloted, but there was little co-ordination ..., little evaluation of the success of initiatives, little development of viable initiatives, and little promulgation of developed viable initiatives (or abject failures) except by way of anecdotes at the operational level' (*ibid*.: 22). The Ombudsman's findings were consistent with the general conclusion that much had been achieved by the Police Service in trying to improve its service to Aboriginal and ethnic communities, but much more needed to be done.

It is difficult to make a clear assessment of what police reforms have achieved in police–minorities relations since Avery's appointment. Certainly, at the top level of the organisation changes have been more noticeable. By the early 1990s, the organisation had worked out a clear sense of direction and was committed to community-based policing as an operational model. A great deal of structural change occurred at the administrative, educational and operational levels. As one's focus moves away from the top level of the organisation, the picture becomes less rosy. Strategic planning remained a preoccupation of headquarters only; at the lower levels it was no more than a paper exercise. Policy and directives from the top could be ignored or bypassed. Few quality control processes operated within the organisation to ensure either that decisions were implemented or that work was properly assessed. Rapid and radical organisational change was effective in breaking up the old culture, but it also left many disaffected and disillusioned. These officers formed the middle ranks which were resistant to change.

Out in the communities, a great deal of consultative activity was apparently taking place. However, much of the consultation was ritualistic and tokenistic. Either communities were not well represented or they had no meaningful input into police decisions. Police attitudes towards visible minorities varied, but the majority felt that police officers were generally not prejudiced. Police were evenly divided between those who agreed with and those who disagreed with the statement that 'arresting criminals is what real police work is about'. Support for the community-based policing concept was similarly split within the organisation, with higher-ranking officers showing stronger support.

Whether the reforms have achieved better service or better police–minorities relations is far from clear. Part of the reason for this confusion is the lack of internal or external monitoring and evaluation. Officers who responded to my 1991 survey were highly positive about their patrol's assessment of policing objectives such as securing community support, crime prevention, increased reporting of crime, reducing fear of crime, maintaining law and order in the community, involving the community in crime prevention, and solving crime. Many of the officers interviewed also offered optimistic assessments of the success of reform. However, the Ombudsman's review, while endorsing the general direction of reform, found a number of shortcomings in policy and practice. There were also numerous highly publicised instances of police blundering and unprofessional conduct which tended to cast doubts on the rosy picture presented by some of the senior officers.

The experience of police reform in New South Wales provides valuable information for understanding the limits and possibilities of reform. An interpretation of this experience and its theoretical implications will be discussed in the next chapter.

Notes

1 The revelations of the Wood Royal Commission have placed the NSW Police Service in a state of serious crisis and sparked calls for even more radical and tough measures of reform. The Royal Commission released an interim report in February 1996; the final report is not due until the beginning of 1997.

2 The Inspector-General was a position created by the Police Board in 1991. The main duty of the Inspector-General was to monitor and review the Police Service's organisational structure, planning strategies and management practices. He or she was also responsible for evaluating the performance of the senior executive officers. The first appointee was a former Royal Canadian Mounted Police Commissioner. Through a reorganisation of the Police Board in 1993, the Inspector-General's position was moved to the Police Ministry. When the incumbent retired in 1994, no further appointment was made to the position.

3 The survey, commissioned by the NSW Police Service, was conducted in September 1993 as a follow-up of an identical survey in 1992. The sample size was 439, out of 500 randomly chosen members.

4 The survey was conducted in August 1994. Questionnaires were distributed to all Senior Executive Service members. Forty-two completed questionnaires were returned from a total of sixty-eight distributed.

5 In 1989, Harry Blackburn, a retired police superintendent, was arrested and charged with numerous sexual assaults. The prosecution case was subsequently withdrawn, following a fresh investigation which found insufficient evidence against Blackburn. A Royal Commission which inquired into the circumstances surrounding the case found that the original investigating officers suppressed evidence pointing to Blackburn's innocence and converted favourable evidence into evidence implicating the accused. The Royal Commissioner criticised the investigating police for 'gross incompetence' and 'blatant dishonesty'. Senior police were also criticised for inadequate supervision of the original investigation and a failure to support the conclusion of the reinvestigation (Lee Report 1990).

6 'White Knights' refer to honest police and 'Black Knights' to corrupt police. See the Lee Report (1990) for an instance where an unsubstantiated rumour of rivalry between the two factions was used to discredit the police officer who reinvestigated the Blackburn case (see note 5).

7 The survey made use of a random sample of police officers stratified by rank, with a higher sampling ratio for senior officers and a lower ratio for probationary constables. The number of respondents was 1082, which gave a response rate of 67.6 per cent.

8 The questionnaire used separate questions for NESB and for Aboriginal communities. However, the pattern of responses suggested that respondents were not making a distinction between the two communities in their answers, since there were very few group-specific community-based initiatives in existence. The figures cited here were taken from the question on NESB; the percentages were similar but lower for the question on Aborigines.

9 The four stages of development relate to: development of the EAPS infrastructure; raising of police and NESB community awareness of the need for cooperation and consultation; the participation of NESB community in the development of police policy and programs; and police practice being sensitive to the needs of NESB community (NSWPS 1992).

10 Many of the officers interviewed were chosen because they had played some part in the reform of the police organisation. Others were chosen because they had direct contact with, or responsibility for the servicing of, visible minorities. These officers were generally positive and optimistic about the outcomes of the organisational change, although not uniformly so. These views, of course, are not representative of everyone within the organisation. However, they show the judgment of a group of concerned and knowledgeable individuals within the organisation.

11 The 40 per cent figure seemed exaggerated. The survey by Stubbs (1992) of NSW police complaint files found that internal police complaints constituted about 20 per cent of the total. These were mostly complaints made by police supervisors regarding their subordinates. A 1987 court decision ruled that even internal disciplinary matters were to be treated as complaints under the *Police Regulation (Allegation of Misconduct) Act* 1978.

12 A larger sample of these comments can be found in Chan (1992a). Most comments were fairly negative, although there were some positive ones. Only the more extreme ones are quoted here to demonstrate the point that racist views existed alongside more tolerant attitudes within the organisation. The quotations are verbatim, with ellipses indicating where text has been omitted to save space.

CHAPTER 10

Changing Police Culture

This book began with a problem often identified as 'police racism', which refers to the processes of stigmatisation, harassment, criminalisation and discrimination against visible or cultural groups by police authorities. I have argued that police racism is a not a simple or clearcut problem: discrimination is inextricably tied to the structural and cultural organisation of police work, as well as deeply embedded in the historical and political positions of minorities in society. It is therefore possible for people to deny the existence of police racism. For example, if one takes the commonsense view that police work is basically reactive, then the issue of differential targeting and over-representation of visible minorities in criminal statistics is largely irrelevant. Police officers, it is argued, are simply doing what is required of them in terms of preventing crime and maintaining order. If there is a problem, it lies within those communities which are more deviant, more disorderly and more criminal than the rest. The trouble with the commonsense view is that it exaggerates the extent to which police officers are mere automatons charged with law-enforcement duties. Decades of police research has demonstrated that both police managers and street-level officers routinely exercise discretion in law-enforcement decisions. The frequent use of public-order offences and the heavy-handed deployment of tactical response police against Aboriginal people, for example, cannot be interpreted as simply reactive policing. Much of the harassing and abusive behaviour of police officers reported by the National Inquiry into Racist Violence certainly cannot be passed off as normal police practice. Research studies using statistical data suggest that discrimination cannot be ruled out, and in some cases differential treatment can be cumulative and injustices are compounded (see Chapter 2).

I have argued, however, that it is unhelpful to take the opposite, but equally mechanistic and simplistic, view that racism is totally and inevitably entrenched in our social and political institutions. If police and other state agencies are no more than instruments of capitalism or, in earlier times, colonialism, then there is not much that can be done about police racism short of a revolution. Even if racism were widespread and openly tolerated within police forces – and there is some evidence that at least the use of racist language is rarely challenged – it could only exist informally. No police force or government in Australia (or in other democracies) has officially endorsed discriminatory treatment of any minority groups. The rhetoric of the 'rule of law' is itself a powerful resource for action against racism, and, ineffective though some of the anti-discrimination legal remedies and legislation may have been, they cannot be dismissed as yet another strand in the seamless web of institutionalised racism. The recent Australian High Court decision regarding *Mabo* and the Labor federal government's initiatives to protect native title through legislation are high-profile illustrations of how anti-racist and racist forces can coexist within one political system. Similarly, many people who work in government or non-government agencies, including some in the police forces, have worked hard over the years to set up structures, guidelines and processes to promote non-discriminatory policies and practices. Such efforts may not have been entirely successful, but it would be insulting to lump these people as part of the undifferentiated racist system.

My conclusion is that a more fruitful way of understanding police racism is to examine the structural and cultural organisation of police work. Because the bulk of police work is directed at street crimes, normal policing is concerned with the control and criminalisation of the poor and the powerless, including the young, the marginal and the visible minorities. This is not to deny that policing has traditionally been done on behalf of the propertied classes and is, to a large extent, dictated by the wishes of the 'respectable' establishment. However, the 'crime problem' is not an exclusively middle- or upper-class concern. There is sufficient societal consensus regarding the content of the criminal law that it is rarely seriously challenged. There is, of course, no reason why policing priorities cannot be shifted to white-collar or organised crime. In Australia at least, these functions are currently taken up by a number of specialised 'elite' policing bodies, while ordinary police forces are left with traditional street-crime work.

Another aspect of the structural context of police work which permits the continued toleration of deviant police practice is the inadequacy of the accountability mechanisms. Unless there is exceptionally strong and corroborated evidence, it is extremely difficult to obtain criminal convictions against police officers for misconduct. Complaints against police, even where an independent Ombudsman exists, are often handled initially by police officers. Members of ethnic or Aboriginal communities are suspicious of such a system; they are reluctant to lodge complaints for fear of reprisals. Young people often find that their accounts are not given credibility, while people with poor English facility face enormous communication barriers. Defendants who have outstanding criminal charges are frequently advised by lawyers not to complain against police abuse for fear of jeopardising their defence.

Apart from the weakness of legal protection against abuse, deviant police practices are protected and perpetuated by negative aspects of the 'police culture', the informal values and practice norms which escape formal scrutiny and accountability. In simplistic terms, not only is the police culture responsible for racist attitudes and abusive behaviour, but it also forms the basis of secrecy and solidarity among police officers, so that deviant practices are covered up or rationalised. Police culture can be a powerful source of explanation for the existence and toleration of racism in police forces; it can also account for the ineffectiveness of police reforms in changing police practice. Unfortunately, the way police culture has been conceptualised is, as I have argued in Chapter 4, theoretically impoverished. Instead of thinking of police officers as being 'socialised' into an all-encompassing, homogeneous and unchanging police culture and being totally dictated by it in values and in action, I have proposed a new framework for understanding police culture, using Bourdieu's concepts of field and habitus. Thus, police practice is to be understood in terms of the interaction between specific structural conditions of police work (the field) and the cultural knowledge accumulated by police officers which integrates past experiences (habitus). The revised model emphasises the active role played by police actors in developing, reinforcing, resisting or transforming cultural knowledge and institutionalised practice. It also resolves the debate regarding whether police reforms should concentrate on tightening the rules or changing the culture (see Chapter 3). The new framework links structural conditions such as legal and administrative rules to cultural knowledge in the production of cultural practice, so that tightening rules cannot be regarded as a separate enterprise to changing culture. However, just as attempts to manipulate police cultural knowledge through education do not automatically lead to change in police practice, efforts at tightening laws and regulations do not guarantee any results either. Much depends on the nature of the rules and the way in which they are interpreted by police, given their 'feel for the game' and other aspects of their work conditions which may or may not reinforce the legitimacy of the new rules.

The New South Wales case study provides a context for examining the utility of this framework for understanding police culture and the consequences of police reforms. As mentioned in the introduction, the NSW experience is important and theoretically relevant: the police force is the oldest and largest in the country, it has undergone almost a decade of quite substantial reforms, and yet it stands out as a spectacular failure in spite of these efforts. The implications of the NSW experience are explored in the next section.

Lessons from New South Wales

The new framework for conceptualising police culture provides a useful set of tools for analysing the New South Wales reform experience. Police racism can be understood in terms of the field and the habitus of policing. I have argued in Chapter 4 that the field of policing visible minorities in New South Wales was complex, with both favourable and unfavourable structural conditions for discriminatory police practices. Politically there was a general lack of public concern and political pressure to scrutinise police practice in dealing with minority groups. Social and economic conditions among Aboriginal people were appalling following 200 years of colonisation and dispossession. There were considerable variations among NESB people in terms of socio-economic status and ability to overcome language and cultural barriers; the most disadvantaged groups appeared to be those who were born in Indo-China and the Middle East. Both the federal and the NSW State governments have implemented policies which outlaw discrimination and attempt to address disadvantage and dispossession, but these policies were limited in effectiveness and not popular among sections of the Anglo-Australian community, including some members of the police force, since minority groups were seen to be given special privilege. In terms of the legal and administrative structures governing police work, the field can be considered wide open since individual officers exercised considerable discretion in their work, legal protection against police abuse was inadequate, and administrative accountability was symbolic rather than real.

The habitus of policing before the Avery reforms consists of many aspects of the 'street cop culture': a sense of mission about police as crime-fighters and crook-catchers (axiomatic knowledge); a tendency to use stereotypes to categorise communities (dictionary knowledge); a routine reliance on 'commonsense' and experience in decision-making, while keeping a posture of chronic suspicion against people and resorting to the use of force or short cuts to take charge of situations (directory knowledge); the adoption of attitudes and strategies which are cynical and defensive: secrecy, solidarity, and scepticism towards police managers (recipe knowledge).

These rather broad-brush descriptions of the field and the habitus may have given an impression of homogeneity which is not intended. As mentioned in Chapter 4, multiple cultures exist in organisations to the extent that stable work groups have developed shared experiences. In other words, where there are variations in the 'subfields' of police work, multiple subcultures will emerge. The distinction made by Reuss-Ianni and Ianni (1983) between the 'street cop culture' and the 'management cop culture' shows that two separate subcultures can exist when the two groups work in two different subfields and develop different sets of habitus. The NSW case study suggests that there was a certain amount of variation in police attitudes between ranks and duties.

The recent history of policing in New South Wales shows that political support for reforms was enhanced by public concerns about police corruption during the years after World War II (Chapter 6). The Lusher inquiry and a major reorientation of the public sector towards efficiency and productivity in the 1980s created favourable conditions for radical changes in the police force. The appointment of John Avery as Police Commissioner in 1984 began a period of major organisational reform. Many of the changes were structural and formal, but Avery's vision was to create a police service free of corruption and in tune with the needs of the community. This required a cultural change. Yet, as the case study has shown, the results of years of reform were uneven and, in some areas, disappointing. The lessons to be learned from the New South Wales experience can be discussed by analysing the reform process in terms of changes in the habitus and the field.

Changing the Habitus

Most of the changes that took place were in relation to the habitus of policing, or what was referred to in Chapter 3 as 'cultural change' strategies. In the terminology of Sackmann (1991), these changes were directed at the dimensions of cultural knowledge.

Shift in Axiomatic Knowledge

Following Avery's appointment, the NSW Police adopted a shift in the basic assumptions about its functions and objectives. The new objectives gave priority to crime prevention, services which are responsive to the needs and feelings of the community, citizens' involvement in policing, and the minimisation of corruption. This defines what Sackmann (1991) refers to as the axiomatic knowledge of the organisation. Once in place, these assumptions guided strategies and processes of reform. Thus, within a short time, community-based policing was adopted by the police force as the principal operational strategy. The implementation of this strategy was achieved through regionalisation, merit-based promotion, changes in recruitment policy, a radical redesign of the training and education program, and the development of a variety of community-based programs, including the appointment of client consultants, liaison officers, the introduction of Beat Policing and other community crime-prevention programs.

According to Sackmann's model, the implementation and realisation of these strategies would influence the dictionary knowledge of police officers. At the same time, the change in organisational objectives led to the enactment of certain organisational processes. For example, the processes of community consultation were designed to help accomplish these objectives. Similarly, the development of performance indicators, the conducting of quality audits and more recently the establishment of customer councils were internal processes which were supposed to ensure that corporate objectives were realised. The process of preparing an Ethnic Affairs Policy Statement was also designed to set in motion strategic planning which involves the participation of operational police.

There are indications from the case-study material that this redefinition of axiomatic knowledge was not widely shared throughout the organisation (see Chapter 9). In fact, results of the 1990 internal police survey and my 1991 officers' survey suggest that the organisation was evenly split between those who supported community-based policing and those who did not, and between those who agreed that 'real police work' was about arresting criminals and those who did not. The pattern, which was replicated to a certain extent in officers' ratings of community-based programs directed at visible minority groups, and supported by impressions of senior members of the organisation, appears to be that the most senior and the most junior ranks were supportive of community-based policing, but this support declined towards the middle ranks – the constables and senior constables according to the survey and the sergeants and senior sergeants according to the interviews. Another pattern is that detectives were less supportive, and beat officers more supportive, of community-based policing than officers on general duty.

Changes in Dictionary Knowledge

The adoption of community-based policing strategies and the implementation of the various programs based on that strategy should inevitably lead to some redefinitions of the situations in which officers find themselves. For example, regionalisation forced patrol commanders to get to know the social, cultural and demographic characteristics of their geographical communities; they were required to allocate resources and plan policing strategies to meet the needs of these communities. Community-based programs were designed to encourage police officers to consult with and be in constant contact with the communities they police, so that they saw them as real people, not stereotypes. Community consultation was also meant to cover all members of the community, not simply the respectable types who support the police. In general, the extent to which changes in dictionary knowledge followed the changes in organisational objectives and strategies depends on the successful implementation of these objectives and strategies.

The case study suggests that, in addition to a lack of widespread support for the concept within the organisation, community-based policing was generally interpreted in a superficial way and was mainly seen as a public-relations exercise (Chapter 9). Apart from the predominance of middle-class, respectable citizens in consultative committees, there was some concern about the tokenistic use of minority community 'leaders' as representing the interests of minority groups, the tendency to exclude operational issues as appropriate for community consultation, and to see the setting up of committees as an achievement in itself. Although there is evidence that some consultative committees were more successful than others, community consultation as a process still left a great deal of room for improvement. Similarly, changes in recruitment and training were only partly successful in changing definitions, since there was a lack of reinforcement once officers came into contact with 'real police work'. Consequently, many of the old definitions still prevailed, and ethnic stereotyping, for example, was still seen as a useful way of categorising citizens at the street level of police work. Examples of such opinions among officers were provided in Chapter 9, together with a recognition that official policies of the Police Service were explicitly non-discriminatory.

Changes in Directory Knowledge

Where strategies were partially implemented and processes had not taken the intended directions, existing ways of accomplishing organisational tasks were not replaced by new ones. Since members found that they could get away with the way things were done in the old days, real changes to police practices were difficult to achieve. In response to minority communities' complaints about police racism, officers justified stereotyping by referring to serious offences committed by members of minority groups while ignoring the discretionary and ambiguous elements in the bulk of police work. Harassment was neutralised in terms of the police mandate to catch criminals, the police duty to be suspicious, and the motto 'if they have nothing to hide, they have nothing to fear' (see Chapter 5).

Where strategies and processes matched the new axiomatic knowledge, for example, in Avery's relentless fight against institutionalised corruption, changes did occur to some extent and these changes led to modifications of members' directory knowledge. Though the Wood Royal Commission has revealed that a great deal of corruption survived the Avery reforms, what Avery's campaign had achieved was to reward honest police work in his system of merit promotion and to allow non-corrupt police to carry out their duties without being challenged (see comments of a police commander in Chapter 9). Changes in directory knowledge in turn affected what officers considered as 'the way things should or should not be done', i.e. recipe knowledge. Such changes would serve to reinforce and maintain the implementation of reform strategies. Conversely, where existing directory knowledge was left unchallenged, reform strategies and processes could be undermined.

Changes in Recipe Knowledge

Changes to what officers perceived as the way things should or should not be done in particular situations followed changes in the other dimensions of knowledge. There was some evidence that the old culture of secrecy and solidarity was beginning to change within the NSW police, with increased willingness among members to 'dob in' (anonymously inform on illegal or improper behaviour) other police officers, or even openly criticise unprofessional police behaviours such as those depicted in *Cop It Sweet* (see Chapters 8 and 9). There was also evidence that the organisation has become more open and less defensive about mistakes and scandals. However, the changes here were certainly not dramatic or universal. Given that many of the strategies and processes outlined earlier had not been adequately implemented, and that neither dictionary knowledge nor directory knowledge had been radically altered, it is not surprising that recipe knowledge was substantially unchanged.

Changing the Field

The key to understanding why almost a decade of reforms has not produced dramatic changes may be the fact that reform efforts were principally directed at changing the habitus rather than the field. Many elements of the field have remained substantially the same during this decade. Although the racist immigration debate has subsided, immigrants are still being blamed periodically for taking jobs away from Australians, especially during economic recessions. In spite of the upward mobility of the social status of some ethnic groups, minority communities are still in relatively powerless positions in society. Aboriginal communities continue to suffer the consequences of dispossession, colonisation and dislocation. Nothing much has changed in the legal context of police work: police still possess wide discretionary powers, and existing legislative mechanisms have been ineffective for changing discriminatory police practices. Complaints against the police still involve an onerous and uncertain process for the complainants. Although the administrative and rank structures of the police organisation have been changed through regionalisation, and senior commanders have been made more accountable through performance contracts, the process of accountability and performance assessment lacked credibility (see Chapter 9). Not only was there little meaningful supervision and quality control of police work, but even Police Board decisions and Commissioner's directives were not always implemented. Regionalisation has also led to unevenness in the development and implementation of programs. Finally, many programs were under-resourced and uncoordinated, and most were not subject to any serious monitoring or evaluation.

Members of the organisation who were interviewed appeared to see a great deal of success in Avery's attempt to minimise police corruption, although the Wood Royal Commission has since demonstrated the limited nature of this success. Nevertheless, an examination of how anti-corruption strategies were implemented and what organisational processes were activated could give some guidance to the recipe for success. The relative success of Avery's anti-corruption campaign may be due to the fact that the campaign did not simply involve an attempt to change the habitus: it was accompanied by a change in the field. In other words, there was genuine and widespread community and political concern about police corruption in New South Wales at the time, and the police administration was prepared to make use of all the available legal and disciplinary tools to pursue the goal of fighting corruption. There has not been the same type of campaign against police racism or police abuse of power.

Pressure external to the police organisation can also cause changes to the field. In Chapter 7, the government-imposed requirement to formulate an Ethnic Affairs Policy Statement and to report progress annually was resisted by the organisation and remained a paper exercise. In contrast, as shown in Chapter 8, the public pressure created by the *Cop It Sweet* documentary did lead to immediate action and more meaningful consultation with Aboriginal communities. These case studies suggest that the media were more successful in changing the power relations between the police and the public than the Ethnic Affairs Commission, mainly because of the relatively weak structure of the EAPS process. Nevertheless, changing the field had some impact on organisational practices, at least at the management level.

This analysis suggests that researchers who emphasise the importance of police occupational culture considerably underestimate the power of the field, i.e. the social, economic, legal and political sites in which policing takes place. Changing police culture requires changes in the field at both management and street levels. These may include the restoration of land rights to Aboriginal communities in recognition of the injustices done in the past; a stronger commitment by the government to monitoring access and equity in policing; a more adequate allocation of resources for community assistance; the enactment of a statutory right to interpreters; the establishment of a more accessible and efficient complaints procedure; and increased internal and external auditing of police practices.

Prospects for Cultural Change

The danger in the current fad in management circles about cultural change is the belief that organisational culture can be readily changed to improve corporate performance (Czarniawska-Joerges 1992; see also Ouchi and Wilkins 1985). Schein (1985: 5), however, has reminded us that 'culture is a *deep* phenomenon' and it is incorrect to assume that 'culture can be changed to suit our purposes'. Schein also warns managers not to assume that they can manipulate culture; more likely, managers are being controlled by culture without even being aware of it. Change can also be traumatic: sociologists who observe the taken-for-granted aspects of everyday life find that prolonged attempts to disrupt accepted norms of behaviour can lead to a breakdown of the apparent orderliness of reality (Garfinkel 1967; Morgan 1986: 129). What, then, are the prospects of changing police culture? To answer this question, we need to examine three aspects of cultural change: the content of cultural change, how change occurs, and how to make change sustainable.

The Content of Change: 'Professional' Knowledge

One of the most frequently advocated models of police reform involves the promotion of 'professionalism' in police work. Professionalism, which emphasises impartiality, accountability, specialised knowledge and ethical standards, is seen as offering an 'alternative set of goals, means, and values to those of the occupational culture' (Brogden and Shearing 1993: 108). This means that it is possible to change police culture if traditional police cultural knowledge can be replaced with 'professional' cultural knowledge. For example, as an antidote to racist policing, professional policing may emphasise an appreciation of social and cultural diversity in society, rather than being informed by stereo-types. However, as Manning has warned, the rhetoric of professionalism has different meanings for different parts of the organisation: 'To patrol-men, the term "professionalism" means control over hours and salary and protection from arbitrary punishment from "upstairs"; to the chief and the higher administrators, it relates to the public-administration notions of efficiency, technological expertise, and standards of excel-lence in recruitment and training' (Manning 1978a: 10). Nevertheless, as Bittner points out, the absence of models or even meaningful discus-sions of what constitutes 'good police practice' ensures that profession-alism remains an abstract ideal: 'presently good and bad work practices are not distinguishable, or, more precisely, are not distinguished' (Bittner 1978: 50). The need to define good police work (see Braith-waite 1992) is in fact as pressing as the need to find ways of controlling police corruption:

> if we are not willing to settle for having physicians who are merely honest, and who would frankly admit that in curing diseases and dealing with patients they have to rely on 'playing by ear,' it is difficult to see why we would devote all our energies to try to make the police honest without any concern whatever for whether or not they know, in a technical sense, how to do what they are supposed to do. [Bittner 1978: 49–50]

Obviously, definition of 'good practice' alone is insufficient for profes-sionalism to take hold in a new set of cultural knowledge. It is therefore important to discuss how culture is developed and transmitted.

How Change Occurs: Organisational Learning

Traditional police cultural knowledge is assumed to have been devel-oped as an adaptive response to the nature and conditions of police work, or as Schein (1985: 312) puts it, culture contains the 'stable solu-tions' to a group's problems of external adaptation and internal inte-gration. According to Schein, culture is transmitted by a group-based learning process either through positive reinforcement of successful solutions to problems ('problem-solving') or successful avoidance of painful situations ('anxiety avoidance') (ibid.: 174).

This distinction between problem-solving learning and anxiety-avoid-ance learning is an important one for understanding police culture. Prob-lem-solving learning is considered positive and rewarding, while anxiety-avoidance learning is negative and defensive: 'avoidance learning is often one-trial learning. Once something works, it will be repeated indef-initely, even if the source of pain is no longer active' (Schein 1985: 177).

Many of the negative aspects of police culture seem to have been developed as anxiety-avoidance mechanisms rather than innovative problem-solving strategies. For example, dictionary knowledge and directory knowledge allow officers to place people and situations they encounter into ready-made categories and standard operational methods. Schein considers 'cognitive overload and/or an inability to decipher and categorize the multitude of stimuli impinging on the senses' as a major source of anxiety (*cognitive* anxiety) for people, so that a stable system of cognitions is 'absolutely necessary' for their own protection and survival (*ibid.*: 179). In addition, police officers' work involves considerable potential for risk and danger, which are sources of *role-related* anxiety. Hence these dimensions of knowledge reduce the level of uncertainty and anxiety in police work and make unfamiliar situations seem more predictable. As Muir points out, police officers are often required to 'form a rapid first impression, to group people quickly according to whether they were likely to behave rebelliously or cooperatively' (Muir 1977: 157). Similarly, recipe knowledge provides a way for officers to reduce *social* anxiety by offering recipes for avoiding trouble and preventing isolation within the police force. By observing the 'code of silence', for example, officers avoid the threat of being ostracised by colleagues and the danger of their withholding of assistance in emergencies.

The consequence of anxiety-avoidance learning, as pointed out earlier by Schein, is that the group has a tendency not to question the original assumptions, even if they were incorrect, because questioning the assumptions would produce anxiety or even pain. Muir provides a good illustration of this attitude among police officers who preferred to be overly suspicious rather than overly trusting when approaching citizens. Officers used a 'minimax' strategy to minimise the maximum risk in their work:

> In the event that an assumption was erroneously suspicious, the policeman ended up unhappy but at least had the consolation that he was alive to appreciate his unhappiness. In the instance where the mistaken assumption was initially trusting, the policeman's mistake was not redeemed by the fact of personal survival. The mistaken oversuspicion meant wasting a citizen; the mistaken overtrust meant death. [Muir 1977: 166–7]

This type of strategy, as Muir points out, provides no incentive for checking the correctness of the initial assumption; such checking would be considered a waste of time. Anxiety-avoidance learning may also result in the group being defensive in the protection of their accepted rituals, beliefs and assumptions. The group may eventually lose its ability to change and innovate. As Sparrow *et al.* (1990) point out, mistake avoidance and resistance to change seem to go hand in hand.

One way to encourage the transmission of a more positive culture, then, lies in establishing a working environment which rewards problem-solving and innovation but also allows people to learn from, rather than be punished for, their mistakes. This requires a cultural change at the management and supervisory levels. While there is no foolproof way of eliminating risk and danger in police work, better training, more thorough knowledge of the communities being policed, and increased contact with the communities in non-stressful situations are all ways of reducing both cognitive anxiety and role-related anxiety in police work. Community-based policing and problem-solving policing strategies provide useful models of this style of policing.

Schein (1985) presented a functionalist model of organisational culture. It suggests that cultural change is resisted when culture is learned through anxiety-avoidance situations because the cost of change is perceived as too high. Another explanation for resistance to change is the absence of sanctions or incentives to induce change. More recently, Zucker has demonstrated through a series of experiments that when social knowledge is highly institutionalised,[1] it 'exists as a fact, as part of objective reality' and becomes highly resistant to change (Zucker 1991: 83). The role of police officers is central to understanding why change is resisted. Since traditional police cultural knowledge is highly institutionalised, it creates a 'reliable' way of looking at the world which is shared by other officers. Any attempt to change this cultural knowledge creates difficulties for officers in carrying out their jobs 'as usual', and questions the assumptions and factual reality which exist in their world. Change is therefore resisted if it challenges existing definitions of the problems, if it makes officers feel more vulnerable and their work less predictable, if it deviates from the accepted methods of how their work is to be accomplished, if it does not accord with 'commonsense', if it violates their collective values, and if ignoring the change has no consequences. It is therefore important to explore ways in which cultural change can be made more sustainable.

How to Make Change Sustainable: Structural Changes

Schein (1985: 271) argues that the prerequisite for cultural change is that the organisation must be 'unfrozen and ready to change, either because of an externally induced crisis or because of internal forces towards change'. Like other writers whose works are directed at managers, Schein's approach is essentially top-down, with a great deal of emphasis on leadership. He suggests that a strategy of 'coercive persuasion' should be used in situations 'where elements of the old culture are dysfunctional but strongly adhered to'. The strategy includes using 'the right incentives' to prevent people valued by the organisation from leaving, relentlessly challenging old assumptions, and providing 'psychological safety' by consistently rewarding the adoption of new assumptions (*ibid.*: 294).

In a sense, that was the strategy pursued by Avery, when in a coercive and directive manner he pushed through a number of major organisational changes in New South Wales. As demonstrated in the case study, however, a decade of top-down reforms did not make a great deal of difference to police racism. Apart from the top-level executives who regularly engaged in the discourse of 'change', there was little evidence that the majority of officers at the operational level were willing or ready for change. This was not unexpected, since studies of police organisations have typically observed a high level of disenchantment and cynicism towards management among operational officers. The impetus for continuing change in New South Wales mainly came from externally induced crises. The *Cop It Sweet* scandal, for example, exposed the gap between the Police Service's espoused policy (community-based policing based on non-racist principles) and operational officers' practice (routine use of racist slurs against Aborigines), forcing the organisation to initiate change (Chapter 8). However, sustainable change requires a more permanent source of pressure to change.

The need for continuing external pressure to change is partly the rationale behind the Mollen Commission's recommendation for an independent external agency to oversight the fight against corruption in the New York City Police Department (Mollen Report 1994: 6–7). In New South Wales, two independent external bodies of oversight already exist: the Ombudsman and the Independent Commission Against Corruption. Both have powers to monitor aspects of police operations and push for change. However, this research has shown that externally imposed changes are often resisted by the organisation, so that change either remains at the damage-control level or is simply a paper exercise. My analysis of the Police Service's implementation of the Ethnic Affairs Policy Statement has shown how difficult it was for an external agency, especially one which did not have a great deal of power, to impose change on the police organisation (Chapter 7). This should come as no surprise, given the embeddedness of cultural knowledge and the ineffectiveness of cosmetic efforts such as policy statements and operational guidelines in challenging assumptions and changing attitudes. What is required to make change meaningful and sustainable is not the establishment of a single structure, but a host of related changes in the field to reinforce the new culture: law reform; external and internal monitoring systems; quality reviews; reward and accountability structures; the empowerment of citizens, especially minority groups, to influence policies; self-determination by Aboriginal people; and even a shift of certain policing functions from the state to civil society (Brogden and Shearing 1993).

The lessons from research are clear: change is traumatic, it has to be directed and continuous, people must be willing to change, and, finally, planned change is difficult to achieve, especially when it is imposed by one group upon another. As Schein observes, the consequences of change may be different from what was intended because 'change agents may have miscalculated the effects of their action or may have been unaware of other forces that were simultaneously acting' (Schein 1985: 301). I have argued that changing police culture requires changes both in the field, the external and internal structural conditions of policing, and in the habitus, the content of cultural knowledge. Finally, I want to re-emphasise what I see as the crucial role of police officers and police managers in organisational change, since there is 'no such thing as spontaneous change' (ibid.: 299). Schein has stressed the role of leadership: 'Leaders create cultures, but cultures, in turn, create their next generation of leaders' (ibid.: 313). However, it would be a mistake to equate leadership with organisational rank or position: leadership is necessary from every level and every division of the organisation, not simply from the top. Obviously, the organisation must create a suitably supportive climate to encourage and reward such leadership.

It is perhaps ironic that a book which has changing police culture as its central theme should end by suggesting that police reformers should reconsider the utility of changing the field, that is, changing the structural conditions of policing. Such a suggestion certainly has many supporters. For example, it would find support among advocates of independent external civilian review of police conduct (see Goldsmith 1991), those who favour tighter control over police misconduct using various administrative, civil and criminal law sanctions (see Lustgarten 1986), those who push for democratic control of policing (see Jefferson and Grimshaw 1984), and those who prefer the use of audit-based monitoring of police conduct (see Brogden and Shearing 1993). Such a suggestion would also be supported by minorities who see self-determination and social inequality as reform issues. It would even find favour among police executives whose activities are dominated by managerialist strategies such as performance indicators, Total Quality Management, continuous improvement and customer focus. As emphasised earlier, changing the field does not guarantee any change in cultural practice. Many regulatory efforts not only fail to gain compliance, but sometimes lead to escalation of the problem, unintended or even perverse consequences (see Grabosky 1995). Nevertheless, changing police culture and improving the relations between police and minorities require changes in both the cultural knowledge and the structural conditions of policing.

Note

1 Zucker defines institutionalisation as both a process and a variable – 'the process by which individual actors transmit what is socially defined as real, and ... at any point in the process the meaning of an act can be defined as more or less a taken-for-granted part of this social reality' (Zucker 1991: 85).

Bibliography of Works Cited

Unpublished Sources

New South Wales Police Service, internal documents.

Periodicals

NSW Police News, 1991–94
Police Service Weekly, 1991–94
Sun-Herald, 1991–94
Sydney Morning Herald, 1991–94

Books and Articles

Alder, C., I. O'Connor, K. Warner and R. White (1992) *Perceptions of the Treatment of Juveniles in the Legal System.* Canberra: National Youth Affairs Research Scheme.

Alderson, J. (1983) 'Community Policing' in Bennett (ed.).

Allison, G. T. (1971) *Essence of Decision.* Boston: Little, Brown.

Aptech (1993) *Cultural Survey Report for NSW Police Service.* Sydney: Aptech Australia Pty Ltd.

Australia. Commonwealth Attorney-General's Department (1990) *Access to Interpreters in the Australian Legal System. Draft Report.* Canberra: AGPS.

Australian Bicentennial Multicultural Foundation [ABMF] (1990) *National Conference on Police Services in a Multicultural Australia: Report.* Victoria Police and the ABMF.

Australian Bureau of Statistics (ABS) (1994a) *Australian Social Trends.*

Australian Bureau of Statistics (1994b) *National Aboriginal and Torres Strait Islander Survey 1994.*

Australian Law Reform Commission (ALRC) (1992) *Multiculturalism and the Law,* Report No. 57. Commonwealth of Australia.

Avery, J. (1981) *Police: Force or Service?* Sydney: Butterworths.

Babbie, E. (1992) *The Practice of Social Research.* Sixth edition. Belmont, Calif.: Wadsworth.

Baldwin, R., and R. Kinsey (1982) *Police Powers and Politics.* London: Quartet Books.
Banton, M. (1964) *The Policeman in the Community.* London: Tavistock.
Bayley, D. H. (1989) 'Community Policing in Australia: An Appraisal' in D. Chappell and P. Wilson (eds), *Australian Policing: Contemporary Issues.* Sydney: Butterworths.
Bayley, D. H. (1992) 'Comparative Organization of the Police in English-speaking Countries' in Tonry and Morris (eds).
Bayley, D. H., and H. Mendelsohn (1969) *Minorities and the Police.* New York: The Free Press.
Bennett, T. (1983) (ed.) *The Future of Policing.* Institute of Criminology, University of Cambridge.
Bittner, E. (1978) 'The Functions of the Police in Modern Society' in Manning and Van Maanen (eds).
Black, D. (1971) 'The Social Organisation of Arrest', *Stanford Law Review,* June 1971: 1109–10.
Bongiorno, B. (1994) 'A DPP's Approach: Some Problems in the Prosecution of Police Officers' in Moore and Wettenhall (eds).
Bourdieu, P. (1990) *In Other Words: Essay Towards a Reflexive Sociology.* Cambridge: Polity Press.
Bourdieu, P., and L. J. D. Wacquant (1992) *An Invitation to Reflexive Sociology.* Cambridge: Polity Press.
Braithwaite, J. (1992) 'Good and Bad Police Services and How to Pick Them' in Moir and Eijkman (eds).
Braithwaite, J., and B. Fisse (1987) 'Self-regulation and the Control of Corporate Crime' in C. Shearing and P. Stenning (eds), *Private Policing.* Newbury Park, California: Sage 1987.
Brockie, J. (1994) 'Police and Minority Groups' in Moore and Wettenhall (eds).
Brogden, M., and C. Shearing (1993) *Policing for a New South Africa.* London: Routledge.
Brogden, M., T. Jefferson and S. Walklate (1988) *Introducing Policework.* London: Unwin Hyman.
Bryett, K., and C. Lewis (eds) (1994) *Un-Peeling Tradition: Contemporary Policing.* Melbourne: Macmillan.
Bull, D., and E. Stratta (1994) 'Police Community Consultation: An Examination of its Practice in Selected Constabularies in England and New South Wales, Australia', *ANZ Journal of Criminology,* 27(3): 237–49.
Bursik, R. J., and H. G. Grasmick (1993) 'Economic Deprivation and Neighbourhood Crime Rates 1960–1980', *Law and Society Review,* 27(2): 263–83.
Cahill, D., and J. Ewen (1987) *Ethnic Youth: Their Assets and Aspirations.* Report of the Department of Prime Minister and Cabinet. Canberra: Australian Government Publishing Service (quoted in Federation of Ethnic Communities' Council of Australia 1991).
Cain, M. (1973) *Society and the Policeman's Role.* London: Routledge and Kegan Paul.
Cashmore, E. (1991) 'Black Cops Inc.' in E. Cashmore and E. McLaughlin (eds), *Out of Order: Policing Black People.* London: Routledge. Quoted in Brogden and Shearing 1993.
Castles, S. (1992a) *Racism: A Global Analysis,* Occasional paper No. 28. Wollongong: Centre for Multicultural Studies, University of Wollongong.

Castles, S. (1992b) *The Challenge of Multiculturalism: Global Changes and Australian Experiences.* Working Papers on Multiculturalism No. 19. Wollongong: Centre for Multicultural Studies, University of Wollongong.

Castles, S., B. Cope, M. Kalantzis and M. Morrissey (1988) *Mistaken Identity.* Sydney: Pluto.

Centre for Applied Research in Education (CARE), University of East Anglia (1990) *The New South Wales Police Recruitment Education Programme: An Independent Evaluation.*

Chan, J. (1992a) *Policing in a Multicultural Society.* Final Report to the New South Wales Police Service.

Chan, J. (1992b) *Doing Less Time: Penal Reform in Crisis.* Sydney: Institute of Criminology, University of Sydney.

Chan, J. (1994) 'Policing Youth in Ethnic Communities: Is Community Policing the Answer?' in White and Alder (eds).

Chan, J. (1995) 'Damage Control: Media Representation and Responses to Police Deviance', *Law/Text/Culture,* 2: 32–60.

Chan, J. (1996) 'Changing Police Culture', *British Journal of Criminology,* 36(1): 109–34.

Cohen, S. (1972) *Folk Devils and Moral Panics.* London: MacGibbon and Kee.

Coldrey, J. (1987) 'Aboriginals and the Criminal Courts' in K. Hazlehurst (ed.), *Ivory Scales: Black Australia and the Law.* Kensington: New South Wales University Press.

Colebatch, H., and P. Larmour (1993) *Market, Bureaucracy and Community.* London: Pluto Press.

Collins, J. (1996) 'The Changing Political Economy of Australian Racism' in Vasta and Castles (eds).

Cunneen, C. (1990a) *A Study of Aboriginal Juveniles and Police Violence.* Report commissioned by the National Inquiry into Racist Violence. Human Rights and Equal Opportunity Commission.

Cunneen, C. (1990b) *Aboriginal–Police Relations in Redfern.* Sydney: Human Rights and Equal Opportunity Commission.

Cunneen, C. (ed.) (1992) *Aboriginal Perspectives on Criminal Justice.* Sydney: Institute of Criminology, University of Sydney.

Cunneen, C. (1994) 'Enforcing Genocide? Aboriginal Young People and the Police' in White and Alder (eds).

Cunneen, C., and T. Libesman (1995) *Indigenous People and the Law in Australia.* Sydney: Butterworths.

Cunneen, C., and T. Robb (1987) *Criminal Justice in North-East New South Wales.* Sydney: Bureau of Crime Statistics and Research.

Czarniawska-Joerges, B. (1992) *Exploring Complex Organizations: A Cultural Perspective.* Newbury Park, Calif.: Sage.

Daniel, A., and J. Cornwall (1993) *A Lost Generation?* Sydney: The Australian Youth Foundation.

Devery, C. (1991) *Disadvantage and Crime in New South Wales.* Sydney: NSW Bureau of Crime Statistics and Research.

Dixon, D. (1993) *Report on a Review of Police Powers in Queensland.* Vol. 1: *An Overview.* Brisbane: Queensland Criminal Justice Commission.

Doob, A., and J. Chan (1982) 'Factors Affecting Police Decisions to Take Juveniles to Court', *Canadian Journal of Criminology,* 24(1): 25–37.

Downes, D., and P. Rock (1982) *Understanding Deviance.* Oxford: Oxford University Press.

Dunphy, D. (1976) 'Behavioural Scientists: The Role of the Consultant', *Australian Journal of Public Administration*, xxxv(1): 9.

Dunphy, D., and D. Stace (1990) *Under New Management*. Sydney: McGraw-Hill.

Elmore, R. (1993) 'Organizational Models of Social Program Implementation' in M. Hill (ed.), *The Policy Process*. London: Harvester Wheatsheaf. (Paper originally published in 1978.)

Ericson, R. (1981) 'Rules *For* Police Deviance' in Shearing (ed.).

Ericson, R. (1982) *Reproducing Order*. Toronto: University of Toronto Press.

Ericson, R., P. Baranek and J. Chan (1987) *Visualizing Deviance*. Toronto: University of Toronto Press.

Ericson, R., P. Baranek and J. Chan (1989) *Negotiating Control*. Toronto: University of Toronto Press.

Ericson, R., P. Baranek and J. Chan (1991) *Representing Order*. Toronto: University of Toronto Press.

Etter, B. (1992) 'The Future Direction of Policing in Australia'. Paper to the Australian and New Zealand Society of Criminology Annual Conference, Melbourne, 30 September–2 October.

Etter, B. (1993) 'The Culture Clash: Police and Multicultural Australia'. Paper to the Australian and New Zealand Society of Criminology Annual Conference, Sydney, 28 September–1 October.

Farrington, D. R., B. Gallagher, L. Morley, R. J. St Ledger, and D. J. West (1986) 'Unemployment, School Leaving and Crime', *British Journal of Criminology*, 26(4): 335–56.

Federation of Ethnic Communities' Council of Australia (1991) *Background Paper on Ethnic Youth Prepared for FECCA's Multicultural Youth Conference*. Sydney: FECCA.

Fergusson, D. M., L. J. Horwood, and M. T. Lynskey (1993) 'Ethnicity, Social Background and Young Offending: A 14-year Longitudinal Study', *ANZ Journal of Criminology*, 26(2): 155–70.

Fielding, N. (1988) *Joining Forces*. London and New York: Routledge.

Finnane, M. (1990) 'Police Corruption and Police Reform: The Fitzgerald Inquiry in Queensland, Australia', *Policing and Society* 1: 159–171.

Finnane, M. (1994) *Police and Government*. Melbourne: Oxford University Press.

Finnane, M. (1995) 'From Police Force to Police Service? Aspects of the Recent History of the New South Wales Police'. Unpublished paper prepared for the Royal Commission into the New South Wales Police Service.

Fishman, M. (1978) 'Crime Waves as Ideology', *Social Problems*, 25: 531–43.

Fisse, B., and J. Braithwaite (1983) *The Impact of Publicity on Corporate Offenders*. Albany: State University of New York Press.

Fitzgerald Report (1989) *Report of a Commission of Inquiry Pursuant to Orders in Council: Commission of Inquiry into Possible Illegal Activities and Associated Police Misconduct*. Brisbane: Queensland Government Printer.

Foley, M. (1984) 'Aborigines and the Police' in P. Hanks and B. Keon-Cohen (eds), *Aborigines and the Law*. Sydney: Allen and Unwin.

Froyland, I., and M. Skeffington (1993) *Aboriginal and Torres Strait Islander Employment Strategy*. Mount Lawley: Centre for Police Research, Edith Cowan University.

Gale, F., and J. Wundersitz (1987) 'Police and Black Minorities: The Case of Aboriginal Youth in South Australia', *ANZ Journal of Criminology*, 20(2): 78–94.

Gale, F., R. Bailey-Harris and J. Wundersitz (1990) *Aboriginal Youth and the Criminal Justice System.* Melbourne: Cambridge University Press.

Garfinkel, H. (1967) *Studies in Ethnomethodology.* Englewood Cliffs, NJ: Prentice-Hall.

Gibbon, J. (1989) 'Police Procedures and Second Language Speakers', *Migration Monitor,* October, 1989: 7–8.

Giddens, A. (1984) *Constitution of Society.* Cambridge: Polity Press.

Goldring, J., and P. Blazey (1994) 'Constitutional and Legal Mechanisms of Police Accountability in Australia' in Moore and Wettenhall (eds).

Goldsmith, A. (1990) 'Taking Police Culture Seriously: Police Discretion and the Limits of Law', *Policing and Society,* 1: 91–114.

Goldsmith, A. (ed.) (1991) *Complaints Against the Police.* Oxford: Clarendon Press.

Goldstein, H. (1979) 'Improving Policing: A Problem-Oriented Approach', *Crime and Delinquency,* April 1979: 236–58.

Gordon, P. (1983) *White Law: Racism in the Police, Courts and Prisons.* London: Pluto.

Gordon, P. (1992) 'Black People and the Criminal Law: Rhetoric and Reality' in P. Braham, A. Rattansi and R. Skellington (eds), *Racism and Antiracism.* London: Sage in association with The Open University.

Grabosky, P. (1995) 'Counterproductive Regulation', *International Journal of Sociology of Law,* 23: 347–69.

Hall, S., C. Critcher, T. Jefferson, J. Clarke and B. Roberts (1978) *Policing the Crisis.* London: Macmillan.

Hawkins, K. (1984) *Environment and Enforcement.* Oxford: Oxford University Press.

Hazlehurst, K. (1987) *Migration, Ethnicity, and Crime in Australian Society.* Canberra: Australian Institute of Criminology.

Heidensohn, F. (1992) *Women in Control?* Oxford: Clarendon Press.

Henry, V. (1994) 'Police Corruption: Tradition and Evolution' in Bryett and Lewis (eds).

Holdaway, S. (1983) *Inside British Police.* Oxford: Basil Blackwell.

Holdaway, S. (1991) *Recruiting a Multi-racial Police Force.* London: HMSO.

Holdaway, S. (1995) 'Constructing and Sustaining "Race" Within the Police Work Force'. Paper to the British Criminology Conference, Loughborough, July.

Hough, M., and P. Mayhew (1983) *The British Crime Survey.* London: HMSO. Cited by Walker 1987.

Hughes, G. (1992) ' Consumerist Policing', *Socio-Legal Bulletin,* 6: 13–17.

Human Rights and Equal Opportunity Commission (HREOC) (1991) *Racist Violence: Report of the National Inquiry into Racist Violence in Australia.* Canberra: AGPS.

Ingram, E. (1991) 'Evaluation Framework and Performance Indicators for Ethnic Client Group Program'. Unpublished paper.

IPC Worldwide (1994) *NSW Police Service PSSES Attitude Survey.* IPC Worldwide Strategic Management Consultants.

James, D. (1979) 'Police–Black Relations: The Professional Solution' in S. Holdaway (ed.), *The British Police.* London: Edward Arnold.

Jefferson, T. (1991) 'Discrimination, Disadvantage and Police-work' in E. Cashmore and E. McLaughlin (eds), *Out of Order? Policing Black People.* London: Routledge.

Jefferson, T. (1993) 'The Racism of Criminalization: Policing and the Reproduction of the Criminal Other', in L. Gelsthorpe (ed.), *Ethnic Minorities and the Criminal Justice System: 21st Cropwood Round Table Conference, 1992*. Cambridge: Institute of Criminology.

Jefferson, T., and R. Grimshaw (1984) *Controlling the Constable*. London: Frederick Muller.

Jefferson, T., and M. A. Walker (1992) 'Ethnic Minorities in the Criminal Justice System', *Criminal Law Review*, 1992: 83–95.

Johnston, E. (1991) *Royal Commission into Aboriginal Deaths in Custody: National Report: Overview and Recommendations*. Canberra: Australian Government Publishing Service.

Jupp, J. (1995) 'Ethnic and Cultural Diversity in Australia' in *Australia Year Book 1995*. Canberra: Australian Government Publishing Service.

Kelling, G., and M. Moore (1982) 'Observations on the Policing Industry'. Harvard University, Kennedy School of Government, Program in Criminal Justice Policy and Management.

Kelly, L. (1993) 'Reconciliation and the Implications for a Sovereign Aboriginal Nation', *Aboriginal Law Bulletin*, 3(61): 10–13. Quoted in Cunneen and Libesman 1995.

Landa, D. (1994) 'Serving the Customer' in Moore and Wettenhall (eds).

Landa Report (1991) *Operation Sue*. Report Under Section 26 of the Ombudsman Act.

Landa Report (1993) *Ombudsman's Report on Allegations of Police Bias Against Asian Students*. Special Report to Parliament.

Landa Report (1995) *Race Relations and Our Police*. A special report to Parliament under Section 31 of the Ombudsman Act.

Lauer, A. R. (1994) 'Policing in the 90s: Its Role and Accountability' in Moore and Wettenhall (eds).

Lee, J. A. (1981) 'Some Structural Aspects of Police Deviance in Relations with Minority Groups' in Shearing (ed.).

Lee Report (1990) *Report of the Royal Commission of Inquiry into the Arrest, Charging and Withdrawal of Charges against Harold James Blackburn and Matters Associated Therewith*.

Lipsky, M. (1980) *Street-level Bureaucracy*. New York: Russell Sage Foundation.

Lucas, D. (1995) 'Breaking the Silence and Silences: A Time of Challenge and Change in Aboriginal–police relations, the 1960s and 1970s', *Current Issues in Criminal Justice*, 7(1): 44–59.

Luke, G., and C. Cunneen (1992) 'Aboriginal Juveniles and the Juvenile Justice System in NSW'. Paper to National Conference on Juvenile Justice, Adelaide, 22–24 September.

Luke, G., and C. Cunneen (1995) *Aboriginal Over-Representation and Discretionary Decisions in the NSW Juvenile Justice System*. Sydney: Juvenile Justice Advisory Council of NSW.

Lundman, R., R. Sykes and J. P. Clark (1978) 'Police Control of Juveniles', *Journal of Research in Crime and Delinquency*, 15(1): 74–91.

Lusher Report (1981) *Report of the Commission of Inquiry into New South Wales Police Administration*. Sydney: NSW Government Printer.

Lustgarten, L. (1986) *The Governance of the Police*. London: Sweet and Maxwell.

MacGregor, P. G. (n.d.) 'Recruitment and Training within Police Services'. Paper to Police, Aboriginal and Torres Strait Islander Peoples' National Conference.

Manning, P. (1977) *Police Work*. Cambridge, Mass.: MIT Press.

Manning, P. (1978a) 'The Police: Mandate, Strategies, and Appearances' in Manning and Van Maanen (eds).

Manning, P. (1978b) 'Lying, Secrecy and Social Control' in Manning and Van Maanen (eds).

Manning, P. (1978c) 'Rules, Colleagues, and Situationally Justified Actions' in Manning and Van Maanen (eds).

Manning, P. (1989) 'Occupational Culture' in W. G. Bailey (ed.), *The Encyclopedia of Police Science*. New York and London: Garland.

Manning, P. (1993) 'Toward a Theory of Police Organization Polarities and Change'. Paper to the International Conference on 'Social Change in Policing', Taipei, 3–5 August.

Manning, P., and J. Van Maanen (eds) (1978) *Policing: A View from the Street*. Santa Monica, Calif.: Goodyear.

Martin, S. (1980) *Breaking and Entering: Policewoman on Patrol*. Berkeley: University of California Press.

McBarnet, D. (1979) 'Arrest: The Legal Context of Policing' in S. Holdaway (ed.), *The British Police*. London: Edward Arnold.

McConville, M., A. Sanders and R. Leng (1991) *The Case for the Prosecution*. London: Routledge.

McDonald, D., and D. Biles (1991) 'Who Got Locked Up? The Australian Police Custody Survey', *ANZ Journal of Criminology*, 24(3): 190–203.

Moir, P., and M. Moir (1992) 'Community-based Policing and the Role of Community Consultation' in Moir and Eijkman (eds).

Moir, P., and H. Eijkman (eds) (1992) *Policing Australia: Old Issues, New Perspectives*. Melbourne: Macmillan.

Mollen Report (1994) *Commission Report: Commission to Investigate Allegations of Police Corruption and the Anti-Corruption Procedures of the Police Department*. The City of New York.

Monaco, J. (1981) *How to Read a Film*. Oxford: Oxford University Press.

Moore, D., and R. Wettenhall (eds) (1994) *Keeping the Peace: Police Accountability and Oversight*. Canberra: University of Canberra and The Royal Institute of Public Administration Australia.

Moore, M. (1992) 'Problem-solving and Community Policing' in Tonry and Morris (eds).

Morgan, G. (1986) *Images of Organization*. Newbury Park, Calif.: Sage.

Morgan, R. (1987) 'The Local Determinants of Policing Policy' in Wilmott (ed.).

Morton, J. (1993) *Bent Coppers*. London: Warner.

Mouzelis, N. (1995) *Sociological Theory: What Went Wrong?* London: Routledge.

Muir, W. K. (1977) *Police: Streetcorner Politicians*. Chicago: University of Chicago Press.

New South Wales Ethnic Affairs Commission (NSWEAC) (1980) *Ethnic Groups and Police: A NSW Survey*.

New South Wales Ethnic Affairs Commission (1985) *New South Wales Government: 'A Decade of Achievement in Ethnic Affairs' 1976–1985*. NSW Government Printer.

New South Wales Ethnic Affairs Commission (1990) *Ethnic Affairs Policy Statement (EAPS) Program: Strategic Plan*.

New South Wales Ethnic Affairs Commission (1991) *Ethnic Affairs Policy Statement*.

New South Wales Ethnic Affairs Commission (1992) 'Policing and Ethnicity in NSW'. Unpublished report.

New South Wales Law Reform Commission (NSWLRC) (1990) *Criminal Procedure*.

New South Wales Office on Social Policy (1994) *New South Wales Social Trends Bulletin*. Sydney: Office on Social Policy.

New South Wales Ombudsman (1991) *Annual Report*. Sydney: Office of the Ombudsman.

New South Wales Ombudsman (1992) *Annual Report*. Sydney: Office of the Ombudsman.

New South Wales Ombudsman (1994) *Race Relations and Our Police: A Discussion Paper*. Sydney: Office of the Ombudsman.

New South Wales Police Board, *Annual Reports*, 1991–92.

New South Wales Police Department (NSWPD), *Annual Reports*, 1985–87.

New South Wales Police Recruit Education Programme (PREP) (1991) *Course Documentation*.

New South Wales Police Service *Annual Reports*, 1988–92.

New South Wales Police Service (1988a) *Ethnic Affairs Policy Statement*.

New South Wales Police Service (1992) *Ethnic Affairs Policy Statement Strategic Plan 1992–1995*.

New South Wales Police Service (1994) *Transition*. Report of the June–November 1994 Working Party Review of Changes to Recruitment Policy and Practice.

New South Wales Police Service (n.d.) *Community Based Policing Papers Nos. 1–8*.

Northern Territory Police (1991) *A Blueprint for the Future*.

O'Neill, S., and J. Bathgate (1993) *Policing Strategies in Aboriginal and Non-English-Speaking Background Communities: Final Report*. Winnellie, NT: Northern Territory Police.

Office of Multicultural Affairs (1989) *National Agenda for a Multicultural Australia*. Canberra: Australian Government Publishing Service.

Office of Multicultural Affairs (1990) *Youth and Multiculturalism: Research Report*. Quoted in Federation of Ethnic Communities' Council of Australia, 1991.

Office of Multicultural Affairs (1992), *Access and Equity Evaluation Report*. Canberra: Australian Government Publishing Service.

Ouchi, W. G., and A. L. Wilkins (1985) 'Organizational Culture', *Annual Review of Sociology*, 11: 457–83.

Patton, M. (1980) *Qualitative Evaluation Methods*. Beverly Hills: Sage.

Performance Diagnostics Services (1990) '1990 Staff Survey. Final Report for NSW Police Service'. Unpublished paper.

Powell, W. W., and P. J. DiMaggio (eds) (1991) *The New Institutionalism in Organizational Analysis*. Chicago: University of Chicago Press.

Presdee, M. (n.d.) *The Effects of Deregulatory Policies on Youth Criminality and the Connections Between Poverty and Crime*. Report for the Criminology Research Council. Project No. 6/88.

Punch, M. (ed.) (1983a) *Control in the Police Organization*. Cambridge, Mass.: MIT Press.

Punch, M. (1983b) 'Officers and Men: Occupational Culture, Inter-Rank Antagonism, and the Investigation of Corruption' in Punch (ed.).

Punch, M. (1985) *Conduct Unbecoming*. London: Tavistock.

Queensland. Criminal Justice Commission (QCJC) (1993) *Recruitment and Education in the Queensland Police Service: A Review*.

Queensland. Criminal Justice Commission (1994) *Implementation of Reform within the Queensland Police Service: The Response of the Queensland Police Service to the Fitzgerald Inquiry Recommendations*.

Rauch, J. (1992) 'South African Police Basic Training: a Preliminary Assessment', *Project for the Study of Violence*, Seminar Paper 4, University of the Witwatersrand. Quoted in Brogden and Shearing 1993.

Reiner, R. (1985) 'The Police and Race Relations', in J. Baxter and L. Koffman (eds), *Police: The Constitution and the Community*. London: Professional Books.

Reiner, R. (1992) *The Politics of the Police*. Second edition. Harvester Wheatsheaf.

Reiss, A. (1983) 'The Policing of Organizational Life' in Punch (ed.).

Reuss-Ianni, E., and F. Ianni (1983) 'Street Cops and Management Cops: The Two Cultures of Policing' in Punch (ed.).

Reynolds, H. (1987) *The Law of the Land*. Penguin.

Roberts-Smith, L. W. (1989) 'Communication breakdown', *Legal Services Bulletin*, 14(2): 75–8.

Ronalds, C., M. Chapman and K. Kitchener (1983) 'Policing Aborigines' in M. Finlay *et al.* (eds), *Issues in Criminal Justice Administration*. Sydney: Allen and Unwin.

Ross, R., and P. Whiteford (1990) *Income Poverty Among Aboriginal Families With Children: Estimates from the 1986 Census*. Sydney: University of NSW Social Policy Research Centre, Discussion Paper No. 20. Cited in Devery 1991.

Royal Commission on Australian Government Administration, Australian Government Publishing Service, 1976.

Sackmann, S. (1991) *Cultural Knowledge in Organizations*. Newbury Park, Calif.: Sage.

Sacks, H. (1978) 'Notes on Police Assessment of Moral Character' in Manning and Van Maanen (eds).

Sampson, R. J., and J. H. Laub (1993) 'Structural Variations in Juvenile Court Processing: Inequality, the Underclass, and Social Control', *Law and Society Review*, 27(2): 285–311.

Scarman Report (1981) *The Brixton Disorders, 10–12 April 1981: Report of an Inquiry by the Right Honourable the Lord Scarman, OBE*. Penguin Books.

Schein, E. (1985) *Organizational Culture and Leadership*. San Francisco: Jossey-Bass.

Shearing C. (ed.) (1981) *Organizational Police Deviance*. Toronto: Butterworths.

Shearing, C. D., and R. V. Ericson (1991) 'Culture as Figurative Action', *British Journal of Sociology*, 42: 481–506.

Sherman, L. (1978) *Scandal and Reform*. Berkeley: University of California Press.

Skolnick, J. (1966) *Justice Without Trial*. New York: John Wiley and Sons.

Skolnick, J. (1972) 'Changing Conceptions of the Police', *Great Ideas Today*. Chicago: Encyclopaedia Britannica. Quoted in Reiner 1992.

Skolnick, J. (1994) 'Police Accountability in the United States' in Moore and Wettenhall (eds).

Skolnick, J., and J. Fyfe (1993) *Above the Law: Police and the Excessive Use of Force*. New York: The Free Press.

Smith, D. (1987) 'Research, the Community and the Police', in Wilmott (ed.).

Smith, D. (1994) 'The Political and Social Constraints to Reform' in Bryett and Lewis (eds).

Smith, D. J. (1983) *Police and People in London, I: A Survey of Londoners*. London: Policy Studies Institute.

Smith, D. J., and J. Gray (1983) *Police and People in London IV: The Police in Action*. London: Policy Studies Institute.

Solomos, J. (1988) *Black Youth, Racism and the State*. Cambridge: Cambridge University Press.

Southgate, P. (1984) *Racism Awareness Training for the Police*. London: Home Office.

Sparrow, M. K., M. H. Moore and D. M. Kennedy (1990) *Beyond 911*. Basic Books.

Staunton Report (1991) *Report of the Police Tribunal of New South Wales to the Minister for Police and Emergency Services Pursuant to an Inquiry under Section 45 of the Police Regulation (Allegations of Misconduct) Act 1978 into Certain Matters Relating to Discipline in the Police Force ('Brennan TRG Inquiry').*

Stubbs, J. (1992) *Complaints Against Police in New South Wales.* Sydney: NSW Bureau of Crime Statistics and Research.

Sullivan, P. S. (1989) 'Minority Officers, Current Issues' in R. G. Dunham (ed.), *Critical Issues in Policing.*

Sutton, J. (1992) 'Women in the Job' in Moir and Eijkman (eds).

Swanton, B., G. Hannigan, and T. Psaila (eds) (1985) *Police Source Book 2.* Canberra: Australian Institute of Criminology.

Sykes, R., J. Fox and J. P. Clark (1976) 'A Socio-Legal Theory of Police Discretion' in A. Niederhoffer and A. Blumberg (eds), *The Ambivalent Force,* second edition. Hinsdale, Ill.: Dryden Press.

Thomas-Peter, K. (1993) 'A Review of the Literature', Appendix Six in I. Froyland and M. Skeffington, *Aboriginal and Torres Strait Islander Employment Strategy.* Mount Lawley: Centre for Police Research, Edith Cowan University.

Tink Report (1992) *Inquiry Upon the Role of the Office of the Ombudsman in Investigating Complaints against Police.* Report of the Joint Committee on the Office of the Ombudsman. Parliament of New South Wales.

Tonry, M., and N. Morris (eds) (1992) *Modern Policing.* Chicago: University of Chicago Press.

Tuck, M., and P. Southgate (1981) *Ethnic Minorities, Crime and Policing.* London: Home Office.

Van Maanen, J. (1978a) 'Kinsmen in Repose: Occupational Perspectives of Patrolmen' in Manning and Van Maanen (eds).

Van Maanen, J. (1978b) 'The Asshole' in Manning and Van Maanen (eds).

Van Maanen, J. (1980) 'Beyond Account: The Personal Impact of Police Shootings', *The Annals of the American Academy of Political and Social Sciences,* 425 (November): 145–56.

Van Maanen, J. (1983) 'The Boss: First-line Supervision in an American Police Agency' in Punch (ed.).

Vasta, E. (1993) 'Multiculturalism and Ethnic Identity: The Relationship between Racism and Resistance', *ANZ Journal of Sociology,* 29(2): 209–25.

Vasta, E. (1996) 'Dialectics of Domination: Racism and Multiculturalism' in Vasta and Castles (eds).

Vasta, E., and S. Castles (eds) (1996) *The Teeth are Smiling: The Persistence of Racism in Multicultural Australia.* Sydney: Allen and Unwin.

Victoria Police (n.d.) *Police Service in a Culturally Diverse Victoria, Strategy Plan.*

Voumvakis, S., and R. Ericson (1984) *News Accounts of Attacks on Women.* Toronto: Centre of Criminology, University of Toronto.

Wacquant, L. J. D. (1992) 'Toward a Social Praxeology: The Structure and Logic of Bourdieu's Sociology' in P. Bourdieu and L. Wacquant, *An Invitation to Reflexive Sociology.* Cambridge: Polity Press.

Walker, J., and D. Biles (1987) *Australian Prisoners 1986.* Canberra: Australian Institute of Criminology.

Walker, M. (1987) 'Interpreting Race and Crime Statistics', *Journal of the Royal Statistical Society,* Series A, 150(1): 39–56.

Weatheritt, M. (1987) 'Community Policing Now' in Wilmott (ed.).

Weick, K. (1979) *The Social Psychology of Organizing.* Reading, Mass.: Addison-Wesley.

Westley, W. (1970) *Violence and the Police.* Cambridge, Mass.: MIT.

White, R., and C. Alder (eds) (1994) *The Police and Young People in Australia.* Melbourne: Cambridge University Press.

Wilenski Report (1977) *Directions for Change: Review of NSW Government Administration.* Sydney: NSW Government Printer.

Wilmott, P. (ed.) (1987) *Policing and the Community.* London: Policy Studies Institute.

Wilson, D., S. Holdaway and C. Spencer (1984) 'Black Police in the UK', *Policing* 1(1): 20–30.

Wilson, P. L., and L. Storey (1991) *Migrants and the Law – The Vietnamese: A Case Study.* Footscray, Vic.: Footscray Community Centre.

Wootten Report (1989) *Report of the Inquiry into the Death of Malcolm Charles Smith.* Royal Commission into Aboriginal Deaths in Custody.

Wootten Report (1991) *Report of the Inquiry into the Death of David John Gundy.* Royal Commission into Aboriginal Deaths in Custody.

Wortley, R. (1993) 'The Limits of Police Education'. Paper presented at the conference Police Education in Australia: The Way Ahead, Brisbane, 6–7 April 1993.

Yeatman, A. (1987) 'The Concept of Public Management and the Australian State in the 1980s', *Australian Journal of Public Administration* 46(4): 339–353.

Yin, R. (1984) *Case Study Research: Design and Methods.* Beverly Hills: Sage.

Young, M. (1991) *An Inside Job.* Oxford: Clarendon Press.

Youth Justice Coalition (NSW) (1990) *Kids in Justice.* Sydney.

Youth Justice Coalition (NSW) (1994) *Nobody Listens.* Sydney.

Zucker, L. G. (1991) 'The Role of Institutionalization in Cultural Persistence' in Powell and DiMaggio (eds), 83–107.

Index